W9-ADG-592

SOUTH AFRICA

SOUTH AFRICA

By

JAN H. HOFMEYR

Second Revised Edition by

J. P. COPE

McGRAW-HILL BOOK COMPANY INC.

NEW YORK   TORONTO

1952

Printed in Great Britain by
Richard Clay & Company Ltd · Bungay · Suffolk

Contents

v

Prefatory Note

I HAVE of set purpose avoided the introduction of footnotes into this book. One result of this avoidance has been my inability to make adequate recognition of my indebtedness to other writers. That indebtedness is considerable—for facts, for interpretations, also for phrases which have stuck in one's mind as a result of one's reading, and are not always easily traceable to their source. To all those upon whom I have drawn in these or other ways I extend my grateful thanks. I cannot mention them all, but I must at least specify the historical works of Professor Walker and Gie, Mrs. Millin's *The South Africans*, and Professor Leppan's writings on South African agriculture. Certain other works are mentioned in the text.

JAN H. HOFMEYR

Foreword

SOUTH AFRICA, Jan Hofmeyr used to say, was one of the world's most fertile fields for human research. In this laboratory of human relationships were all the most difficult problems that could be found in our modern age. Yet when Hofmeyr wrote his book on South Africa in 1930 it seemed that at least one of these problems—the vexed question of English and Afrikaans assimilation into a united nation—was in sight of solution.

' South Africa ', he believed, ' has learnt that it must make an end to the old feuds and the old controversies, must leave past disputes honourably at rest, either side admitting that part at least of the error and the blame attaches to itself. It realizes that there must be no more talk of the domination, the superiority of one element in the European population over the other; that on the basis of mutual recognition of language rights and distinctive sentiments, they should have equal weight in the councils of the land.'

That was the mood of our leading statesmen—of Smuts, Hertzog, Hofmeyr, and others—in 1930. It was a declaration of faith which Hofmeyr himself sought with all the force of his eloquence and intellect to fulfil. But history was against him. Great events in the world at large shook South Africa to her foundations, kindling animosities that had never really died, and loosing new and dangerous ideas that boded ill for the future. The war imposed severe political strains, and traditional ways of living were disturbed by an industrial revolution for which the nation was ill-prepared.

When Jan Hofmeyr died on 3rd December, 1948, it seemed that the ideal of co-operation for which he and Smuts and others had striven, was falling about him in ruins. And yet, even at the end, he himself refused to despair. He regarded the present chapter in the history of South Africa as a sombre interlude between two great and promising eras.

Whether he was right or not remains to be seen. Meanwhile it is, perhaps, appropriate that Jan Hofmeyr's book on South Africa should end in 1930, and that another pen should add the last chapters, bringing the rich chronicle up to the present day. For Hofmeyr himself had a powerful and pervading influence on events between 1930 and 1948, and he was too modest ever to have given due acknowledgment to his own significant rôle.

In editing Jan Hofmeyr's contribution, which forms the major portion of this volume, I have brought his statistics up to date. I have added a relevant fact here and there, as in Chapter 11, which deals with the Constitution, and Chapter 14, discussing problems of colour. I have eliminated those portions in which Hofmeyr wrote of the immediate future and which have become redundant through the passage of time. For the rest, it is remarkable how little has required amendment or amplification.

In the four chapters at the end of the volume I have described the more important political and economic events in South Africa between 1932 and 1952. And as Hofmeyr did in his original volume, I have indicated the main trends that seem likely to shape the immediate future of South Africa.

J. P. COPE

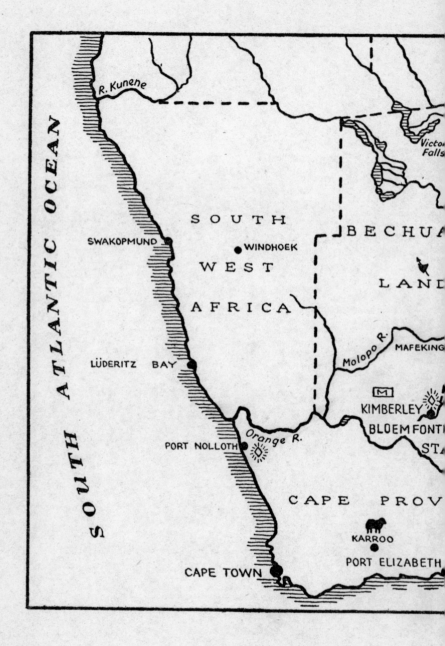

KEY

NATIVE RESERVES

COAL

GOLD

DIAMONDS

WOOL

MANGANESE

STEEL

SOUTH AFRICA

Scale of Miles

0   100   200   300   400   500

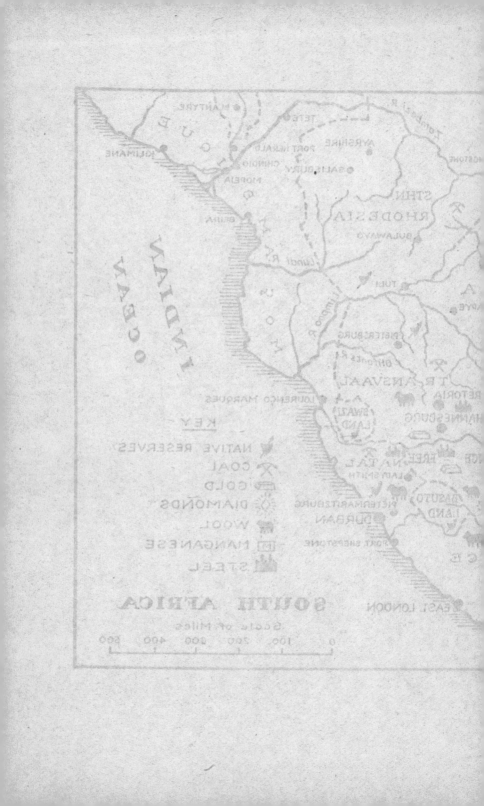

BOOK ONE

Chapter 1

Introduction

THERE are competent modern geologists who assign to the continent of Africa a central position in the southern hemisphere. From it they believe other land-masses have been dislodged and drifted away—South America to the westwards, Madagascar, India, and Australasia to the eastwards. But whatever may have happened in remote periods of geological time, certainly in comparatively recent centuries the central position of Southern Africa, its importance for Westerners who sought to journey eastwards, and later for Easterners who travelled westwards, has been a significant factor in history. That fact of its position made of it a meeting-place of men of diverse races and nations, and so stamped its history with what has been its most enduring characteristic.

Time was when the Cape was known as the Tavern of the Seas. To it there came Portuguese and English and Dutch and Germans and French, seeking rest and refreshment from the hardships of their voyages. In their train followed slaves from West Africa. To it also there came Malays from the East, and men from Madagascar and distant Batavia. But in time it became more than a tavern; men chose it as a dwelling-place and a home. Those who settled there, Dutch and German and French, fused into a single Afrikaner stock, speaking a common language, and alongside of them there grew up out of the intermingling of Malays and Bantu slaves and the indigenous Hottentots of the country, together with an infusion of white blood, what looked like becoming an equally homogeneous coloured people. For the two peoples there was, so it seemed, space enough in the land. There was no lack of elbow-room. Certainly after a hundred years of settlement there appeared to be nothing insoluble in the problems caused by the meeting of men of different stocks in Southern Africa.

But the following century had a different picture to reveal. The Cape passed under British rule. Men of British birth were brought to make their home in Southern Africa. So there came into juxtaposition two powerful self-conscious nations, the descendants in either case of men who had made great sacrifices for civil and religious liberty, the possessors of distinctive traditions which neither would readily see destroyed. There arose differences of outlook, divergences of opinion, conflicts of sentiment. Thus were born controversy and strife, and out of that strife unity could be built up only by means of painful and toilsome effort.

Thence, too, came threads which have their place in the design of South African history, a design in which there has been no lack of colour and diversity. Yet that strife accounts only in part for the complexity of the South Africa of to-day. South Africa has not only been the meeting-place of Dutch and British; in it there have also come together European and African, Westerner and Oriental. To its tangled skein black Africa and yellow Asia have contributed many a thread, and much of the difficulty of modern South African problems arises from the very fact that, while men fixed their gaze on what seemed to be the main pattern, the relations namely between British and Dutch, the complication of the central design, the relations between men of diverse colours, was proceeding almost unnoticed. And although it is of great importance for the British Commonwealth of Nations that men of English and of Afrikaans speech should resolve their differences and attain unity of nationhood in the Union of South Africa, the establishment of a system whereunder European and African and Asiatic shall live together to the common advantage of all, is not only of more abiding significance for South Africa itself, but also compels the interested attention of the inhabitants of a far larger area of the earth's surface. It is, indeed, no exaggeration to say that in South Africa to-day are to be found the issues of good and evil for hundreds of millions of men throughout the world.

In this book the attempt will be made to show how men of diverse nationalities have come to meet in South Africa, and what have been the results of their meeting. So perhaps light will be cast on the historical forces which have produced

the South Africa of to-day, and have determined its significance for the modern world. We shall pass in review the
elements which went to the making up of the Afrikaner
people, and the circumstances which gave to it its predomi-
nant characteristics. Then we shall follow up the results of
the coming to South Africa of men of British stock, the enlargement of its boundaries, its dissidence into fragments, the
long struggle for the re-establishment of political unity, the
even slower growth of the tender plant of national unity.
And in the background we shall see the stage being set for the
main drama of Africa, the struggle to avoid the occurrence
of a tragic clash of colour. So then, having considered
the forces which have been at work, we shall be able to
regard South Africa in relation to its own national and
economic future, in relation to the continent of Africa, in
relation to the British Commonwealth of Nations, and in
relation to the world-problem of inter-racial relationships.

But first it will be necessary for us to examine the geographical environment in which the complex which to-day
we call South Africa has assumed its form, being not un-
mindful of the importance of physical factors in shaping the
lives of nations as of individual men.

Chapter 2

The Physical Background

I T IS on a large stage that the drama of South African history has been enacted. The area of the Union alone is eight times that of England and Wales, although its population of men of all colours is still under twelve millions. Spaciousness, a sense of freedom, the lavishness of nature in the exercise of her creative powers—these are the prevailing features of the South African scene. It is a land where great elemental natural forces have been at work, a fitting stage for the play and inter-play of no less elemental historical forces. And so, for all its magnitude, its structure admits of simple description. It is a great plateau, tilted up at its eastern end, so that the approach to it from the south or from the east is by a series of sharply-graded terraces to a mountain barrier, from beyond which it dips gradually to the Western ocean. Into relation with that general description may be brought a factor, special in character, but of fundamental importance for South Africa. As the plateau sinks, so the rainfall decreases. It is in the mountain belt, and on the southern and eastern terraces, that the precipitation is greatest. To westward of the mountains the rainfall becomes less and less as the Indian Ocean recedes, and in most of the western portion of the sub-continent arid and semi-arid conditions prevail.

Let us observe some of the physical features of the land which have done most to determine its history. First there is the central position of Africa in relation to the other great land-masses. That central position made of South Africa a meeting-place of nations, but it led also to its being regarded as a stage in the journey to other lands, rather than as a land to which men came for its own sake. It was as a half-way house to the treasures of the Indies that it was thought of, not as a final goal of endeavour, and when first men were sent from Europe to dwell there, they came, not as colonists, but simply to minister to the needs of those who passed it on their journeyings to and from the wealthier East. When the name Cape of Good Hope was first used, it was not with any reference to the land itself, but merely to the hope which it held out of a safe and profitable passage to the Indies. The history of South Africa as a settled community is not much shorter than that of the United States—the first cause of its relatively slow progress lies in that conception of it which, because of its central position, came to prevail in men's minds.

To this conception the land itself was slow in providing a corrective. It is no land of easy access, inviting entry into its interior. Its coastline consists very largely of cliffs and sandhills, and its river-mouths are for the most part blocked by bars of sand. Its shores are uninviting and dangerous, and are girt by stormy seas and strong currents. In natural harbours, like the continent of Africa as a whole, it is for the length of its coastline singularly deficient, and the best of those that it has are either on the west coast, where the rainfall is scantiest and the population least, or beyond that point where the Union ends and Portuguese East Africa commences. Like the rest of Africa, too, it suffers from lack of inland waterways. The courses of nearly all the African rivers are interrupted by cataracts; only a very few are navigable for more than 100 miles from the sea; none of these few are to be found in South Africa. On the eastern slopes of the mountains, where the rainfall is heaviest, the rivers are numerous, but they drop rapidly down the terraces to the sea. The greatest of these eastern rivers, the Limpopo, is impeded by falls 100 miles from its mouth, and is of little use for navigation. The western rivers make a more gradual descent, but for the most part they drain an area of slight and uncertain rainfall, and are therefore useless as waterways. Even the Orange, the largest of them all, actually loses more in evaporation in the last 800 miles of its course than it gains from the country through which it flows. Nor is the lack of navigable rivers made good by indentations, such as those which lend access almost to the heart of the continent of Europe. The ratio of length of coastline to area of territory is in the case of South Africa abnormally low.

These facts help us to understand why in South Africa settlement lagged so far behind discovery, why the traveller was encouraged in his desire to pass it by rather than to remain. Similar in its effect was the internal configuration of the country. If in the early days there was little to encourage men to land upon the South African coast, it was no easy matter for them, having once landed, to make their way into the interior. Within the coastline there presented themselves a succession of mountain ranges, and these run parallel to it, and not in such manner as to strike it at right angles, and so leave natural avenues of entry between them. For the early pioneer it was a toilsome approach to the interior plateau. From the west the ascent was by comparison gradual and easy, but the country to be traversed was barren and waterless. From the south and east range after range, standing out sheer and precipitous for the most part, had to be surmounted. Few lands have presented greater initial obstacles to colonization than has South Africa. Compare it with North America, and one notes the importance, in the case of the latter, at once of greater proximity to Europe, and of the innumerable lakes and rivers, which, with the Gulf of St. Lawrence, have been the highways of colonization, lending easy access to a plain that stretches unbrokenly to the Rocky Mountains. Compare it with Australia, and one observes how much better that continent is served with harbours, and how much less formidable are the obstacles which its mountain ranges present.

In other ways also geography has determined the history of the land and the character of the people of the land. Its physical characteristics have not encouraged its habitants to become a seafaring people, to find in the waterways the ways of their expansion. That explains why the South African nation of to-day, descended though it be from the sea-dogs of Holland and of England, has essentially a continental outlook, can with no measure of truth be described as a maritime people. The configuration of the land made the early Dutch settlers turn their backs upon the sea, and the adventurous spirit of the Dutch sailor, who had braved hostile attacks and the uncharted dangers of strange coasts, found a new embodiment in the pioneer for whom savage

foes and wild beasts had no terrors, whose response to the
call of the unknown opened up a great new era for European
settlement.

In that spirit, in due season, men forced their way up
the mountain terraces from the south-western coastlands on
to the interior plateau; and when they had reached it, the
land again imposed itself upon their life and character.
For its physical features led them to spread themselves over
a wide area, made isolation and solitude their portion, and
developed in them that resolute individualism which was to
become a determining factor in South African history. The
plateau, with its absence of marked natural features, encouraged men to roam at will over its wide expanse; moreover it offered but scanty opportunity for that intensive
agriculture which provides the basis for men's congregation
together. That portion of the plateau into which the
pioneers first came is an area of low rainfall—the average is
some fifteen inches annually, but over much of it the fall is
under ten inches. What rainfall there is, is variable and
intermittent. There is great difference between one year
and the next; evaporation is considerable; and most of
the rain comes in the form of heavy thunder showers with a
quick run-off. Furthermore, the rivers are of little value for
purposes of irrigation, save on a large and costly scale.
Most of them alternate between flood and drought, and run
in deep channels. So then it was that the first inhabitants
of the plateau turned to pastoral pursuits, confining their
cultivation of the land within the narrowest of limits. They
passed beyond the range of community influences, learnt to
' desire loneliness,' came to love the life of restless wandering.

In such circumstances the settlement of the interior could
not be rapid—nature had, so it seemed, done but little to
assist its colonization. It is true that the portions of the
plateau which lay nearer the eastern mountains and enjoyed
a more generous rainfall, those portions where grasslands
take the place of the stunted Karroo-bush of its southern and
western areas, offered considerable inducement to agricultural development, but they were not reached until well
into the nineteenth century. It is true also that the soil of
the plateau is on the whole rich, and that in limited areas it
admits of exploitation by irrigation projects, but such

advances could not be made until the nation had grown in
numbers and in material resources, till the engineer had
provided the means of communication which nature had
withheld, till the increase of urban population offered inland
markets for the products of agriculture.

For the satisfaction of these conditions nature in South
Africa also had the means at her disposal. Though she had
not endowed the land with agricultural wealth admitting
of easy exploitation, she was certainly prodigal in the gifts of
mineral wealth. Both in precious and in base metals the
sub-continent has great resources, and when in the fulness of
time its diamond mines and its gold mines were discovered,
there were created at once the necessity and the means for
the building of railways into the interior; large urban
centres sprang up; money became available for irrigation
projects and other schemes of development. Thus were
laid the foundations of agricultural prosperity, and in this
way nature, which had placed so many difficulties in the
way of South Africa's advance, also provided the means of
resolving those difficulties. But since its mineral wealth
had for the most part been stored, not in those regions in
which European colonization first established itself, but in
the inaccessible interior, the difficulties remained unsolved
until South Africa had fallen behind in the race with other
lands, where the records of settlement go back to the same or
to an even less remote date.

Many of its physical disabilities South Africa shares with
the rest of the African continent; in one respect, of great
importance for history, it enjoys a considerable advantage—
that is, in the healthiness of its climate. The bulk of the
African continent is tropical. Of its eleven and a half
million square miles of area only four millions, mainly
desert, lie outside of Cancer and Capricorn. In most of
the remainder intense heat and tropical diseases have
impeded colonization, though not necessarily exploitation.
But South Africa falls mainly in the South Temperate Zone,
and it must not be forgotten that the South Temperate
Zone is, in general, cooler than its northern counterpart.
The summer heat of Capetown, lying 34 degrees south, is
considerably less oppressive than that of Tripoli, which is
equally far north; for its equivalent we must go close on

twelve degrees still further north, to South Central France. Of the Union of South Africa only a relatively small portion is tropical, and though all of Rhodesia lies within the tropics, much of it is high-lying, and therefore healthy. The plateau region in general—and three-fifths of the total area of the Union lies between 3,000 and 5,000 feet above sea-level—offers no climatic disabilities to the European settler and the European worker. The dryness of the plateau air and its height above the sea temper the heat of summer; moreover, it has the characteristics of what is known as a continental climate, in that it is subject to greater extremes of temperature than are found in regions exposed to maritime influences. The nights are nearly always cool—in winter they may be very cold. On the Witwatersrand, within three degrees of the tropics, and in the region between it and the eastern mountains, snow is by no means uncommon, and winter frosts are regular. But rain seldom falls in winter on the plateau. The winter months offer almost unbroken sunshine. Johannesburg enjoys seventy-three per cent. of the possible hours of sunshine in the twelve months as against London's twenty-nine. In the coast-belt the rainfall is greater—in the west and south-west more rain falls in winter than in summer—and the climate is damper and less bracing, but it is not until Zululand is reached that it begins to threaten the health of the European. In Portuguese East Africa, and in the lowveld areas of the Transvaal, which lie to the east of the mountains, fever is still an enemy. But it recedes steadily, as European settlement advances.

So, then, South Africa is predominantly a healthy land, a land also of prevailing sunshine, where men live naturally in the open air, but with a diversity bracing enough to promote physical and mental health. The South African youth grows rapidly to maturity, is sturdy and self-reliant, inclined to give his affection rather to outdoor activities than to intellectual pursuits, but gaining from his contact with nature much that in other lands he would miss. As for the South African of maturer years, since, as the country has become more thickly populated, he has developed gregarious instincts, the opportunities which climatic conditions provide for the satisfaction of those instincts have made him, perhaps, as politically-minded as is the citizen of any country

in the world. There is, indeed, much in South Africa—
especially in the countryside—to recall the political-minded-
ness of the ancient Greeks, which sprang from the fact that
they, too, were a people of the open air.

Enough has been said in this brief sketch of its physical
characteristics to suggest that South Africa is a land of great
variety and diversity. As constitutive factors in that
diversity there are, not only its extent, but also the fact of its
division into areas of summer and winter rainfall, with great
variations in the amount of precipitation within each of those
areas, and the considerable elevation of a large part of its
interior. Of its two largest cities, one is at the coast, the
other at a height of close on 6,000 feet above sea-level.
The traveller journeys inland from Capetown through the
smiling valleys of the Western Province, well-watered by
mountain streams, and enjoying a good and on the whole
well-distributed rainfall. The train struggles up a mountain
pass, and he finds himself in a portion of the Karroo, where
semi-arid conditions prevail, and sometimes year succeeds
year without more than an inch or two of rain falling on the
thirsty land. Or he starts out from Pretoria, and travels
over a high table-land with only gentle undulations, bleak
and frost-bitten in winter, green and restful to the eye in
summer, but with no natural trees to lend it diversity.
Then he starts descending. In sixty miles he has dropped
4,000 feet, and he finds himself in a different world, a world
of tropical heat and vegetation, combining wonderful
mountain scenery with the rich growth of valley and plain.
Perhaps he will stand on a high peak in the mountain-knot of
Basutoland. Eastward he will see the green land of Natal,
falling in terraces to the sea, endless in its variety of hill and
wooded gorge and pleasant river-valley, the most English
portion of South Africa in some aspects of its scenery, as in
other things; westward he looks out over the endless plains
of the Free State, which nature seems to have forgotten to
diversify.

These are the chief characteristics of the land as a whole.
It will perhaps be most convenient to indicate at this point
the main features of its constituent parts, taking for ease of
reference the political sub-divisions which exist to-day.
Of the four Provinces into which the Union of South Africa

is divided, the Province of the Cape of Good Hope is the largest and the oldest in European settlement. In its diversity it is almost as remarkable as is South Africa itself. Most of the Union's coast-belt, and therewith three of its four harbour-towns—Capetown, Port Elizabeth, and East London—fall within its limits. In that coast-belt are included some of the best-favoured parts of South Africa. In most of it, though not in the north-western strip, the rainfall is good, but there are considerable stretches where adequacy of rainfall is neutralized by deficiencies of soil. Yet it embraces the Western Province, with its wealth of wine and fruit and corn, the fertile and well-watered Transkeian territories, and the most thickly-peopled districts of the Eastern Province. Away from the coast-belt stretch the mountain terraces and the plain of the Karroo, regions where, save in times of unusual drought, sheep thrive on the stunted Karroo-bush, an area, therefore, of vast sheep-runs, diversified, however, by agricultural settlements, where irrigation has made it possible to turn the rich soil of the plateau to its due account. Towards the north of the plateau, beyond the Orange River, lies Kimberley, the one considerable urban community of the Cape Province away from the coast, the town of diamond mines, with its hectic past, its uncertain future.

The other coast province, that of Natal, is far smaller than the Cape. It is a pleasant, well-watered land, with, as it rises sharply to the mountains from one terrace to the next, a great variety of climate in a comparatively limited area, and therefore a wide range of productivity. It yields tropical and sub-tropical crops as well as the fruits and cereals of the temperate zone, while over considerable areas sheep-raising and cattle-farming are pursued with success. It is also relatively well-timbered, and has in its northern districts a large coalfield. Moreover, its port of Durban, which has a considerable share of the trade of the interior, brings it much wealth. But not least important of its geographical features is its isolation. A semicircular mountain-range separates it from the interior. For all too long in its history it tended to be sundered from the rest of South Africa by mutual ignorance and mountains.

Of the interior provinces, the Orange Free State is the

smaller. It consists almost entirely of an extension of the
interior plateau running up to the eastern mountains. In
the south its plain is covered with Karroo-bush, in the north
with grass. For the most part it is a vast grazing ground,
but the eastern portion of it, where the rainfall is good, and
to a less extent some of the central districts, have lent themselves to the development of agriculture; maize, and in the
south-west wheat, are grown with considerable success.
In the Free State until recently, when an area of rich gold
reefs was discovered, there was little mineral development.

Larger and of greater diversity is the Province of Transvaal, with its gold-mining industry, the largest in the world,
which has created the vigorous community of the Witwatersrand, its great diamond mine, the Premier, near Pretoria,
the Union's administrative capital, its rich coal belt, and all
its other resources of base metals, the exploitation of which
is only beginning. The southern portion of the Transvaal consists of grasslands, offering good pasturage, and
admitting, especially as the rainfall improves to the eastward, of the profitable cultivation of maize. Northwards
the plateau descends gradually into bushveld, with richer
and more varied vegetation, affording excellent grazing for
cattle, and in parts inviting tillage, especially of tobacco,
cotton, citrus, and wheat. North-eastward, below the
mountain ranges, stretches a considerable area of lowveld,
much of which is well supplied with water, and capable of
extensive irrigation. In that area the danger of fever has
impeded the intensive development of agriculture, but in
recent years the danger has been almost entirely eliminated.

Attached to the Union is the mandated territory of South-
West Africa, which is itself six times as large as England and
Wales. It rises from a desert coastal strip, through a series
of grassy terraces, to a plateau of Karroo type, changing to
the northwards first into park-like grasslands, and later into
dense bush. Primarily it is a cattle-raising country.

There should be mentioned the three Protectorates of
Basutoland, Bechuanaland, and Swaziland. Of these,
Basutoland consists almost entirely of a jumble of mountains,
producing grain in rich, well-watered valleys, and raising
cattle, sheep, and horses; Swaziland has, in addition to a
mountainous region, a productive lowveld area on its

eastern side; Bechuanaland, by far the largest of the three, falls entirely within the interior plateau of South Africa; in the east it is fairly fertile and occasionally well-wooded, towards the west mainly sandy and waterless. Basutoland is about the size of Belgium, Swaziland is nearly as large as Wales, while Bechuanaland has three times the area of Great Britain.

Finally must be mentioned the Union's neighbours to east and north, Portuguese East Africa, a fertile low-lying land, and Southern Rhodesia, which reproduces many of the features of the country to the south of it, while it marks the transition to more tropical conditions.

Such in its vastness and its diversity is South Africa, no easy oyster for men's opening, rich indeed in mineral and agricultural potentialities, but not laying out its store to be carried away save after long and toilsome effort; a pleasant, health-giving land, but one which has imposed the endurance of hardness as a condition of the enjoyment of its best gifts; a land of many difficulties and much questioning, always perplexing, sometimes discouraging, but a land wide, free, expansive, varied in its beauty, liberating in its atmosphere, challenging in its prospects, and in the last resort no ungenerous rewarder of those who give themselves to its service.

Chapter 3

The Tavern of the Seas

I T WAS the strife of men, strife between peoples, strife between religions, that first brought European civilization to South Africa. Its coming was part of the reaction to that mighty onrush of Islamism, which carried it northwards and eastwards into Asia, southwards down Africa's eastern coast, westwards into the Mediterranean area, and up through the Iberian peninsula into the plains of France. Gradually the tide receded. Step by step Spaniards and Portuguese won back their homeland from the Moors. In 1415 the reaction carried them into enemy country. In that year, the year of Agincourt, the Portuguese took Ceuta, twin guardian with Gibraltar of the Mediterranean gate. Europe had resumed the exploitation of Africa.

The spirit of the Crusades, which constant struggle with infidel Moors kept alive in Portugal and Spain long after it had spent itself elsewhere, kindled enthusiasm for the continuance of the enterprise. That spirit found embodiment in Prince Henry, soon to be called the Navigator, second son of Portugal's King, and grandson of John of Gaunt. The attack on Ceuta had been a success, but the cost was heavy, and the difficulty of a frontal attack on Islam had been revealed. It seemed obvious strategy to outflank the enemy, to open a way round Africa, to make touch with the Christian King, Prester John, of whose power and magnificence men spoke with bated breath, to tap the rich wealth of the Indies, whence came much of Islam's strength. So would great work be done ' for the glory of God and the profit of Portugal.'

To that work Prince Henry gave himself. He withdrew from the Court, built an observatory on the promontory of Sagres, established a maritime research station, and organized voyages of discovery to the southward. A toilsome and disheartening enterprise it proved to be. Many a voyage ended in disaster; the ships that returned mourned many a comrade lost; and it was not without reason that Pope Nicholas V granted absolution in advance to all who took part in the new Crusade. When the Prince died in 1460, Sierra Leone was the furthest point of his captains' voyagings. On his death followed a period of stagnation. Twenty years later King John II of Portugal resumed the enterprise. In 1485 Diego Cam reached the mouth of the Congo; next year Bartholomew Diaz rounded the southernmost point of Africa, and only the timidity of his sailors prevented him from continuing his voyage beyond Algoa Bay to the goal of the Navigator's desires. More fortunate was Vasco da Gama, who on Christmas Day, 1497, gave its name to Natal, and a few months later cast anchor off the coast of India. It was a great achievement—it is made no less so by our acceptance (and there is no adequate ground for doubt) of Herodotus's story of the circumnavigation of Africa by Necho's Phoenicians 2,100 years before.

So, then, it was Portugal that first among the nations of modern Europe came to Africa, and before long she was mistress of its eastern and western coasts. True, the Portuguese made but few contacts with the harbourless and relatively unproductive lands to south and west of Delagoa Bay. They had come to Africa to fight the infidels of the Crescent. They found them on the east coast as far south as Sofala, hardly in any numbers below that point. That region was, therefore, the first goal of their endeavours. To it, having displaced the Arabs, they directed their outward voyages. And the death of their great Viceroy, Francisco d'Almeida, at the hands of Hottentots on the shores of Table Bay in 1510, gave them additional cause, if such were needed, to avoid the stormy and uninviting southern coasts. Yet it is not without its significance in the history of South Africa that Portugal should have been the pioneer in African waters. For Portugal was but a small nation, too weak for schemes of land dominion, but keenly alive to commercial opportunity. Of effective colonization in Africa there could be no question; the exploitation of its resources was all that mattered; to that end the labour of African slaves provided the obvious means. That conception of the development of Africa came to prevail in men's minds, and to it much in modern South Africa goes back.

Religious strife had brought the Portuguese to the south and the east; religious strife gave the impetus to the next step in the opening up of Africa. It started with the struggles between Philip of Spain, who in 1580 annexed Portugal, and the Protestant nations of the north. These struggles established the maritime greatness of England and Holland, and sent forth their mariners on adventurous voyages to break the Spanish and Portuguese commercial monopolies. In 1580 Drake rounded the Cape of Good Hope; in 1591 James Lancaster set foot ashore in Table Bay; four years later Cornelis de Houtman, first amongst the Dutch, sailed round the Cape to Java. It is not without its significance for the future that, while Diaz had named the Cape of Good Hope the Cape of Storms, d'Almeida had been murdered in Table Bay, and Portuguese mariners had for a century dreaded and avoided the southern shores of Africa. Drake in his Journal denied the Portuguese report of the dangers of the Cape, calling it ' a most statelie thing, and the fairest Cape we saw in the whole circumference of the earth.' Lancaster spoke appreciatively of the ' goodlie baie ' at the base of Table Mountain, and de Houtman's men reported with enthusiasm on the beauty and the attractions of the new land of the south. And indeed that land held far more in store for English and Dutch than for its Portuguese discoverers.

These voyages laid the foundation of the systematic exploitation of the Indian trade. In 1600 the English East India Company was founded; two years later various competing Dutch companies merged into the Dutch East India Company, with its four Chambers representing six different towns, its capital of over £500,000, as compared with the English Company's £30,000, and its powerful governing body, the Council of Seventeen. It might almost have been described as the Dutch nation organized for purposes of commercial expansion, and great indeed was the power which it secured. Spaniards and Portuguese were all but driven off the Indian Ocean; with the English there existed an alliance, but their thoughts were divided between the trade of North America and that of the East, and to an increasing extent they were limited, as far as the East was concerned, to what the Dutch regarded as the less attractive sphere of exploitation offered by the Indian Peninsula.

For these Dutch and English mariners, and for the Frenchmen who followed in their wake, Table Bay assumed steadily growing importance. The route which they found most convenient for the outward voyage lay along the west coast of Africa to Sierra Leone, then across to Brazil, down the South American coast, and thence eastwards to the southern extremity of Africa, leaving St. Helena hundreds of miles to port. And while the Portuguese had sailed up the south-east coast of Africa, and availed themselves of its harbours to the northwards, the Dutch, and in the first instance the English, had as their goal not East Africa and South India, but the East Indian Islands, and to reach that goal their best course lay well to the south of Madagascar. Those were days when ships were small and voyages long, when therefore, on so extended a run as that between the South American coast and Batavia, some place must be found to take in fresh water and meat, and to seek relief and refreshment from the toil of seventeenth-century seafaring. For all this there was no place so convenient as Table Bay. For Dutch and English therefore it held an inducement which it lacked for the Portuguese, and so it became a fixed point on the outward voyage. As for the homeward voyage, the route followed was different, and St. Helena might have been a convenient port of call, but at Table Bay alone could contacts be made with those who brought news from the homeland. To that latter end it came to be customary to leave letters under so-called ' post-office stones,' to be called for by ships that voyaged in the opposite direction.

It was natural enough, then, that the project of establishing a permanent post in Table Valley should have come up for discussion, and again it is not without its significance for future history that in 1619 the Council of Seventeen should have discussed with the Directors of the English Company the possibility of a joint settlement. Nothing came of it, and in 1620 two officers of the English Company, Shilling and FitzHerbert, annexed the coasts abutting on Table Bay and the land beyond in the name of King James I. But His Stuart Majesty had other things to think of, the annexation was not confirmed, and in the years that followed, as the

English Company's main interest in the East shifted from the islands to the Indian Peninsula, and its ships therefore began to follow the old Portuguese route up the East African coast, Table Bay became of less importance to it. It was left for the Dutch to found the first European settlement on South African soil.

That did not, however, take place until 1652. Holland was then at the height of her political and commercial power, and of her intellectual and artistic greatness. In 1648 the Peace of Munster had set the seal on her eighty years of struggle for freedom, and Holland held her place among the leading powers of Europe. Her commercial fleet was larger than that of any other nation. The wealth of the East she held in fee. For the launching of a new enterprise the time was more than opportune. So then when, in 1649, the shipwrecked company of the *Haarlem*, which had spent a year in Table Valley, brought back favourable reports on the possibility of a settlement, the Seventeen decided to establish there ' a rendezvous and a stronghold.' As leader of the enterprise with the title of Commander, they chose a ship's surgeon, Jan van Riebeeck, young in years, but old in journeyings, keen, vigorous, practical, but with a vision and an imagination not unworthy of a people which had marked out the whole wide world for its activity. On Saturday, 6th April, 1652, the three ships that bore van Riebeeck and his men, *Dromedaris*, *Reiger*, and *Goede Hoop*, anchored in Table Bay.

It is no part of the plan of this book to tell the whole story of the Cape under the Dutch East India Company, or, indeed, of any subsequent period of its history. It will be sufficient to seek to follow up those historical forces which are important for the understanding of the South Africa of to-day. First, with that end in view, it will be necessary to consider the conception of the settlement in the minds of its creators, and the extent to which that conception was modified with the passing of the years.

It must not be forgotten that the settlement at the Cape was not the enterprise of a colonizing nation. The Dutch community was small—it had no surplus population to send forth for the founding of new homes in strange lands. And in its oversea activities its policy was directed, not by the national government, but by a commercial corporation. However patriotic that corporation was, it was bound to regard commercial gain as its primary object. It was purely to serve commercial ends that the settlement in Table Valley was founded. Its success in meeting those ends, its effect on the Company's balance sheet—these were the factors to be considered in determining its character and in shaping its future.

The purpose of the Company in sending van Riebeeck to the Cape was the establishment of a refreshment station for the men sailing on its ships to and from the Indies. With that end in view his instructions were expressed with due precision. He was to build a fort for the protection of the water supply, and for the accommodation of a garrison and of such sick sailors as might, from time to time, be landed in Table Bay. He was to lay out gardens and orchards, so that there might be no lack of refreshment for the ships. He was, by friendly barter with the natives, to provide for an adequate supply of meat for that same purpose. And finally he was to keep expenditure as low as possible, and, if he could, find the means to show a profit.

These ends, including the provision of agricultural and pastoral products, the Company thought, could all be achieved by the labour of men in its direct employment. All those whom it sent out with van Riebeeck were its own servants—no one of them was to have the freedom of the colonist to strike out for himself in a new land. Colonization was not part of the Company's programme. Its efforts in that direction in the East had not been successful. What mattered to it was trade, and it had no desire that there should be anyone who might threaten its monopoly. But official farming in the first few years of the settlement was not successful. The supplies of cattle offered by the natives for barter were uncertain; the production of corn by the Company's officers was inadequate, and food had to be imported. Table Valley, it was clear, could not produce all that was required. It was imperative that the settlement should be extended round the mountain to the south-eastwards. That, however, meant an increase in the number of defenders necessary for its protection; it meant also an increase in the number of productive workers. In the interests of economy, therefore, van Riebeeck recommended that grants of land should be made to free burghers, and the Company adopted his recommendation. In 1657 the first nine land-grants were made to men who had come out in the Company's service, and the settlement became a Colony. But adequate steps were taken to safeguard the Company's interests. The free burghers were to do garrison duty; on their produce the Company was to have first call at fixed prices; what the Company did not take they might dispose of to visiting ships, but only after the Company had enjoyed a selling monopoly for the first three days after arrival; they were restricted in the bartering of cattle from the natives, for fear that under competition the price to the Company might rise; they were forbidden to grow tobacco, lest the Company's profits from importation and sale might decline.

It is not to be wondered at that in circumstances such as these the growth of the Cape as a Colony was slow. The Company's restrictions were severe; the number of visiting ships was small; such trade as was free was most precarious. Already in 1658 there was what might be described as a strike of the free burghers to protest against being, as they described it, ' slaves of the Company.' As late as 1672 there were not more than sixty-four of them, none dwelling beyond the limits of the Cape Peninsula. Of immigration to South Africa of Colonists from Holland and elsewhere there was still no question; the free burghers were all recruited from the ranks of the Company's servants at the Cape.

But in the last quarter of the century there came a change in the policy of the Company. The Seventeen began to look with favour upon projects of colonization in the East and elsewhere; at the Cape the Company's farming operations did not yet yield satisfactory results; cattle-barter with the natives was still precarious; the production of the free burghers was not yet sufficient for the needs of the settlement and of visiting ships. Moreover, the war with Louis XIV made it necessary to increase the number of the Cape's defenders against a possible French attack, and on financial grounds it was desirable that such an increase should be effected without the expansion of the already costly garrison. So, then, a policy was adopted which aimed at the extension of the Colony, and an increase in the number of Colonists; and as the instrument of that policy Simon van der Stel was appointed Commander in 1679. Already in the previous year a tentative commencement had been made with the grant of grazing rights to free burghers outside of the Cape Peninsula. Van der Stel, who was fired with the ideal of a new Holland in the south, advanced vigorously in the direction indicated to him. Shortly after his arrival, he founded the village of Stellenbosch in the Eerste River valley, and apportioned the district round it in farms. To the task of securing suitable Colonists he applied himself with enthusiasm. Settlers from Holland were given free passages, and Company's servants, whether in the Cape command or on their way to or from the Indies, were encouraged to take their discharge and, with it, a grant of land. The result was a steady annual increase in the number of Colonists. By 1687 the free burgher population had grown to 573; by 1707 to 1,641.

But the results of the van der Stel policy were not satisfactory in all respects. True, the desired increase in production was secured, and the free burghers proved themselves well able to meet all the Company's needs, so much so that its own agricultural activities were steadily restricted, and even the right of cattle-barter was eventually given to the burghers with a view to their supplying the meat that was required. But the market for which they were producing was an inelastic one, and before long supply began to outrun demand. The number of consumers resident in the settlement, other than those for whom the Company purchased, was small. The inadequacy as a harbour of Table Bay, with its 2,000 deaths by shipwreck between 1650 and 1800, militated against its popularity, and on the average there were only forty-four visiting ships each year. High freights made competition in the markets of Europe and the East Indies exceedingly difficult. Moreover, the incurably monopolistic tendencies of the Company seriously hampered the free development of trade. Quite apart from the special protection of its own interests as a purchaser, it embarked upon a policy of letting out concessions for the right of retailing various commodities, and so still further restricted the activities of the free burghers.

B

The economic difficulties which resulted from all these circumstances led to the first serious political disturbance in the history of the Colony, and through it to the abandonment of the policy of colonization. Simon van der Stel, whose post had been raised to the rank of a Governorship, was succeeded in 1699 by his son, Willem Adriaan, and he, though in many respects an enlightened ruler, pursued a course of action which could not but precipitate a crisis. Together with his chief officials and members of his family, he embarked on large-scale farming undertakings, and secured the most important contracts and concessions for his own creatures. To the free burghers, hampered as they already were by the restrictions on their market, the competition of the Governor and his associates, producing under specially favourable conditions with freedom from taxation, was the last straw. A movement was launched to secure his recall. Van der Stel countered it by arresting Adam Tas and other leaders, and deporting some of them to Holland and Batavia. But when the facts had been investigated by the Seventeen, they gave their decision in favour of the Colonists, and in 1707 van der Stel's Governorship was terminated.

The struggle had been one between the officials, who represented the original conception of the settlement's purpose, and the Colonists, who stood for the enlarged view of it which had come to be held. For the moment the Colonists won, but to the policy of Colonial expansion their victory brought a definite set-back. To the Directors it seemed as if the difficulties in which they had been involved were the result of the despatch of immigrants to the Cape. It was a mistake, so it seemed to them, which must not be continued, and the policy of assisted immigration was definitely terminated. Immigrants, it is true, still continued to trickle through to the Cape until the end of the Company's rule, but they came on their own initiative, and the growth of the free burgher population was mainly in the form of natural increase.

Yet during this period of Colonial expansion (1679–1706) the character of the settlement had been definitely fixed. It had been founded as a revictualling station, and nothing more; it had become a Colony, and the course of evolution had been set which was to end in the acknowledgment of its free nationhood in the British Commonwealth. It had been started upon a path from which there could be no recall. The economic difficulties of the Colonists continued to be great—the monopolistic policy of the Company endured until the end, and until the end also, though the home market gradually improved, high freights hampered the export trade—but their steady growth in numbers, in prosperity, and in the sense of national distinctiveness could not be checked. Van Riebeeck, when he pressed for permission to make land-grants to free burghers, van der Stel, when he secured the despatch of immigrants for the building up of a Colony, took determinative steps in the history of South Africa, and laid the foundations of a structure far greater than they could ever have contemplated.

But if the Cape was to be a Colony, it was to be a Colony built on a foundation of black labour. In this new land, with its Mediterranean climate, there was no physical reason, any more than was later to be found in Australia, to prevent development on a purely European basis. But there was the Portuguese tradition, which made men think of Africa as a continent in which only black men could do the hard manual work, and there was the fact that in the East the Company had become accustomed to the employment of slaves. It was the custom of the age to exploit negro labour. The institution of slavery spread therefore almost without question to the Cape. During the first few years of the settlement's existence the manual work was all done by Europeans, with only a negligible amount of assistance from hired native labour. Then the monopolistic policy pursued by the Company in relation to the free burghers precipitated the issue. One of the grievances of the ' strikers ' of 1658 was that the prices fixed by the Company as payable by itself for their produce were too low in relation to the cost of labour. A substantial increase in price van Riebeeck refused to contemplate; it seemed far more economical to approach the difficulty from the other end, to cheapen the cost of labour by the importation of slaves. So it was that in 1658 ships were sent to the Guinea coast for slaves; pending their return, a cargo of Angolese from a captured Portuguese vessel was readily snapped up. Some slaves the

Company kept for its own use; others it issued to the free
burghers on a credit basis. Thus were the foundations of
South African agriculture laid in the shifting sands of slave
labour.

The first experiment in the importation of slaves gave only
limited satisfaction. To the West African natives the
prospect of reaching their homes overland seemed far from
remote, and many of them fled their masters. But importation continued, and slaves from Madagascar and the East,
chiefly from the Malay Archipelago, took the place of the
runaways. Steadily the number grew: in 1687 there were
274 adults and 36 children; in 1708 there were 1,107 adults
and 151 children. The form of slavery was on the whole a
mild one. The Government punished owners who ill-used
their slaves; it was part of its policy to Christianize them;
manumissions were frequent; and those who were skilled
tradesmen were given the opportunity to earn money
wherewith to buy their freedom. As an institution slavery
at the Cape gave every promise of stability; yet there were
those who doubted whether its continuance was in the best
interests of the Colony.

The troubles between Willem Adriaan van der Stel and
the burghers forced the Directors of the Company to give
more thought to the affairs of the Cape than they had done
for many a day. Of the working of the settlement they took
careful stock, and as the result of their consideration they
submitted in the year 1716 various questions to their
Governor, Mauritz Pasques de Chavonnes, and his Council,
with a view to the determination of future policy. One of
their questions was whether European farm-hands and
agriculturists would not be less expensive than slaves. It
was a question of far greater significance for the future of
South Africa than the Lords Seventeen ever dreamed. For
though to them it arose merely as a matter of financial
policy, at the root of it lay the issue whether free white or
servile coloured labour was to be the foundation of the
Colony's economic structure.

On this point de Chavonnes and his Council were all but
unanimous. They confined themselves to a strict interpretation of the question as put to them, and on that basis they
proceeded to answer it. The annual charges in respect of a

slave were, so they said, on a high estimate sixty gulden; the
free labourer would cost in food and wages, at the very
lowest, three times as much, and 'a European's wages
would have to be raised from time to time, and thus cost our
Masters more and more.' Moreover, there was in the matter
of obedience and pliability a great difference in favour of
the slave; European labourers were lazy and addicted to
drink, and 'we are amply provided with drunkards to keep
our hands full'; they would not be as useful as slaves in
farm work, 'especially in the daily menial tasks; besides it
is more fitting that slaves rather than Europeans should be
used.' 'I cannot,' wrote one of the Councillors, 'understand who has dared to trouble our Masters with such a
useless suggestion.'

One there was, however, whose voice was as of one crying
in the wilderness. He was the Governor's brother, the
officer commanding the garrison, Captain Dominique de
Chavonnes. With sound insight he saw that at the root of
the Colony's economic difficulties was the inadequacy of its
home market. For that the remedy could only be found in
an increase in its European population. 'If the further
importation of slaves were prohibited,' he wrote, 'and
people were gradually to accustom themselves to employ
Europeans or Dutchmen born in this country, as farm
labourers, etc., I am certain that it would be of advantage
to the Company, the country, and the inhabitants. . . .
These wage-earners all contribute to the revenue of the
Company, and the welfare of the country. The money
spent on slaves, on the other hand, goes out of the country
to its loss, and no money transactions can be expected from
slaves. . . . They [the wage-earners] would help the
Colonists by increasing the money-circulation, which is the
foundation of every country's prosperity.' Other advantages he proceeded to point out—two Europeans could perform the work done by three slaves, and they required less
supervision—their employment would produce greater
tranquillity, and facilitate a reduction in the garrison with,
of course, a saving to the Company—not least important,
it would make for the breaking up of the large farms into
small holdings, for 'generally speaking, the inhabitants have
much larger properties than they can conveniently manage.'

When the commander of the garrison wrote these wise words, the economic structure of the Colony was still plastic. Slavery was not yet deeply rooted; the native of the country had not yet become an indispensable servant of the white man; a white man's country in the full sense of the term could still have been built up in this land with its temperate climate. But Dominique de Chavonnes was a century, or more, before his time, and the views of the majority prevailed. Not only did the Company adhere to the policy of giving no encouragement to European settlement; it allowed the institution of slavery to take firm root, and the slave population grew steadily, until the number of slaves exceeded the number of free burghers. Of the result Baron van Imhoff, Governor-General of Batavia, who visited the Cape in 1743, may be left to speak. ' There is,' he wrote, ' another serious drawback to agriculture, which in my opinion cannot be easily remedied. I refer to the want of ordinary farmers or labourers and farm hands. The want is general, and by reason of the high wages and heavy expenses entailed by keeping so many slaves on the plantations it becomes a burden to the whole community.' He went on to point out that the apparent cheapness of black unskilled labour has as its complement excessively high wages paid to the European skilled worker, ' who does not do as much as a half-trained artisan in Europe.' He continued : ' It is a burden this Colony cannot bear, and it certainly has a prejudicial effect on agriculture. I believe it would have been far better, had we, when this Colony was founded, commenced with Europeans, and brought them hither in such numbers, that hunger and want would have forced them to work. But having imported slaves, every common or ordinary European becomes a gentleman, and prefers to be served rather than to serve. We have in addition the fact that the majority of the farmers in the Colony are not farmers in the real sense of the word, but owners of plantations, and that many of them consider it a shame to work with their own hands.'

Thus wrote de Chavonnes and van Imhoff before the middle of the eighteenth century. In the nineteen-twenties very similar statements were destined to be made about South African economics, and sometimes the enthusiasm

which ordinarily attends the proclamation of a new truth
has characterized the making of them. For though slavery
passed away, the white man's prejudice against what had
come to be regarded as work which the black man should do
endured, and, indeed, it was strengthened by the largeness
of the number of the black men who were available to do
that work. The introduction of slave labour was perhaps
the most fateful event in South African history.

So, then, there developed two elements in the population
which gathered round the Tavern of the Seas—on the one
side, a European people of Company's servants, farmers,
traders, and skilled artizans, on the other side, coloured men
whose lot it was to be the hewers of wood and the drawers of
water. For the understanding of the South Africa that was
to be, it will be necessary to consider each of these elements a
little more closely. Neither was homogeneous in origin;
both became so as the years advanced.

Right from the start the European population at the Cape
was of a mixed character. Holland, as has already been
said, had no large population to draw from, and the East
India Company found it increasingly difficult to recruit all
the men it needed from within the United Provinces. As a
result men of many nations entered its service. Germans in
particular were numerous, but there were also Swedes and
others from Northern Europe, including some from the
British Isles. From its earliest years, therefore, there was at
the Cape a cosmopolitan community, and wide also were the
contacts with the outside world which the sea gave to it.
Steadily, if slowly, the number of English, French, and
Danish vessels casting anchor in Table Bay increased, and
the flags of other nations were also seen.

Of the first nine free burghers of 1657 some were Germans,
and that was true also of their successors. When with the
appointment of van der Stel a policy of assisted immigration
was adopted, and the Directors were hard put to it to persuade men to leave prosperous Holland and settle in an undeveloped land, they were glad to find a number of Germans
who were willing to go out. Quite naturally, also, they
availed themselves of the opportunity presented by the
Revocation of the Edict of Nantes to strengthen the Colony's
population by the despatch to it of Huguenot refugees. To

these Huguenots the offer was made of free passages for themselves and their families, on the understanding that they would settle at the Cape, and earn a living there, either by farming, or by the fruits of their industry, knowledge, handiwork, or trade. To those who took up farming there was further offered as much land in freehold as they could cultivate, and the loan of all necessary articles for farming, such as seed-corn and oxen, to be repaid in corn or other produce, as occasion might offer. On this basis not quite 200 Huguenots came out; their coming meant much to the infant Colony. For, small though the number might seem, it was large relatively, since it represented an addition of about one-quarter to the existing free burgher population. The new immigrants who, by virtue of their history, might be regarded as picked men, had no fatherland to return to, and this brought stability to the settlement. Their influence was, therefore, quite disproportionate to their numbers.

Simon van der Stel cordially welcomed these industrious settlers, many of whom were skilled viticulturists, and established them, some in the Eerste River valley, but most further inland at Drakenstein, in the valley of the Berg River, from where in due course they spread still further afield to Wagenmakers Vallei (Wellington), and the ' Land van Waveren ' (Tulbagh). He and his son were, however, determined to maintain the Dutch character of the settlement, the more so as war with France was an ever-present danger, and when the Huguenots had come to constitute what they thought was a sufficiently high proportion of the population, they pressed the Directors to send out no more Frenchmen. As a result aided French immigration came to an end, although until 1706 Dutch and German settlers were still assisted to go out.

After the cessation of the main stream of immigration the ranks of the free burghers continued to be recruited from amongst the retired servants of the Company, together with occasional settlers from Europe. Of these newcomers some were Frenchmen; Swedes also there were, and Danes, and other North Europeans; but most came from Holland and Germany. Actually more Germans than Dutch arrived to settle in the Colony during the whole period of Company rule, but many of them were advanced in years, and the number of German women who came was small. It has been estimated that the proportion of Dutch blood in the European population of the Colony at the end of the eighteenth century was just about one-half—the Germans contributed twenty-seven per cent., the French seventeen per cent., and other elements the balance.

Yet diverse as were the European stocks which came to be represented at the Cape, they were none the less fused in course of time into a single national type, possessing distinctive characteristics and speaking a single distinctive language. Certainly, the heterogeneity of the early settlers did not provide matter for later controversy and struggle. From the outset the settlement was regarded as Dutch in character; from that character the Seventeen were determined that there should be no substantial variation, readily agreeing to limit the number of French immigrants in order to ensure its maintenance; and those who would come to the Cape must needs be willing to assimilate themselves to its spirit. In the case of the Germans that was easy enough, for the line of demarcation between them and the Netherlanders was none too deep to start with; in the case of the Huguenots it was not so simple a matter, and the process of assimilation requires at least a passing reference.

As condition of their acceptance as Colonists was prescribed the taking of an oath of allegiance, and it was further laid down that they were to be considered as born Netherlanders. That they should remain a distinct national unit was never the intention of the Company—that, indeed, could hardly have been expected in view of the spirit of the age and of the relations which then prevailed between Holland and France. On arrival, therefore, the refugees were interspersed amongst Dutch and German Colonists, so as to ensure the breaking down of their distinctiveness, and they were at first even denied the right of having their own church and congregation. Against such an accelerated absorption the Huguenots protested, but on the main point the Seventeen stood firm. They definitely refused to allow the Huguenots all to live together in a single area, but they permitted them to form their own congregation at Drakenstein, with the right to use their own language, and they were also given their own schoolmaster. His duty, however, it was to teach not only French, but also Dutch, ' in order to unite our nation by this means.' In due course Dutch became the only language both of church and school, the Seventeen having, in 1701, made a declaration of policy, that ' the language (French) should in time die out, and be as it were banished.' To that policy there was some resistance, but the gradualness of its enforcement helped to smooth out difficulties, and in fact Dutchmen and Frenchmen had more in common than geographical contiguity to make them mix freely. Some of the Huguenots had lived for long enough in Holland to be able to speak Dutch; their children grew up with a good knowledge of the language, intermarriage was frequent, and social intercourse developed on easy and natural lines. All but a few of the grandchildren of the original settlers spoke Dutch, and Dutch alone. The Abbé de la Caille in 1752 found no one under forty years of age who spoke French, unless he had actually come from France.

There was one historical event which undoubtedly did much to hasten the process of assimilation. In the struggle between the Colonists and Willem Adriaan van der Stel, Frenchmen and Dutchmen stood side by side in a common cause. That struggle gave solidarity to the farming community, and made them forget differences of origin. Of the sixty-three signatories of the memorial which set forth their grievances, thirty-one were French; of the nine whom the Governor banished, three were French, three were Hollanders, and three were of South African birth. It has been remarked that, while at its commencement the diary which Adam Tas kept during the period of the struggle reflects the prevailing mistrust of the French, in its later pages they are spoken of in the most cordial terms. From that time onwards the assimilation may, as far as community of spirit went, be said to have been all but complete.

So, then, there was produced in South Africa during the eighteenth century a single European type. Because of its assimilation with other stocks, because also of its isolation from Europe, it developed a character of its own, diverging more and more from the character of the people of Holland. Influences which caused rapid and profound changes in Holland were inoperative in South Africa, and on the whole the Dutch-speaking South African of to-day is nearer to the

Netherlander of the seventeenth century than is the modern Hollander. Yet in their turn the influences of the land and of those other peoples who came to dwell in it have not failed to leave their mark on the South African of to-day. Not least distinctive is the language which he speaks. Based on the language of those who went down to the sea in ships, rather than of the settled urban communities, divorced in large measure from contact with cultural developments in the motherland, and exposed to the influences of a very different social environment in a new country, subjected moreover to the ' clipping ' effects of the admission into the speech-group of men who spoke French and German, as well as of Hottentots and slaves, it acquired, in form rather than in vocabulary, a character and a strength of its own. The Afrikaans language, so men called it, became a worthy vehicle for the expression of the thoughts of those who were to open up the greater part of Southern Africa.

In respect not only of the European, but also of the coloured inhabitants of the Cape, was the period of Company rule characterized by the emergence of a steadily increasing measure of homogeneity out of great initial diversity. When van Riebeeck came to Table Valley he found two native stocks in the country, though he does not seem to have distinguished very clearly between them. Of the two the one that went furthest back was that of the Bushmen, who had roamed over Southern Africa for many centuries, gradually being dispossessed by immigrant peoples of a higher level of culture. They were a nomadic race of hunters, the natural enemies of those who had reached the pastoral stage of development, and that enmity was their undoing. At the time of van Riebeeck's coming they were already a vanishing people. Their cattle-stealing proclivities harassed the early Colonists, but they were soon dispersed, and they steadily declined in numbers. To-day there are only a few Bushmen left, living in the remotest parts of South Africa, and even of these most are of mixed blood.

More numerous, even at that time, were the Hottentots, a pastoral people, but unversed in the arts of agriculture, who dwelt in scattered clans in the western and southern coast-belt. With some of these clans van Riebeeck came early

into conflict; one of the incidents of his commandership was
a Hottentot ' war.' They were, however, of more abiding
importance to the Company as the owners of the cattle
which were to be acquired by barter for supply to its ships
and its servants in Capetown. Upon these Hottentot tribesmen the European incursion had a disintegrating effect.
Some were soon drawn into the European sphere. Detribalized natives became part of the population of the settlement. The lack of marriageable women among the
Europeans led van Riebeeck to encourage mixed marriages,
and servants of the Company duly wedded Hottentot wives.
Soon there were to be added to the population slaves from
West Africa and from the East. Malays also were sent to
the Cape from the Indies to serve terms of imprisonment, and
others came in their train. Of these foreign importations by
far the most were men. The mingling of races therefore
went on unchecked, though by degrees intercourse between
white and coloured came to be viewed with disfavour. As a
result of that mingling there emerged what to-day is called
the Cape Coloured folk, with its infusion of white blood,
which is smaller, perhaps, than men tend to think, and for
the rest the blood of many dark-skinned peoples.

Not all, however, of the Hottentots were so speedily detribalized. Certain of the clans withdrew before the
approach of the white man, and made their way into the
interior, where some remain in comparative racial purity
until to-day. Others hovered about the borders of the
settlement, trading with the white man, sometimes raiding
his cattle, rarely entering his service, seeking with varying
measures of success to maintain their tribal organization.
But resistance to the process of disintegration was in the long
run of little avail. Steadily the proximity of the white man
broke down old allegiances and old traditions. On the
frontiers, to which the wilder spirits amongst the settlers
tended to drift, miscegenation continued to take place.
Finally the white man's diseases completed the process.
In 1687 there was a fever epidemic; in 1713 and again in
1755 small-pox ran riot. Leprosy followed, and arrack and
brandy carried on the work. So the tribes were broken up,
and their assimilation was hastened with the Cape Coloured
folk which was growing up in the heart of the settlement.

From the point of view of the Colonists the Hottentots as a distinctive race, as a source of danger to colonization, had ceased to be. In their place there was now a people of mixed blood, developing common characteristics, and speaking the Dutch language. One distinguishing feature of importance alone remained within that people of mixed blood. Some of those who were of Asiatic descent remained true to the religion of the Prophet. They are to-day still spoken of as Malays. The rest became Christians, at least in name.

Such, then, were the foundations of the Colony as they were laid during the earlier periods of Company rule, and from the manner of the laying of them many of the difficulties of the future took their origin. It remains to speak of the extension of the Colony's boundaries, and so to prepare the way for the understanding of a further set of historical forces, which were destined to be of great constitutive significance.

The free burgher had quite early in the history of the settlement shown signs of a preference for cattle-raising over the tillage of the soil. It held out to him a pleasanter life, there was on the whole a more assured market, the returns were less uncertain. Even the earliest free burghers kept some cattle, and the Company's prohibitions of cattle-barter with the natives soon became dead letters, and were by the end of the century withdrawn. As the boundaries of the Colony were extended, the custom began to prevail of farmers of any substance having cattle-runs on the frontiers, in addition to the farms on which they dwelt; a race of hardy frontiersmen, active, adventurous, masters in the use of fire-arms, inured to hardship and privation, began to grow up. Against this tendency to burst the bounds of the Colony Simon van der Stel, intent as he was on the development of a compact agricultural settlement, fought hard, but ineffectually. After his retirement a new expansion movement started, for which the controversy between his son and the burghers provided the occasion, if not the cause. As there grew in the minds of the farmers a sense of hostility to Capetown and its Castle, their thoughts turned naturally towards the interior. The inelasticity of the Cape market for agricultural produce and its inability to keep pace with the increase of the farming population had a similar effect.

The decimation of the Hottentots by the small-pox epidemic of 1713 removed some of the obstacles in the way. In the decades which followed there was a steady stream of colonization into the interior, a large part of the natural increase of the population being caught up in its flow.

First the stream made its way chiefly to the northwards along the western coast-belt, but when it reached the arid region of Namaqualand, its progress was stayed. More attractive was the southern coast-belt, and when the Hottentots Holland mountains had been crossed, the Colonists moved eastwards rapidly. In 1745 the advance made was consolidated by the establishment at Swellendam of a magisterial centre for the new area. Other pioneers again made their way over the mountain ranges which bound the coast-belt, and found themselves on a wide spreading plateau, which seemed to entice them ever onward. The provisions which were in force in regard to land-tenure stimulated this tendency. The Company had adopted a system of granting *lenings-plaatsen*, great blocks of land of 6,000 acres and upwards, which were held on lease nominally for a year at a time. To the award of such a farm each Colonist regarded himself as being entitled; but the insecurity of his tenure made him loath to improve his farm, and encouraged him to move further on in the hope of finding a more suitable place for his abiding. So there grew up an almost nomadic, pastoral people, accustomed to isolation, self-reliant, impatient of control, intensely individualistic. No better pioneers of a new land could have been desired than these Trek-boers, as they came to be called, but they were no easy people to bring within the scope of ordered regular government. Vainly the Company sought to check the dispersion. The edicts which it launched to bid its people go no further were ignored. The amendments it proposed to the system of land-tenure came too late, and produced no effect. The one abiding result of its activity was a growing tendency to regard the Government as a thing of no account. Again and again the Company was compelled to extend the boundaries of its territories in order to keep some hold over its frontiersmen, and so in effect to recognize the expansion which it had sought vainly to prevent.

Steadily men advanced ever further into the interior. Isolated ivory-traders and adventurers went on in advance of the main body. In 1760 the first European crossed the Orange River. At an even earlier date an officer of the Company had visited the Transkei. The main stream, of course, advanced more slowly; in 1760 it reached the site of the future Beaufort West, ten years later the future Somerset East. Those Hottentot clans which sought to maintain their identity retired before it; those who allowed themselves to be detribalized came into the service of the farmers. Bushmen alone offered active resistance; but their numbers were comparatively small, and their desperate defence of their hunting-grounds was soon crushed. At length a boundary was fixed which was destined to endure for a considerable period. In 1778 Governor van Plettenberg visited the eastern districts of the Colony. Near the site of the present town of Colesberg he planted a beacon, further south he appointed the Fish River to be the Colonial boundary, and to serve as a barrier between the Colonists and the advancing Bantu peoples which they met there. A few years later a new magistracy was established at Graaff-Reinet. Within this new frontier the tendency towards a nomadic life was for the moment arrested, and at least the semblance of a settled community established.

In this way, then, there was added to the Colony a vast area with a small population, which mountain ranges and the unequal distribution of water divided into many scattered units. It was a necessary step in the development of South Africa, and on the whole it is, perhaps, as well that men took that step when they did. But heavy was the price which these pioneers and their children had to pay for the taking of it. The disabilities under which they suffered were summed up in these words written in 1802 by Commissary de Mist: ' The long distances which separate these lonely homesteads from Capetown, sometimes between one hundred and fifty and two hundred hours by ox-wagon; the lack of social intercourse with civilized individuals; the monotonous life of the herdsman which tends to retard civilization to the same extent as the cultivation of the soil encourages it; the daily hunt; the continual diet of meat and of the flesh of wild animals; the war (we might almost

term it an organized hunt) conducted for some years against
the Bushmen and Kaffirs, which taught our people to shoot
down a fellow-being with as little compunction as they
would a hare or a wolf; real or imaginary reasons for dissatisfaction with the Cape Government, which, under a
mistaken idea of what was required of it, consistently
pursued a policy of severity rather than of tolerance and
persuasion; all combined in fostering the demon of
discontent.'

In large measure, then, these early frontiersmen lost
contact with the organized State, with the organized church,
and with education. Had they been men of less force of
character, of less determination, they would have sunk low
indeed in the scale of civilization. In the maintenance of
their standards they were, in fact, amazingly successful, and
their hardships did not, in fact, merely bring them loss, for
there were developed in them the qualities of courage and
persistence and self-reliance, which were to fit their descendants to fill the rôles of pioneers on an even vaster stage.
Yet their isolation caused them to be limited in their outlook, impatient of the restraints of civilized government,
difficult to unite in effective co-operation. Moreover, the
magnitude of the area over which they were dispersed made
its administration from an outlying capital a task of insuperable difficulty, and so added to the complexity of the
problems which the fact of their dispersion created.

Sufficient has been said to indicate the main characteristics of the South African community towards the end of
the eighteenth century. Like Saul, who went out to seek
his father's asses and found a kingdom, the Dutch East
India Company had aimed at a revictualling station, and
it had created a Colony, covering an area half as large again
as that of England and Wales, with some 15,000 European
inhabitants, a Colony which, moreover, had its feet firmly
planted on the road that leads to free nationhood. The
Colony fell into three parts. First there was Capetown,
with its 5,000 inhabitants, a town of charm and beauty,
drawing its vitality partly from the fact that it was the
capital and the Company's headquarters, partly from the
ships that put into the port of Table Bay. At times it was
rich and prosperous, especially when during periods of war

great fleets visited it and gave to it a cosmopolitan character—'little Paris' men called it in the seventeen-eighties—at other times again it suffered stagnation and distress. Then there were the agricultural areas of the coast-belt near to the Cape Peninsula, where, in the main, men enjoyed a limited prosperity, and life was easy and spacious, though not very luxurious. The Company's monopolistic system stood in the way of the acquisition of great wealth, but emigration to the interior had reduced the surplus of supply over demand, and made the market for agricultural produce a relatively easy one. Lastly there was the pastoral population of the remoter coast-belt and the interior plateau, living restless and uneasy lives, exposed to the dangers of cultural degeneration which isolation brought with it, creating new problems of government, but playing a worthy part in the building up of the greater South Africa. In all three areas the Europeans were in essence an aristocratic community, employing slaves and native labourers to do the menial work, regarding it as 'more fitting that slaves rather than Europeans should be used' for such tasks. To the composition of the European population several stocks had made contribution, but it had easily and speedily attained homogeneity, while it diverged considerably in language and in character from the people who dwelt in the Netherlands. And in its midst there lived in peaceful subjection people of mixed blood, Hottentots mainly, and Malays, and West African negroes, and the rest, not without a European strain, who were acquiring, though less rapidly, a similar homogeneity, and becoming the Cape Coloured folk.

Of such a character was the Colony, but from two quarters clouds were commencing to obscure its clear sky. Across the Fish River gathered threatening Bantu hordes. In Europe men were thinking new thoughts and devising new forms of government, pregnant with possibilities of change over a great area of the earth's surface.

Chapter 4

The Coming of Briton and Bantu

WITH the passing from the eighteenth to the nineteenth century two new actors made their entry on
to the South African stage, each destined to add
greatly to the complexity of the plot. First in historical
order came the Bantu, a native race far more powerful than
Bushmen or Hottentots, an agricultural as well as a pastoral
people, blessed with remarkable powers of adaptation, one
of the most vigorous, indeed, of the coloured peoples of the
world. Its strength and vigour go far to account for the
distinctive position which South Africa holds to-day among
lands where white and coloured peoples have met. It is
one of the few such lands where the coloured peoples have
not been destroyed or submerged as a result of the coming
of the white man, but have grown in strength as distinct
entities.

Then there came the British, successors in title to the Dutch
East India Company, settlers, colonizers, sharers in the task
of opening up the interior, participators in the more comprehensive South African nationhood of the future. But
they came as a distinct element. Their political dominance,
as well as their sharply defined national characteristics, prevented their absorption into the growing South African
nation, as French and Germans had been absorbed. It was
just as unnatural that they on their part should absorb the
enlarged Dutch element in the population, which was the
stronger numerically, and had just as sharply defined
national characteristics of its own. Dutch and British
were to find that they had many a bond of union, many a
common sentiment and tradition that might serve as the
basis of co-operation and friendship. But they were to
find also how strong was the individuality which each of
the two elements inherited from its past, and to learn that
it was only on the basis of equality, equality of status and

equality of esteem, that their comprehension in a greater whole could be effected. But these lessons only long and bitter experience could teach South Africa.

Of the manner of the coming of the Bantu little need be said. Aboriginal to the land they were no more than the Europeans who came to dwell there. No one can say with certainty what their original homeland was, but it is known that they moved gradually southward by way of the Great Lakes. Into parts of what are now Rhodesia and Portuguese East Africa they entered perhaps 1,000 years ago, possibly even earlier. Towards the close of the sixteenth century they commenced the effective penetration of the future Union of South Africa. Steadily they moved onwards, plateau tribes like the Damaras and the Hereros on the West, highlanders like the Barotse and the Bavenda in the centre, the Nguni coast peoples on the east. It was these Nguni peoples that advanced furthest south. A portion of them, Xosas and Tembus, made their way through the land which Vasco da Gama had called Natal, across the Umzimkulu and the Umzimvubu, exterminating the Bushmen, partially absorbing the Hottentots. At the commencement of the eighteenth century the Xosas were on the Kei; as the century progressed their advance hunting parties began to meet cattle-traders from the Cape. For long it was but a meeting of outposts, an affair of cattle-barter and of hunting. Then in the seventeen-seventies the main streams of the two migrations came together in the valley of the Fish. That clash was one of the circumstances that prepared the way for a change of regime at the Cape and for the coming of the British.

The Dutch East India Company had slowly, but steadily, been verging towards its fall. The seventeenth century was its period of greatest prosperity, as it was also the period of greatest glory in the history of Holland. Great was the wealth of eastern trade which its flotillas brought it. To 20,000 Netherlanders it gave employment. It paid large dividends. Its shares rose to seventeen times their nominal value. But towards the end of that century it began to decline. First came commercial struggles with the English, and the passing of the financial centre of the west from Amsterdam to London; then increasing French competition in the East, the expansion of the activities of the English East India Company, the long and exhausting struggles which ended with the peace of Utrecht. Throughout the eighteenth century the financial position of the Company went steadily back. The wars which sprang from the American Declaration of Independence and the sweeping of Dutch shipping off the seas by British fleets hastened the end. In 1782 it paid its last dividend. In 1794 it declared its bankruptcy with a shortage of £10,000,000.

To the troubles of the Company's declining years the Cape contributed its share. In the books it had always been a liability, showing year after year a deficit. In part, it is true, that was the Company's own fault. Its monopolistic policy restricted the free development of trade, which might have provided a sounder basis of public finance; to its officials it paid starvation wages, and then it left administrative corruption to grow almost unchecked. As the Company declined, the financial and administrative dissolution of the Colony advanced rapidly. In 1782 an inconvertible paper currency was issued. Only the fictitious prosperity brought by the French fleet, which virtually occupied Capetown for three years in the 'eighties, and subsequently stimulated by the extravagances of Governor van der Graaff, delayed the crisis. It was the more serious when it did come. At last the Company decided to send special Commissioners to Batavia and the Cape to seek to save its falling fortunes. The Commissioners made drastic changes, even going so far as to modify the Company's monopolistic policy. But any relief which this might have brought to the Colonists was more than neutralized by the imposition of additional taxation and by the fall in the value of the paper currency, and in the long run little was achieved save the exacerbation of the tempers of the people.

There was much, indeed, that served to prepare the ground for an outbreak. Those were days when, in the old world, as never before, old ways of thought were being changed, and old institutions being shattered. The teachings of Locke and Rousseau had led men to challenge the ideas and conventions of centuries. On every hand there was ferment and unrest and revolt. To the Cape also there came the doctrine of ' natural rights.' Reason enough there was for complaint in maladministration and extortion. The Company had broken its ' contract.' Why should free burghers in Africa submit, when Colonists in America had successfully raised the standard of revolt? So men murmured, and in the last years of Company rule rebellion and anarchy were never far off.

Actual revolt did, indeed, take place on the frontier. There the problem of relations with the Bantu was beginning to be pressing. For the moment it was merely a frontier problem, but a frontier problem of more than ordinary complexity. In 1778 a boundary had been drawn, and it had been ratified by a treaty with some Xosa chieftains. But it was a treaty that brought an uneasy peace, as, indeed, was to be the case with all treaties between European and Bantu. On the one side there was the restlessness of the Trek-boer; on the other the instability in the Bantu political structure, which made it most difficult to discover where authority really lay, and so robbed any agreement of much of its value. To that was added the fact that the Bantu conception of land-holding was based on status rather than on contract, which had the effect of making the alienation of land, from the native's point of view, an impossibility. Again and again a chief would receive presents from the white man in a land transaction. To the white man it meant a transfer of the ownership of the land to himself; to the black man merely the concession of the right to use the land in a certain way, while his own right to use it similarly remained unimpaired.

So, then, disputes and conflicts were of frequent occurrence along the eastern frontier. Already in 1779 the first Kaffir War broke out. There was cattle-lifting. Xosa clans spread themselves over the land to westward of the Fish. The Colonists organized the defence, first on their own account, later with authority from Capetown, the natives were driven back, 5,000 head of cattle were taken, and again there was peace. It was the first of many similar episodes.

To the Governor and his Council away in distant Capetown this new problem of the frontier was one of which they understood but little, one from which, indeed, they withheld attention, save in so far as it forced itself upon them. They had laid down a frontier, again and again they issued proclamations forbidding the burghers to cross it, but they maintained no military force for its protection. In the isolation of the capital they only heard of frontier disturbances weeks after the event; all that they did was to supply the burghers with ammunition, and to send a few officials to Graaff-Reinet. And of these the chief was one Maynier, who in the spirit of the age descanted on ' natural rights,' and spoke of the virtues of the ' noble savage.' The frontiersmen had also heard of the new doctrine of Liberty, Equality, and Fraternity, but though Liberty was very much to their taste, they had little patience with Maynier's conception of Equality and Fraternity as covering the destroyers of their farms and the robbers of their cattle. And when, in 1789, he permitted the Xosas, who had crossed the Fish, to remain in occupation of the Zuurveld, which is the name given to the rectangle formed by the river where it deflects its course and flows eastwards for some sixty miles before it finally turns southward to the sea, their indignation knew no bounds. Four years later there was again trouble in the Zuurveld and to the west of it; farms were burnt, farmers were killed, and cattle were carried away. The course of the First Kaffir War repeated itself, but in the end the Xosas were allowed to remain in the disputed territory. To the burghers on the frontier the failure of the Government to give them adequate protection seemed to be a violation of *their* ' natural rights,' too serious to be tolerated. In 1795 they rose in revolt, expelled the Company's officials, and established their own Government at Graaff-Reinet. The burghers of Swellendam followed suit almost immediately, and summoned a ' National Assembly.' For the moment the Colony was broken into three parts. The fissiparous tendencies born of the isolation in which the Trek-boers lived were beginning to evidence themselves.

The revolt at Swellendam coincided almost to a day with the appearance of nine British ships-of-war in Table Bay. It was the disturbances in Europe, of which those at the Cape were in a sense the complement, that brought the British to South Africa. The Cape was still the half-way house on the road to the East, and with France, its rival for the trade of India, Britain was now at war. The Dutch East India Company had gone into liquidation. Holland was in a state of dissolution. A new Batavian Republic was being formed in alliance with France, and the Prince of Orange had taken refuge in England. It was with the backing of a mandate from him that the expedition was sent to the Cape, to secure it against a French annexation. After a short struggle the Colonial Government capitulated, and the rule of the Dutch East India Company was ended.

In this manner, then, the British came to South Africa. At first they came merely as temporary occupants, representatives of the Prince of Orange, guardians of the passage to India against a French attack. By the Peace of Amiens their occupation was terminated, and the new Batavian Republic assumed direct control. To organize the Government it sent out Commissary de Mist, one of the most interesting figures in South African history. He was a Liberal and a visionary, yet possessed of all the shrewdness and practicality of his race; a worthy representative of the enlightenment of his age, yet a man who believed in the virtues of a strong Government, and was determined to repress the unlimited freedom of the individual citizen; a convinced champion of the theories that inspired the French Revolution, yet frank in his admission of facts that limited the validity of those theories; and in his case there seemed to be nothing one whit unnatural in the blending of those seemingly contrasting elements. In his ordering of the affairs of the Colony there is much to attract favourable attention. But the test of time was not applied to his work. War between Great Britain and France with its Batavian ally was soon resumed. Again the key of India was regarded as a major strategic point in the struggle. In 1806 the British were back in Capetown, this time not to retire. Under the peace settlement of 1814 the Cape was formally ceded to Great Britain by the Kingdom of the Netherlands. Save for British Guiana, it was the only one of the Dutch Colonies taken in the war that was retained. The rest, including the rich East Indian islands, were returned. And as part of the whole transaction Holland was credited with an amount of £6,000,000.

For weal or woe, then, British and Dutch had been brought together in South Africa. For a time the relationship between them was mainly as between ruler and ruled.

As such it was in the first instance a happy relationship, though after a while clouds began to gather, as the complexity of South Africa's problems asserted itself. Later there came a modification in the relationship, when, with the planting of British settlers, the British stake in the country increased, the numerical disparity was diminished, and by the association of British with Dutch in the category of the ruled the way was prepared for closer co-operation on the basis of common interests and a common responsibility.

In the days of the first British occupation the rulers proved to be on the whole not unpleasing to the ruled. The new Government started with the advantages that accrued from its predecessor's unpopularity. It wiped away the monopolistic system; it reformed abuses; its coming and the prevailing war conditions stimulated trade. The new order met on the whole with ready acceptance. Even on the frontier disaffection ceased, though only for a time. Then the old difficulty of shaping frontier policy from Capetown reasserted itself. In their dealings with the Xosas the British were as vacillating as the Company has been. They were in danger of becoming almost as unpopular when the Peace of Amiens intervened.

The second British occupation was less cordially welcomed than the first had been, but it made on the whole an excellent start. The Government was, indeed, despotic, and there were no popularly-elected representatives to exercise restraint—in the reaction from the spirit of the French Revolution it would have been strange indeed if such a concession had been made—but the despotism was ably, even sympathetically, administered. Rulers and ruled found that they had much in common. It was a conservative community that dwelt at the Cape, and the new rulers were essentially conservative in their outlook. In system and personnel the administration of the Colony was at first left practically unchanged, and there was a minimum of interference with old customs and traditions. The Cape remained a Dutch Colony in spirit, though its rulers were British. There was no deliberate policy of Anglicization. That the early British Governors were content to leave to time. So the opposition was disarmed, and a general

atmosphere of contentment began to prevail. On the
eastern frontier there was a general tightening up of the
administration, and, after renewed troubles with the Xosas,
the Zuurveld was finally cleared. The frontiersmen hailed
with acclamation the abandonment of the policy of vacillation and *laissez-faire* which had made previous governments
unpopular. Everywhere the omens seemed good for cordial
co-operation between Dutch and British. Then from the
presence of the coloured races in the South African complex
circumstances arose which disturbed the harmony.

Among the features of the enlightenment which characterized the later eighteenth century had been the birth of
the modern missionary movement, and the banding together
of men of liberal views in philanthropic enterprise. The
slave trade was one of the abuses which chiefly challenged
reforming activity, and so drew men's attention to the
position of coloured peoples throughout the world, free as
well as slave. In 1807 Great Britain passed the Abolition
Act, and though there were inevitable difficulties of enforcement, the supply of slaves to the Cape soon failed, and the
European population, which had hitherto been smaller
than the slave population, now began to overtake it, and
rapidly outstripped it. One effect of the reduction in the
number of slaves was an increase in their value, and, as a
result, in the owners' solicitude for their welfare. Slavery
as an institution at the Cape had always been comparatively
free from the abuses that prevailed in other slave-owning
lands. In its later years standards perhaps as humane as
the nature of the institution permitted prevailed practically
throughout the Colony. It is significant also that the abolition of the trade aroused but little opposition. But indirectly
it led to much conflict. For since it made the farmers more
dependent on the labour of free Hottentots and coloured
folk, it created matter for dispute between them and the
missionaries, who had taken up the task of Christianizing
these peoples, and, in the process, of protecting them from
what they regarded as exploitation by the Colonists.

Missionary activity in South Africa had been initiated
by the Moravian Brethren in the second quarter of the
eighteenth century. But it did not establish itself firmly
until the final decade. Then there followed, in the wake of

the Moravians, missionaries from Holland, Denmark, later France, but chiefly from England, with the London Missionary Society playing the most important part. Among the first of that Society's representatives was a Hollander, Jacobus van der Kemp, an eccentric but able and energetic man, who in 1803 founded a missionary institution for the Hottentots at Bethelsdorp, near the future Port Elizabeth, which was destined to play an important part both in the religious and in the political life of the Colony.

Between missionaries, especially those of the London Missionary Society, and farmers there soon revealed itself a difference in outlook which was to have far-reaching effects. It was not a difference between a specifically Dutch and a specifically British conception, for as British settlers came to South Africa they speedily adopted the farmers' view-point; but since the missionaries were for the most part British, and the farmers were, in the first instance, almost entirely Dutch, the seeds of conflict between Dutch and British were most regrettably sown. The missionary view was based on the conception of all men's equality before God; starting therefrom, and paying all too little regard to present differences between a civilized people and those who were still emerging from barbarism, they emphasized ideas of social and political equality which could not be acceptable to those who had, as a result of their practical experience, convinced themselves of the black man's inferiority. It was natural enough that the missionaries should regard themselves as the protectors of the people to whom they ministered, but the conception which inspired their advocacy of the cause of these people made it just as natural that there should be a conflict between them and the employing farmers. To the farmers, suffering in the days after the abolition of the slave trade from a shortage of labour, the presence at the mission stations, which came in effect to be native reserves on a small scale, of unemployed Hottentots served as an abiding irritation. The readiness of the missionaries to accept the stories told them by their charges against their masters, the manner in which, so men believed, they incited those charges to disobedience, added bitterness to their anger.

The conflict of ideas was first brought into relief in 1812.

The new Government had instituted a Circuit Court to visit the outlying areas and try important cases. To this Court during its second Circuit was referred the investigation of charges which the Bethelsdorp missionaries had made against the frontier farmers on the score of cruel and inhuman treatment of the Hottentots, and of further complaints against the officials to the effect that they had failed to follow up the charges. The Government was determined to investigate the matter fully. The missionaries were given every opportunity of substantiating their specific complaints. Large numbers of witnesses, European and Hottentot, were summoned; the frontier was aroused to a state of intense excitement. Most of the charges broke down. The over-gullible missionaries were rebuked by the Court. But that was not the end of the episode. It had far-reaching consequences. The suspicion and dislike of the missionaries in the minds of the Colonists were intensified. Moreover, the ardour of the officials in taking up petty charges and summoning large numbers of witnesses, often at great inconvenience, which had been inspired by the desire to rebut the missionaries' attack upon themselves, was interpreted as an indication of approval of and participation in what was looked upon as a campaign of persecution. And before that impression had been effaced there came a tragic incident which stirred men's feeling yet more profoundly.

The clearing of the Zuurveld was evidence of the new Government's changed conception of its duty in relation to frontier policy. It was one side of the introduction of the reign of law on the frontier, which was to apply both to white man and to black man. Soon the other side was revealed. In 1815 two European officers with a dozen Hottentot soldiers were sent to arrest a frontiersman, Bezuidenhout by name, who had for two years been refusing compliance with repeated summonses to appear before the court on a charge of cruelty to a coloured servant. He resisted arrest, fired on the party, and was himself shot. It was an incident such as in those days might have occurred on the outposts of any new land. But again the consequences were far-reaching. Bezuidenhout's brother and his friends swore vengeance, and tried to raise the frontier in revolt. But—and it was thus shown that most of the frontiersmen were essentially law-abiding—the rising did not spread, and was speedily crushed. The ringleaders were brought to trial, were sentenced to death, and five of them were hanged at Slachter's Nek.

In the light of the fact that no one of the prisoners had been guilty of actual bloodshed, the sentence was by modern standards a harsh one, though it was in perfect accord with both the letter and the spirit of the law of the time. The authorities might have appealed with confidence, either to the English or to the Roman-Dutch Law. But that they committed a mistake time was destined to show with unhappy conclusiveness. For the men who had been executed came to be regarded as martyrs, Slachter's Nek became a symbol of British oppression, enduring in the minds of the people, and men of subsequent generations were to declare that ' they could never forget Slachter's Nek.' The memory of it was destined to be potent in dividing asunder peoples who had so much in common that should have kept them at one.

The Slachter's Nek episode coincided with a change in the attitude of the British rulers towards their new Colony, a change which was to have an important effect on the future relations between the two white peoples. Until 1814 it was felt that there was a measure of uncertainty in the position. The Cape had been given back in 1802—perhaps when peace came it might be given back again. That consideration quite naturally checked both innovations in the form of government and the tendency to regard the Colony as a field for British settlement. The British residents were virtually confined to the senior officials in Capetown, the military and naval establishments, and a few merchants and missionaries. The peace of 1814, however, removed all uncertainty, and projects of assisted immigration began to be actively canvassed. A few private enterprises prepared the way for a Government scheme of colonization on a considerable scale.

That scheme represented a response to the concurrence of two necessities. At the Cape never-ending trouble with the Xosas had made it clear that for the adequate protection of the frontier there was necessary the close settlement of the border area of the Zuurveld by a large body of men with a

stake in the soil. In Great Britain the post-war reaction had
brought with it unemployment and distress, and men's
thoughts turned naturally to emigration as a cure of those
ills. So it was that in 1819 the British Government was
induced to vote £50,000 to assist emigrants to settle in the
Zuurveld. Assistance was to be given, not to individuals,
but to parties of not fewer than ten adult males, on the
basis of free passages and a grant of 100 acres to each such
adult, and applications were invited from those who were
willing to take out parties. The response was excellent,
and eventually fifty-seven heads of parties were selected.

In this manner the so-called 1820 Settlers were brought to
South Africa, some twenty ship-loads of them. They
landed for the most part in Algoa Bay, and by their landing
they virtually created the town of Port Elizabeth. From
there they scattered over the Zuurveld and beyond.
Coming from settled English towns and the trim orderliness
of the English countryside, they found themselves in a rough
and undeveloped land, where they were threatened with
constant danger to life and property from the attacks of
barbarian neighbours. It was their task to create farms out
of virgin soil, though for the most part they possessed but
little knowledge of agriculture. Moreover, nature in the
early years of the settlement was not in her kindliest mood.
Yet they faced the situation with courage and determination, and though for some time their position continued to
be difficult, even precarious, and though some of the
immigrants proved to be unsuited to the strange conditions
of their new home, most of them in time won through, and
the project was crowned with success. Between March
1820 and May 1821 close on 5,000 men, women, and
children from the British Isles took up residence in the Cape
Colony. They and their descendants were to play a great
part in the making of South Africa. And in the composition of the Colony's population, small as it then still
was, their coming wrought a significant change. No longer
was it to be a Colony of British rulers and Dutch ruled.
Among farmers and frontiersmen were now to be found
British as well as Dutch. The basis of equal co-operation
had been laid.

Chapter 5

The Dividing Asunder

THE history of South Africa is richer in those events that fire the imagination than is the history of any other Dominion. It is so largely because at an early stage of its development it fell apart into fragments, and out of disunion arose conflict and strife and the colourfulness of stormy happenings. It is of the tragedy of history that such should have been the lot of South Africa. The land is not one of those that geography seems to mark out for disunity, where great natural barriers keep men apart and create divergences of interest and outlook, where it costs a long and painful struggle to overcome those physical forces before unity can be achieved. Nor is there any fundamental difference between the two chief elements in the European population. British and Dutch in South Africa have far more in common than have British and French in Canada. Religion, which is so potent a cause of strife in many lands, has played no effective part in driving men asunder in South Africa. Dutch and British speak kindred languages, they come from a common stock, they cherish similar ideals. Yet fate and cruel circumstance divided them, and over a period of close on a century South African history is, inevitably, largely a tale of the way in which that division was brought about, and then of the slow, laborious, often painfully ineffective endeavours that were made to bring the scattered members into conjunction once again. The painfulness of that process has done much to determine the character and the outlook of the South African of to-day. In that sense the history of much in South Africa's past is truly contemporary history. Only in the light of that history can its present politics be understood.

For several years, as has already been remarked, relations between British ruler and Dutch ruled were, in the main, happy. And when with the 1820 Settlers there came into being a class of British ruled as well as of Dutch ruled, the mingling of the two elements did not lead to friction. On the eastern frontier intercourse between Dutch farmer and British settler was consistently friendly. It did not take long before the newcomers found themselves in accord with the Dutch pioneers on most of the issues that affected them. Yet their coming provided the occasion for a change in Government policy which was the source of much future discord. Hitherto the Colony had continued to be, in the main, a Dutch Colony under British rule. English had gradually come into use as an official language alongside of Dutch, but the older Colonists retained their full language rights, and the political institutions to which they were accustomed remained practically unaltered. The British immigration had, however, brought an important new element into the population, as yet only one-seventh of the whole, but, judged by the standards of those days, it provided ample ground for the adoption of an active policy of Anglicization.

In 1822, therefore, a proclamation was issued, which provided for the gradual substitution of English for Dutch as the official language for all administrative and judicial purposes. By 1828 the substitution had become fully operative. In that year also there came into force a new ' Charter of Justice,' which remodelled the judicial system of the Colony. On the whole it was a well-conceived reform, but one of its features was the replacement of the old Dutch system of ' landdrosts ' with their representative ' heemraden ' by the English system of magistrates. At the same time the old Burgher Senate, which had dealt with certain aspects of local government in Capetown, disappeared. In church and school a similar policy of Anglicization was pursued. Even in the matter of currency a change was made, the Dutch rix-dollar being replaced by British silver, a change which brought serious loss to many. The intentions of the rulers of the Colony were clear—it was to be an English Colony, administered by a centralized English bureaucracy, in the spirit of the Tory reaction of the eighteen-twenties. For that day and generation it was perhaps a natural policy. But it took all too little account of the strength of the Dutch Colonists' attachment to their language and traditions, and it created grievances, which for all that they hardly found expression at the time, made deep lodgment, and added greatly to the acuteness of future discontents.

These discontents were the consequence of the presence in South Africa of the third great element in its population —the coloured races. In quick succession the relations of the white man with Hottentots, with slaves, with Bantu tribes, provided cause for grievance.

The old-established farmers of the west met their labour requirements largely by the use of slaves. The eastern frontiersmen, slenderly equipped with capital, had few slaves, and were dependent on the labour of the Hottentots, now rapidly merging into the Cape coloured folk. Of the scarcity and inefficiency of this labour, and also of the predatory tendencies of unemployed Hottentots, the farmers made constant complaint. The aims which they set themselves, therefore, were the imposition of checks on the freedom of movement of the Hottentots, the enactment of vagrancy laws, the exercise of pressure on them to offer their labour, the maintenance of the powers of masters over their servants. Against these aims the missionaries contended with vigour. Their object was the conversion of the Hottentot into a landowner, so far as might be possible, but at least to the extent that he would be able to bargain freely with his labour. In the reaction from the Circuit of 1812 the policy of the farmers had prevailed, and various restrictive Ordinances had been passed. But gradually, with the rising tide of Liberalism, the missionaries and the philanthropists, led now by the redoubtable Dr. John Philip of the London Missionary Society, grew in influence. The struggle was long and bitter, but in 1828 the policy of the missionaries triumphed in the passage of the famous Fiftieth Ordinance, which secured the civil rights of the free coloured inhabitants of the Colony, cancelling all the restrictive enactments of an earlier date. In the minds of the eastern frontiersmen, in particular, keen resentment was aroused. To them the Ordinance meant scarcity of labour, the weakening of the white man's authority and prestige, the dangers of vagrancy in the case of a still almost barbarian people. But its effects went further. It exacerbated feeling against the missionaries, and it threw into relief the difference between their conception—a conception now beginning to be adopted by the British rulers—of the equality of coloured man with white man, and the view of the pioneer which refused to admit such equality either as a present fact or as a future contingency. Between the undiscriminating idealism of Exeter Hall and the hard, but not in essence unkindly, pragmatism of the frontiersman there was, indeed, a great gulf fixed.

There followed the emancipation of the slaves. The Colonists foresaw its coming, and sought to anticipate it with proposals, which they submitted from time to time with a view to making its application gradual. And even when, in 1833, those who held the view 'What thou doest, do quickly' prevailed, they made no protest against the principle of emancipation. But there were attendant circumstances that created a bitter sense of grievance. Prior to emancipation certain regulations had been framed, restricting the rights of the owner in the use of his slaves, which rankled deeply. They were regulations which, so men said, might have been necessary in the West Indian plantations, but certainly not at the Cape, with its very much humaner standards. And then the ruffled feelings were violently agitated by the way in which effect was given to the principle of the Emancipation Act. For while it was enacted that emancipation should be accompanied by compensation, it appeared later that for the slaves in the Colony, whose value was assessed at close on £3,000,000, only a sum of £1,250,000 was to be paid out. Moreover, all claims had to be proved in London, where payment was to be made partly in cash, and partly in three and a half per cent. stock, with the result that many of the farmers, having no option but to sell their claims to agents, received only a small fraction of the value of their property. The material loss of the Colonists was considerable, and the sense of grievance was made yet more acute by the fact that there was now no law against vagrancy, and therefore no security against possible depredations by the newly liberated slaves.

Finally the Bantu. On the frontier there was still no lack of trouble. The British Administration had cleared the Zuurveld, and made the Fish River an effective boundary.

C

For the protection of that boundary it had brought out British settlers. Then it had pushed the native tribes back from the Fish to the Keiskama, and sought to make a buffer neutral belt of the land between. But the end in view— peaceful relations between white man and black on opposite sides of a fixed frontier line—was not attained. Cattle-thieving gave unceasing trouble; even in a time of nominal peace 3,600 head of cattle were carried off in eighteen months. And in 1834 peace gave way to war. A great wave of Bantu invaders swept across the frontier, burning, destroying, massacring. The material losses sustained by the Colonists were estimated at £300,000. There followed a short, sharp struggle. From the burghers the Governor of the day, Sir Benjamin D'Urban, received vigorous and valued assistance. The invaders were driven back, and D'Urban decided that a better frontier line must be found. Accordingly he annexed the territory between the Keiskama and the Kei as the Province of Queen Adelaide, and pro-claimed that all hostile tribes should be driven out of it across the Kei, while Europeans and friendly natives were to be settled in the vacant lands. To the burghers, who had lost severely and fought effectively, he held out the hope of compensation in the form of land-grants in the new Province.

The D'Urban policy was popular in the Colony. But it aroused the wrath of the philanthropists, and the proposed ' extermination ' of the hostile tribes across the Kei gave force to their attack. With Lord Glenelg, the Secretary of State for the Colonies, they prevailed, the D'Urban policy was reversed, and the Province of Queen Adelaide was abandoned. For the Colonists it meant that all hope of compensation for the losses which they had sustained was gone; to their injury was added the sense of insult, when it came to be known that the Colonial Secretary had made it perfectly clear, that he considered that ' in the conduct which was pursued towards the Kaffir nation by the Colonists and the public authorities of the Colony through a long series of years, the Kaffirs had an ample justification of the war into which they rushed.' The frontiersmen's indigna-tion knew no bounds. The Glenelg despatch was the deciding factor in the minds of many who participated in the Great Trek which followed it, and gave to that movement the magnitude which was to lend it historic importance.

In a sense the Great Trek was but a continuation of the migration which had in the eighteenth century spread European farmers over the interior plateau as far as the Fish River. To further expansion the Bantu had presented a barrier, which effectively held up the main stream. But in the minds of the frontier farmers the spirit of the Trek still lived, and economic factors maintained its vitality. For them as cattle-farmers under South African conditions large ranches were a necessity. But marriage came early, and families were large, and the pressure of the need of new farms steadily increased. Changes in the system of land-tenure and the introduction of a quitrent stimulated the desire to seek new land beyond the borders. The abandonment of the Province of Queen Adelaide dispelled the hope that the conquered territory would satisfy the farmers' wants.

So far, however, we have only a very incomplete explanation of the causes of the Trek. It was no mere bursting of a dam which could no longer hold the increasing pressure of pent-up waters within. Along these lines one cannot account adequately either for its magnitude or for the relative completeness of its organization and the spirit in which it was undertaken. This was no mere random spreading over a new land such as there had been in the eighteenth century. There was preliminary investigation of the land to be occupied; there was the organization of parties, each under its leader; there was a large measure of understanding and co-operation between the several parties. And it was no mere land-hunger that sent forth this body of Voortrekkers, as they came to be called. Many of them abandoned settled farms at great loss to themselves with no apparent prospect of advantage. Rather was it a definite feeling of dissatisfaction with the conditions in their homeland, and a desire to be free of the Government which was held to be responsible for those conditions. 'We quit this Colony,' wrote Pieter Retief, foremost among the Voortrekkers, in a manifesto which he issued on departure, ' under the full assurance that the English Government has nothing more to require of us, and will allow us to govern ourselves without its interference in future.' It is true that not all the Voortrekkers went forth in this spirit. Many of them were still not unwilling to regard themselves as British subjects, and to accept the extension of British rule over the new lands into which they went. But it was certainly not so with most of them, and therein lies the significance of the Great Trek in South African history—its clearly defined aim was the dividing asunder of what had, till then, been joined together, it meant the alienation of Dutch from British, it meant the breaking-up of political unity. And though legally the Voortrekkers remained British subjects, until after much vacillation and uncertainty their independence was formally recognized, in fact their moving forth initiated a process of disruption, which may be said to have reached its culminating point, when, in 1857, there were in existence within the limits of the future Union of South Africa no fewer than eight civilized governments, five Republican and three Colonial.

So then it was that some 5,000 of the Colonists in all, men, women, and children—' the flower of the frontier farmers,' Sir Benjamin D'Urban called them—moved forth to brave the dangers of a largely unknown land. Both in their actual achievement, and in the manner in which they faced suffering and privation, they left a splendid legacy for the South African nation of the future.

The Trek, as has been said, was not undertaken without organization and preparation. In 1834 three commissions of investigation were sent out; one went to Damaraland in what is now South-West Africa, one to the Zoutpansberg in the Northern Transvaal, one to Natal. They came back with reports of the existence of much good and, withal, thinly populated land to the north-eastwards. Then in 1835 the first two parties of Voortrekkers left. They moved on as far as the Limpopo, but they fared ill in their journeyings. One party was completely destroyed by natives, the other was almost exterminated by fever in an attempt to open up for the new state that was to be founded a passage to the sea at Delagoa Bay. Then in 1836 the main body of emigrants crossed the Orange.

They entered the great plains beyond the river at an opportune time for settlement. The first part of the nineteenth century was a period of constant warfare and destruction for the Bantu peoples. Among the Zulus, between the mountains and the sea, a great chief, Tshaka, had risen to power, and had used the magnificent military machine which he devised practically to exterminate rival tribes on the Natal terraces. And on the plateau west of the mountains Moselikatse, one of Tshaka's generals, who had broken away from him, had similarly spread red ruin. It was the period of the *Mfecane*, the crushing, and so the Voortrekkers found large stretches of the land which they entered lying relatively empty, the former inhabitants having been decimated and scattered. All that was necessary for them, if they would secure an assured title, was to dispossess Moselikatse and his Matabele tribesmen. The issue was soon decided. The Matabele at once attacked the immigrants, harrying them constantly, destroying their cattle, and massacring isolated parties. But fire-arms easily prevailed over assegais, and Moselikatse gave up the struggle, retiring across the Limpopo.

As a result parties of Voortrekkers were able to spread over the plateaux which lie to the north of the Orange and the Vaal, and some established themselves in the lower and less healthy regions of the northern and north-eastern Transvaal. But it was below the mountains in Natal that they first set about the organization of an ordered community. There Englishmen had settled for the carrying on of commerce at the port of Natal away back in 1824, but the British Government had consistently refused requests for annexation, even after the settlement had been given the name of Durban in honour of the Governor. To Retief and his followers there seemed to be no reason why they should not in this fair land build up the state of their desire without interference, and negotiations were set on foot with Dingaan, Tshaka's successor, for a cession of territory. At first Dingaan received Retief favourably, but after he had made the grant of land asked for, he treacherously murdered him with some sixty companions at his kraal, and then burst upon those of the emigrants who had followed him down the mountains, cruelly massacring men, women, and children.

For long the fortunes of the Voortrekkers looked dark;

in further fighting with the Zulus heavy losses were sustained; there was talk of abandoning Natal. But the arrival of a new leader, Andries Pretorius, brought fresh vigour and inspiration. On 16th December, 1838, a day ever since commemorated in South Africa as Dingaan's Day, a great victory was won at Blood River. Soon after Dingaan was expelled by a Zulu faction, under Panda, whom Pretorius supported, and the Republic of Natal could be definitely launched, with the Tugela River as the frontier between the Zulus and itself. At the new town of Pietermaritzburg, reminiscent in its name of Pieter Retief and Gerrit Maritz, another leader who had lost his life, a *Volksraad* (People's Council) commenced to function as legislative, judicial, and, in many respects, executive authority of the new state. It was the first effective breach in the political unity of South Africa.

But the Republic of Natal proved to be short-lived. By the British authorities the emigrant farmers were regarded as subjects who happened to have gone beyond the borders, but still owed allegiance to the Crown, and Pretorius addressed himself to the task of securing a formal recognition of independence. For a time it looked as if he might succeed. Two tendencies struggled for the mastery in British policy. An aversion from Colonial expansion was a feature of the prevalent political philosophy, but a countervailing force was provided by the desire of the philanthropists to protect the native peoples against possible oppression by the emigrants. In this instance commercial influences were also brought to bear, and the philanthropists won. In 1842 a British garrison was despatched to Durban. It was promptly besieged by the forces of the Republic, but timely succour came. In 1843 the Volksraad submitted. Two years later Natal became a Province of the Cape Colony under a detached Lieutenant-Governor. Political unity was restored.

But there remained the Voortrekkers on the plateau, reinforced as they now were by most of those who had settled in Natal. To these latter, British rule, and the principle of equality between the white and coloured races which the new Administration espoused, were unacceptable. They moved back again over the mountains and left Natal to become a predominantly British Colony. In the plateau regions the dispersion of the emigrants was greater than it had been in the comparatively restricted area below the mountains. They had two chief centres, Winburg, south of the Vaal, and Potchefstroom to the north of it, but their lack of political experience, their resolute individualism, their impatience of restraint, which had been born of the isolation of successive generations of frontiersmen in the old Cape days, made the evolution of a settled Government a slow process. For a time Winburg and Potchefstroom had been loosely linked up with the Natal Volksraad and with one another, but distance made the bonds of union loose and ineffective, and when Natal was annexed they ceased to exist, and the plateau communities began to fall apart into detached units.

For a time, however, it seemed as if here again the action of the British Government might restore political unity. In this case also there was a conflict between the philanthropist and the non-expansionist views on the question whether responsibility should be assumed for the government of the emigrant British subjects. That conflict expressed itself in hesitancy, vacillation, and compromise. Such a compromise was the adoption of the policy of treaties with native chiefs beyond the frontiers, in terms of which they undertook, in return for a British subsidy, to keep order in their territories, and to send European criminals to the Colony for trial. Agreements of this nature were, in 1843, concluded with Adam Kok, the head of the half-breed Griquas who lived in the south-eastern portion of the later Orange Free State, and with Moshesh, who was building the tribes scattered in the *Mfecane* into the Basuto people in the mountain knot between the Free State and Natal, and in the plains and valleys to west of it. These treaties, which meant in effect that large numbers of the emigrants were placed under the jurisdiction of native chiefs, created an essentially unstable position, which could end only in the assumption of direct responsibility by the British Government. Gradually, almost despite itself, it was drawn across the Orange. First, while native sovereignty was retained, a European resident was stationed at a new centre called Bloemfontein, as virtual administrator of the Europeans

between the Orange and the Vaal. Then in 1848 Sir Harry
Smith, Governor of the Cape, formally annexed this area,
though not without a struggle. Many of the farmers rose
in revolt. Pretorius, who was now living at Potchefstroom,
came across the Vaal to lead them. He was defeated in a
battle at Boomplaats, and the Orange River Sovereignty
was able to start on its career. The process of making South
Africa's political union effective had, so it seemed, advanced
a further stage. It remained only to compel the Queen's
subjects who dwelt beyond the Vaal to acknowledge the
authority of the Queen's Government.

But reaction was close at hand. So far in the conflict of
policy the expansionists had prevailed. Now there was a
turn in the struggle, and the victory began to go to the non-
expansionist Liberals, who believed in the development of
free political institutions, and saw no virtue in the retention
of unwilling subjects. And that victory meant that the
tendencies towards political disunion were left to run their
course freely and without control.

Events in the new British dependency between the rivers
provided the occasion for the change of policy. The Orange
River Sovereignty had a precarious existence. It came into
being amid boundless possibilities of trouble—the dissatisfaction of many of the burghers, the restlessness of its
northern neighbours, the wiliness of Moshesh, its boundary
difficulties with various native tribes. If it was to establish
itself securely, it was essential that for some time at least it
should be able to dispose of a strong military force. Then in
1850 came disturbances on the Cape's eastern frontier, which
necessitated the concentration of all available troops in that
area. The Sovereignty was denuded. The Basutos began
to make trouble. Soon a crisis developed. To the Resident's call to arms the burghers responded in small numbers
and with obvious reluctance. A defeat was sustained. It
became clear to the British Government that it would be a
long and costly undertaking to assert its authority over the
lands beyond the Orange. The policy of abandonment was
decided upon.

As a first step the independence of the emigrants north of
the Vaal was formally recognized. In 1852 Major Hogge
and Mr. C. M. Owen, Special Commissioners of Her

Majesty, signed the Sand River Convention, whereby the British Government guaranteed to ' the emigrant farmers beyond the Vaal River the right to manage their own affairs and to govern themselves according to their own laws, without any interference on the part of Her Majesty the Queen's Government.' The Convention further provided that ' no encroachment shall be made by the said Government on the territory beyond to the north of the Vaal River.' The Sovereignty survived yet a while longer, but a further check sustained at the hands of the Basutos hastened the withdrawal of the British Government. Many of the burghers protested against abandonment, some because they were reconciled to British rule, other because they objected to being left to face the victorious Basuto power without British aid, but in 1854, by the Convention of Bloemfontein, the full independence of the Orange Free State was recognized.

But the process of disruption was not yet complete. In the Free State the burghers faced their responsibilities in a spirit of harmonious co-operation, and devised a constitution for their Republic, which soon gave evidence of efficient functioning. But in the Transvaal, where the more restless among the Voortrekkers had congregated, where distances were greater, and the difficulties in the way of the establishment of a strong Government more serious, it proved to be no easy task to build up the fabric of a centralized administration. There was much that worked in the direction oj keeping men apart. The Trek had been organized on the basis of separate parties, each under its chosen leader. After the Trek the power of the military leader, with whom his followers desired to retain some measure of personal contact, survived. In such circumstances society tends to become patriarchal, and unified control over a large area a contradiction in terms. Fissiparous tendencies were encouraged, the effect of which on the national character is not yet spent. So, then, in the Transvaal rival leaders struggled for pre-eminence, and ecclesiastical controversies complicated political disputes. The example of the Free State did, indeed, give inspiration to constitution-building, but it did not bring unity with it. When, in 1857, the new constitution of the ' South African Republic ' became operative, with the son of Andries Pretorius as its first President, and the newly founded Pretoria as its capital, the burghers of Lydenburg in the north-east promptly declared their independence, while those of Zoutpansberg in the north did so by implication. And to the south-east, on the borders of Natal and Zululand, another little state, the Republic of Utrecht, maintained its separate existence.

There were then five Republics in South Africa in 1857. But there were also three Colonies. For in 1847 Sir Harry Smith had re-annexed the old province of Queen Adelaide between the Keiskama and the Kei, not, however, this time as a part of the Cape Colony, but as a direct dependency of the Crown under the style of British Kaffraria, and in 1856 Natal became a separate Crown Colony with a Legislative Council of its own. The climax in the process of dissolution had been reached. For some time, indeed, the people of the eastern districts of the Cape Colony pressed for separation and for their constitution as a distinct unit, but their efforts were not crowned with success.

One result of this process of dissolution was a great expansion of the area under European rule. Ultimately that was to make for the building of a greater South Africa, but in the first instance it was a source of weakness rather than of strength. European civilization was spread far too thin over too wide an area to ensure the adequate maintenance and advancement of its cultural standards. The intensive development of the territories originally settled was retarded, and in the new lands weak Governments, assailed by difficulties of all kinds, not least of them financial, were unable to provide educational facilities, the lack of which was yet to cost the nation dear.

For the later developments in the breaking up of South Africa's political unity the ascendancy of Liberal ideas in Great Britain was responsible. But that same Liberalism was responsible also for the creation of the nucleus round which the *disjecta membra* were in time to coalesce. In accordance with its policy of developing free political institutions it gave a Parliament to the Cape Colony, and so prepared the way for the greater self-governing Union of South Africa. The Colonists had for long been pressing their claims to a measure of self-government, but in the first half of the century progress was slow. In 1825 the autocratic power of the Governor was tempered by the institution of a Council of Advice of six members, three official and three nominated, and in 1833 there was established in its place a Legislative Council, with greater powers, but a similar constitution. There for the moment advance was stayed, although in the development of local self-government there was steady progress on sound and healthy lines, which, as in mediaeval England, did much to prepare the way for the growth of parliamentary institutions. Then in 1848 Earl Grey, Lord John Russell's Colonial Secretary, decided that the time was ripe for constitutional advance. There was discussion interminable, draft succeeded draft, a change of government caused delay, but at last in March 1853 an Order-in-Council was issued which gave a Parliament to the Cape Colony, and next year the first Cape Parliament met.

The new constitution was of a liberal character, though it stopped short of Responsible Government. Its franchise provisions made no distinction on grounds of race or colour, a low property or salary qualification being imposed. Save for the Chief Justice of the Colony, who was to be President of the Upper House or Legislative Council, the electorate was to choose all the members of Parliament. But the Executive was not to be responsible to Parliament. It was to consist as before of officials, who were to have the right to participate in debates, but whose salaries were secured by a reserved civil list, so that they were not subject to Parliamentary control. Therein, of course, as in the case of Canada, lay the germ of conflict and discontent, but there was also the promise of further constitutional advance, and the way of advance which led to a Parliament of a South African Dominion lay open and prepared.

Chapter 6

Ebb and Flow

I N 1857 the dissolution of the political unity of South Africa was complete. It was the result largely of differences of view on matters of policy, and of controversy and disputes which drove men to establish isolated new communities. But it was also due, in part, to the vastness of the land, and to the inadequacy of its facilities for inter-communication. By 1857 Europeans had spread themselves, for the most part in widely scattered bands, over practically the whole of what is now the Union of South Africa, a territory, be it remembered, eight times the size of England and Wales, poorly favoured with natural facilities for traffic and intercourse, with roads over its mountain ranges only just beginning to be built, and railway construction not yet commenced. For a single government to have ruled the land at that stage of its development would have been no easy task. Yet these natural difficulties in the way of political unity were certainly not insuperable. In 1859 the construction of the first lines of railway was in fact started. Thereafter the essential geographical unity of South Africa steadily asserted itself. Centripetal, in addition to centrifugal, tendencies began to become effective, and they were in no wise the less powerful.

In 1858 the Zoutpansberg accepted the constitution of the South African Republic; in that same year the Republics of Lydenburg and Utrecht joined hands. In 1860 the two groups north of the Orange Free State united. In the years that followed, the union of the South African Republic and the Free State was almost achieved, and for a time Pretorius was, in fact, President of both Republics, joining them in a personal union. Then in 1866 Kaffraria was united to the mother Colony. The evils of disunion, so clearly stated by Sir George Grey when in his Federation despatch written as Governor of the Cape Colony he

declared that ' South Africa appears to be drifting by not
very slow degrees into disorder and barbarism,' had impressed themselves upon the minds of many, and the tide
seemed to have set definitely towards political union. But
such union was not easily to be attained. Progress there
was, but it was slow, and there was ebb, as well as flow, in
the movement of the tide.

That in its turn bears close relation to the fact that,
though the dissolution of the political unity of South Africa
had reached its climax, the similar process in the case of the
feeling of national unity, the sense of participation in a
single South African nationhood, was not yet complete.
In 1857 relations between Dutch and British in South
Africa were on the whole friendly. The grievances of the
pre-Trek period had spent themselves. Even in those who
had felt them most keenly, time had assuaged their bitterness. The Cape Colony was progressing steadily towards
prosperity as the production of wool advanced by leaps and
bounds, and the grant of a liberal constitution did much to
reconcile those who might yet have had grounds for political
discontent. In the Orange Free State there was much good
feeling towards the British, and especially towards Great
Britain's chief representative, Sir George Grey, and any
proposal of federation with the Cape Colony under the
British flag was assured of considerable support. The South
African Republic was, indeed, sturdily independent, but
the Sand River Convention had done a great deal to remove
the old grounds of complaint. In general there was a
solid foundation of goodwill on which statesmanship might,
so it seemed, erect the national union of the future. And yet
the building of that structure was destined to be long
delayed. While in the latter half of the century there was,
despite the tide's ebb and flow, on the whole an advance
towards political union, in respect of national union there
was retrocession rather than progress. In that respect also
there was ebb and flow, and at times progress was made,
but controversies and conflicts arose which more than
annulled the progress, and by the end of the century men of
Afrikaans and of English speech were far more sharply
divided than they had been in 1857. Only in 1902 was the
climax in the dissolution of national unity finally reached.

It was Sir George Grey who first made comprehensive proposals for the political federation of South Africa. In 1858 he was asked by the Secretary of State to submit a report on the possible federation of the Cape, Natal, and British Kaffraria. But Grey had found that there was also in the Free State a strong feeling in favour of closer union— its Volksraad had, indeed, passed a resolution affirming the principle and asking for a Conference to consider details. In this knowledge he proceeded to write his historic despatch, in which he emphasized the evils of disunion, showed in particular the necessity of the native question being dealt with by a single, strong government if it was not to be a source of growing perplexity and trouble to each of the states, and recommended that some form of federal union should be devised which would embrace the three Colonies and the Free State, leaving it to the Northern Republic to come in later, as it doubtless would. Having sent off his despatch, Grey promptly asked his Parliament to give sympathetic consideration to the Free State's request. But he had gone too fast and too far. The Imperial Government refused to consider the resumption of ' sovereignty in any shape or form ' north of the Orange River, it censured Grey for having raised the matter in the Cape Parliament, and it recalled him. The next Government reappointed him, but it was with the clear instruction that Federation was to be regarded as falling outside the limits of practical politics.

So ended Grey's project, though it was launched at a time when the feelings between British and Dutch in South Africa were such as to provide ground for hope of success in the attainment of national as well as political unity. The next effort was to be made from Downing Street itself, but in the meantime events took place which made the ideal of national unity far more difficult of attainment.

The Convention of Bloemfontein had left the Free State to deal with the problem of the Basutos on its own account. The small State, with its inadequate financial resources, found it no easy task to cope with the wiles and the numerical strength of old Moshesh. These difficulties, indeed, had much to do with its willingness to enter into a federal union with the British Colonies. At length, how-

ever, in 1865 under a new President, Jan Brand, one of the
great men in South Africa's history, it resumed the struggle
with the determination to advance it to a final issue. This
time it was successful, and Moshesh next year signed a
treaty, in which he ceded large tracts of land to the Republic.
But the very completeness of the success won contained the
germs of weakness. Moshesh had been left with territory
which seemed to be far from adequate for the needs of his
tribesmen. To force them to leave the ceded territory he
was unable, and, doubtless, unwilling. Moreover, the
threatened over-population of Basutoland, and resultant
dispersion of landless Basutos in search of land elsewhere,
constituted a menace to the security of the Cape Colony's
frontier, and attracted the attention of Grey's successor,
Sir Philip Wodehouse. To Wodehouse it seemed clear that
the policy of the Conventions was a wrong policy, and that
British authority would again have to be asserted in the
territories beyond the Orange. When, then, non-com-
pliance by the Basutos with the treaty of 1866 led to a
renewal of the war—a war full of difficulties for the Free
State—the Governor took steps to intervene. In 1868 he
annexed Basutoland, regardless of the protests of the
Republic, although in the Bloemfontein Convention the
intention of Her Majesty's Government to enter into any
treaties with native tribes to northwards of the Orange had
been specifically disclaimed. He then went on to set aside
the provisions of the treaty of 1866, and though later he
modified his attitude to some extent in points of detail, the
fact remained that the Bloemfontein Convention had been
broken, and that lands which the Republic regarded as the
fruits of toilsome struggle were taken away from it, and
handed back to the native tribes.

The annexation of Basutoland marks the commencement
of a new phase in British Imperial policy. It is true that
Wodehouse had not secured either a ready or an uncondi-
tional consent from the Colonial Office for the policy on
which he embarked, yet a change of attitude was clearly
coming in Downing Street. The policy of the Conventions
was now held to have been a mistake, and the extension of
British rule in South Africa was receiving tentative approval.
Of that change of attitude the motive was not so much a

desire for Imperialistic expansion, as the wish to remove possible sources of friction between European and native in the interior, and to prepare the way for a strong united South Africa under Responsible Government, which would relieve the British taxpayer of responsibility for the cost of its defence. But, whatever the motive, it meant the birth of the new Imperialism in South Africa.

That was, however, not the only respect in which the annexation of Basutoland was significant; for it also did much to create what may be described as the new Republicanism. Certainly it aroused bitter feelings in the Free State, strengthening the determination of those of its burghers who desired that it should tread the path of isolation, and it likewise stirred up pro-Republican and by implication anti-British sentiments among men in other parts of South Africa to whom community of descent gave a community of interest with their Republican cousins.

Before there was time for this bitterness to be allayed, another incident took place which stirred men's feelings even more profoundly. In 1867 diamonds were discovered in Griqualand West, to westward of the Free State. It was an event of profound significance in both the economic and the political history of South Africa. It marked the effective commencement of the era of mineral development, bringing to the land population and wealth, and the means of creating those facilities for inter-communication which were to break down the barrier walls of isolation. But it brought with it also a renewal of strife between Dutch and British. The diamondiferous lands lay north of the Orange River, on both sides of the Vaal. The lands to the south and east of the Vaal, and the south-western portion of the lands to the north and west of it, were claimed by the Free State and also by a petty Griqua chief, Waterboer by name, through his agent, David Arnot. Arnot induced Waterboer to ask for British protection, the request was favourably entertained, and so the dispute developed into one between the British and the Republican Governments. The Free State's claim to the country between the Vaal and the Orange, which contains what are to-day the mines of Kimberley, was, on the evidence now available, incontestable; on the evidence then submitted, it was exceedingly strong. But the officials at Capetown were set on the annexation of the diamond fields. In 1871 Griqualand West was proclaimed British territory. In the first instance its affairs were directed by a separate administration. In 1880 it was to be incorporated in the Cape Colony.

Across the Vaal a similar dispute developed between the South African Republic and various native chiefs, including Waterboer again, but the British Government did not enter quite so directly into the controversy. In this case a court of arbitration was constituted, with Lieutenant-Governor Keate of Natal as final umpire. His award went very definitely against the Republic. It assigned to native tribes much that was unquestionably Republican territory, but on the evidence submitted it could hardly have been otherwise, for the Transvaal's case was very inadequately presented.

The loss by the Republics of the diamond fields led to important consequences. In the Transvaal the sense of grievance was not so much against Britain, which had no interest in the greater part of the area affected, though even so some of its actions provided cause for complaint on the score of contravention of the provisions of the Sand River Convention. It was rather against the President and his advisers that public anger was directed. The Volksraad repudiated the award, and forced Pretorius to resign.

But in the Free State it was the British Government that bore the sole weight of men's wrath. The Republic was convulsed with indignation. Only President Brand's moderating influence prevented the burghers from rushing on a hopeless war. For years, however, there was a bitter dispute, and though it was settled in 1876 by the payment of £90,000 to the Republic, the feelings which it aroused rankled deeply in the minds of men of the older population throughout South Africa. The cause of national unity had received a serious setback.

These events then marked the abandonment of the policy of the Conventions and the resumption of active interest by the British Government in the affairs of the territories, which lay beyond the borders of its South African Colonies. One other event of this period, which was in itself an evidence of this renewed interest, was destined to have important

results in later South African history. On the east coast
of Southern Africa there is no port with natural advantages
as great as are those of Delagoa Bay. It was, moreover, the
port nearest to the South African Republic, the port which
had, from the days of the Voortrekkers, been regarded as its
natural outlet to the sea. But to this port both Portuguese
and British had staked their claims. In the early days of
African exploitation it had unquestionably fallen within the
Portuguese sphere, but there had not been continuous
occupation, and Britain contended that the Portuguese
claim, at least to the southern portion of the Bay, had lapsed.
By way of assertion of British rights possession was, in 1861,
taken of certain islands in the Bay in the name of the Queen,
the main motive being the desire to prevent the South
African Republic from establishing itself on the coast.
Seven years later President Pretorius did, in fact, proclaim
Republican sovereignty over a large area of country, which
included a strip of the foreshore of Delagoa Bay. But when
the British Government sternly protested, Pretorius withdrew, admitting that the question was one between Britain
and Portugal. That question was at last referred to the
arbitration of President MacMahon of the French Republic.
His award, given in 1875, was in favour of the Portuguese,
but it conceded to Britain a pre-emptive right. It was an
important decision. A double barrier was imposed to the
advance of the Republic to the coast, but a perplexing and
difficult foreign factor had been definitely introduced into
South African affairs.

The annexations of Basutoland and of Griqualand West,
and the enforced withdrawal of President Pretorius from
Delagoa Bay, were all symptomatic of the change in British
Imperial policy. It was now accepted that the drift towards
political disunity must be checked, that steps taken in that
direction in the past must be recalled, that the ideal of a
United South Africa under the Union Jack must be pursued.
In the pursuit of these ends Downing Street resumed the
work, which not very long before it had compelled Sir
George Grey to abandon. Unhappily it adopted, in its
striving after political unity, a course of action which greatly
increased national disunity.

Upon the annexation of the diamond fields there followed

historically and logically the Confederation proposals of
Lord Carnarvon. In February 1874 Carnarvon succeeded
Kimberley at the Colonial Office. He soon found that
South Africa yielded much to occupy his attention. The
Delagoa Bay dispute was coming to a head; there was
trouble with natives in Natal, the result of the purchase by
them of guns out of the proceeds of their earnings at the
diamond fields; the disputes over the ownership of Griqua-
land West and the boundaries of the Republics were
still dragging on. Recollections of the consummation of
Canadian Confederation during his previous tenure of the
Colonial Office made Carnarvon think that the solution of
South Africa's troubles was to be found along similar lines.
As a first step he asked the historian, James Anthony Froude,
to visit South Africa, as an unofficial observer, during the
course of a voyage to Australia which he was contemplating.
Froude's reports were to provide the basis for future action.

In those reports Froude quite definitely took the side of
the Free State in the diamond fields dispute, emphasizing
the injustice which had been done to it by Britain's representatives. He stressed also the difficulty of native problems
in South Africa, and the importance of their bearing on the
inter-relations of the South African states. Carnarvon had
got what he wanted. He sat down forthwith to write his
famous Confederation despatch.

The primary aim of that despatch was to bring about a
settlement of the Griqualand West question, in regard to
which Carnarvon was satisfied that the Free State had been
unfairly treated; its ultimate purpose was a South African
Confederation, similar to that of Canada. To neither of
these objects, however, could the Colonial Secretary give
pride of place in his despatch. And so he emphasized the
advisability of securing greater homogeneity in the native
policies of the various South African states, and to that end he
proposed the holding of a Conference of delegates in South
Africa. But the Conference might also discuss related
questions, such as the position of Griqualand West, and the
boundary question, and ' if in the course of the free inter-
change of communications between the representatives of
the different States concerned, that all-important question
of a possible Union of South Africa should arise, Her

Majesty's Government will readily give their favourable attention to any suggestion that may be made.'

The intentions of the Secretary of State were admirable, but good intentions are sometimes very far from being enough. In creating the machinery to bring his project into effect, Carnarvon most unaccountably forgot that there was now in South Africa a Colony with Responsible Government, and a Cabinet of its own. For in 1872 the Cape Colony had attained an enhanced constitutional status, and Sir John Charles Molteno had become its first Prime Minister. It would have been ordinary political wisdom for Carnarvon to take Molteno into his confidence, before he gave publicity to his schemes. Not only did he fail to do this, but he went so far as to indicate who he thought should represent the Colony at the proposed Conference, and one of those whom he suggested was a political opponent of the Administration in office. In this way Carnarvon right at the outset antagonized the Responsible Government of the most important of the states which he wished to confederate. Significantly enough, the reception of his proposals in the Republics was by no means unfriendly—even after the annexations of Basutoland and Griqualand West the breach in South Africa's national unity could still have been repaired without undue difficulty—but Molteno's opposition determined Carnarvon on a change of policy. He cancelled the proposals set forth in his original despatch, held a partially representative Conference in London, settled the Free State's claim in respect of the diamond fields by a money payment, and decided to approach his goal of Confederation along a different route. Having passed a Permissive Confederation Act through the Imperial Parliament, he initiated the policy which led to the Annexation of the Transvaal.

The South African Republic had once again fallen upon evil days. After the resignation of Pretorius in 1872 it had elected the Reverend T. F. Burgers, a prominent minister of the Dutch Reformed Church in the Cape Colony, as its President. Burgers was a man of idealism and energy, but he lacked discretion. Full of great schemes for the Republic, he launched out upon a progressive policy, but in doing so he failed to take account of the conservatism of his people. In consequence he alienated their sympathies, and lost their confidence. His attempt to suppress a native rising failed ignominiously. Financial chaos was upon him. The fabric of government seemed to be crumbling beyond the Vaal, and the resultant native unrest threatened to have serious consequences for the rest of South Africa. To Carnarvon it appeared that there was sufficient justification for the settlement of the Transvaal problem by the short cut of annexation. So also, he thought, would he advance a further stage towards his goal of Confederation. Sir Theophilus Shepstone, who had won distinction by his administration of native affairs in Natal, was appointed ' Special Commissioner to enquire respecting certain disturbances which have taken place in the territories adjoining the Colony of Natal.' He was given secret instructions, authorizing him to annex the South African Republic. On the 12th April, 1877, he exercised that authority.

The annexation of the Transvaal stands out as one of the black spots in South African history, the event which did more than any other, save the Jameson Raid, to exacerbate feeling between Dutch and British, and to delay the attainment of national unity. It was a flagrant violation of solemn treaty obligations, but the tragedy of it is heightened by the reflection that, had Great Britain held her hand, there is a strong probability that the Republic would, in the position in which it found itself, before long have applied to her for friendly aid, and of its own volition consented to a scheme of Confederation. As it was, the exercise of force produced the inevitable result. The opposition to the annexation grew steadily in strength. Protest followed protest. At last, when Gladstone seemed to have forgotten his Midlothian speeches, recourse was had to force. And though the policy of Liberalism prevailed in Downing Street, it did not do so until Majuba had been fought, until the impression had been created in the minds of many of the simple burghers of the Republic that they had been able to extort by force the freedom which appeals to justice could not secure, until Britain had once again come to stand in their minds as the enemy and the aggressor, against whose attacks they must be prepared to defend their liberty with all the power that in them lay.

But the effects of these events, leading as they did to war and bloodshed, went far beyond the limits of the Transvaal. Throughout South Africa, wherever men of Dutch speech were gathered together, bitter sentiments were expressed. Dutch national consciousness was awakened. A sense of Dutch nationhood, embracing Republicans and Colonists of kindred stock, became a powerful motive and inspiration in political action. British and Dutch were driven into sharper antagonism than at any previous period in South African history. Once again the tide was on the ebb, away from the goal of union, and it was hard to foretell where its outflow would be checked. In the years that followed Majuba, new States again began to come into existence in South Africa, most of them, indeed, soon to be absorbed into larger units, but by the fact of their emergence illustrating the strength of the fissiparous tendencies that were at work; and withal there was the danger of the development along lines of increasing hostility of two conflicting national sentiments, British and Dutch.

Those years are among the most interesting years in South African history, and that not least because it is before all others the period when individual personalities command the attention, the period when the interest passes from bodies of men to individuals, from systems and policies and traditions, which determine the actions of individuals, to the individuals who create, destroy, or revivify those systems and policies and traditions. It is a period the history of which is best understood as the interplay of forces, which find their embodiment in individuals of dominating personality. There were three men—Kruger, Rhodes, and Hofmeyr—who filled the stage during those years, and rarely in the history of any nation have three such men made simultaneous appearance. And so for the understanding of the events of those years, as also for the appreciation of much that is still vital in the South Africa of to-day, it is necessary first to seek to understand these men and what they stood for.

It is natural to consider first the oldest of them, Paul Kruger. He was one of those who left the Cape Colony as participants in the Great Trek. Too young, indeed, to take an active part in the exploits of the Voortrekkers, he was yet old enough to catch the inspiration of that great

adventure, to share in the sorrows caused by the murder at
Dingaan's kraal, to rejoice in the victories over the hordes of
Zulu and Matabele. On the young lad the significance of
those great days was not lost. He caught the meaning of
the Voortrekkers' ideal of a wide, free land, an ideal which
he never lost; and when a new generation sprang up, that
knew not of the deeds of its fathers, it was he who kept alive
the inspiration of the past. In the toilsome task of settling
the Transvaal he, in his turn, played a great part. In
clearing the land of wild beasts, in fighting the Republic's
native foes, in many a distressful civil war, he was ever in
the van.

So he laid the foundations of his great influence with his
people. Shrewd and cool, with the doggedness and determination that refused to despair even when the clouds that
enveloped the infant Republic were at their darkest, pre-
eminent in strength and courage even among those early
pioneers, he won affection and honour throughout the land.
At the same time his life on the veld gave him confidence in
himself, and a knowledge of how best to deal with his fellow-
men. Above all, he was typical of the people amongst
whom he lived, and that is the chief reason why he, though
his education was limited to what he had picked up at his
mother's knee, and during three months of desultory school-
ing, was to succeed where his predecessor, Burgers, the man
of European culture, who seemed almost to have passed
into a different century from those over whom he ruled, had
failed.

Yet though Kruger, already in the eighteen-seventies,
had considerable influence over his fellow-countrymen, he
gave little indication, at that time, of the greatness of the
part that he was to play; no one dreamed that he was
destined yet to attract the attention of Europe and the world.
It was the call of a crisis that gave him direction, a policy,
something for which to fight; it was in that emergency that
he may be said to have found himself. That crisis came with
the Annexation of 1877. It was characteristic of the slow-
thinking man that the full significance of the event did not
at once become clear to him, that for a spell even he
acquiesced in the new order of things in the Transvaal.
But time for reflection brought a change of attitude. He

had been present as a young man when the Sand River
Convention was signed. To him, therefore, its iniquitous
violation came home with more than ordinary force. All
the feelings of the Voortrekker stirred within him again,
feelings which the lapse of time and the deadening of the
old sense of grievance had pushed into the background—so
much so that in 1872 he had supported the candidature for
the Presidency of an Englishman from Natal. And so,
when to the farmers out on the veld there gradually came
the same awakening, Kruger was their natural leader.

There followed the years of the British occupation of the
Transvaal, during which he developed the diplomatic gifts
that were to make him a match for the statesmen of Europe.
His task was a difficult one—to hold back his people from
premature action, yet not to damp their ardour; to arouse
the sympathy and secure the co-operation of kindred South
Africans outside the Transvaal, to drive the Imperial
Government by degrees into an untenable position, and then,
at the right moment, to act. He succeeded. His election
to the Presidency, after the Retrocession had taken place in
terms of the Convention of Pretoria, followed naturally.

His policy as President was a logical response to the
events which had gone before. It was a frankly separatist
policy. The South Africa of which Kruger dreamed, if
South Africa was to become a single unit, was a purely
Dutch South Africa. If the Cape Colony would not join
him in such a policy, then he would content himself with the
union of the two Republics. Round them he would build a
ring-fence, political and economic, and to secure his communications with the world he would revive the policy which,
when Burgers championed it, he had opposed, the policy of a
Delagoa Bay railway, and, if possible, a port for the Republic
on the east coast. That was what he desired for his people.
And his people meant those of the same stock as he was—
men of English birth and English speech were, and must
needs remain, a people apart.

These were the thoughts that passed through Kruger's
mind after the war of 1881. They did not definitely
crystallize into a policy until some years later, but thereafter they gave the impulse to his activity, and in that
conception which he held of South Africa we find the one

constant element that lent simplicity, vigour, and cohesion
to his statesmanship.   And in that activity and that policy
were embodied tendencies that did not make for the con-
sumation of national unity in South Africa.

From Paul Kruger it is an easy transition to the more
complex character of Cecil Rhodes.   Dissimilar as they were
in many ways, the seventeenth-century Puritan farmer-
statesman and the Capitalist prince of the modern world,
who saw in money the means to power, in one respect they
were alike.   Each had a great, an outstanding personality.
Even those whose dislike of Rhodes is most intense, testify,
by the very strength of their aversion, to the forcefulness of his
personality, to the portentous energy of a character that was
to affect the world so deeply for weal and woe.

Strange was the training which Cecil Rhodes received for
his life-work.   For he graduated simultaneously at the
universities of Oxford and of the diamond diggings, in the
academies of thought and of action.   While Kimberley and
its life of ceaseless activity and struggle gave him the same
concreteness of vision which the taming of the wild Transvaal
gave Kruger, there was always in him something more,
some trace, evanescent perhaps at times, of a dominating
idealism.   Oxford fired him with enthusiasms, encouraged
him to champion forgotten, even apparently lost causes;
Kimberley endowed him with the ability and the means to
translate enthusiasm into action.   But the days of strangely
varied life on the diggings left a yet deeper impress on him.
The keenness of competition gave him the never-to-be-
effaced desire, always to be getting the better of some rival.
The rapidity of his success filled him with confidence in
his own strength, and with an eagerness fully to satisfy all
the latent possibilities of his being.   The vastness of the
transactions in which he came to play a part led him to
find glamour in a big idea just because of its bigness.   But
there was one other thing that he acquired at Kimberley—
his attitude towards life as a game, which was so potent a
factor in his later political career. 'I should not care
greatly, if I lost all I have; it is the game I like,' said he in
his Kimberley days.   Many years later, when near to
death, he declared that the game had been worth the
candle, but the great fault of life was that, just when one

was beginning to learn the game, one had to stop. It was just this feeling, and the speculative instinct which it encouraged, that made Rhodes venture on projects from which others would have shrunk.

Therein also lies the reason why, in him, we seek in vain for the simplicity, the directness, the unity of policy, which we find in Kruger. To some that may seem a strange saying. It is, perhaps, not in accord with the still prevalent conception of Rhodes. There are many who do think that they find in him simplicity and unity of purpose and ideals. Ordinarily he is still represented as the great antitype of Kruger, the exponent of the ideal of a purely British South Africanism, as Kruger was of Dutch South Africanism, and foremost champion of the creed of the Jingo Imperialist. In support of that conception of Rhodes it is possible to adduce a great deal of evidence. If one reads for instance that remarkable first will of his, wherein he bequeathed his fortune yet unmade for the purpose of extending British rule throughout the world, one is reminded of Punch's almost contemporaneous definition of Imperialism as the policy that would

> Defy mankind from China to Peru,
> And then annex from Afghan to Zulu.

If again one turns to the speeches of his later years, the impression produced is on the whole similar. But in the Rhodes of the intervening period one meets with a different man—the Rhodes who jests with the idea of the Empire on which the sun never sets, the Rhodes who threatens to hoist ' his own rag ' in Zambesia, the Rhodes who is the quintain at whom all approved Imperialists tilt as ' an English-speaking Dutch Boer.' It is true that all through this period Rhodes claimed to be, and was, an Imperialist—in a sense—that he retained his belief in the virtues of British rule, that he continued to dream of a world wherein the ideals and the government would be determined by a dominant Anglo-Saxon Federation. But in the application of these ideas to South Africa there had come a vital change. That change had not yet commenced in 1881. He was then still in his first phase, ' a rabid Jingo,' as he himself later expressed it, with sore feelings at the issue of the

Transvaal War of Independence, with a determination to paint all South Africa red, with no friendship for his Afrikaans-speaking fellow-colonists at the Cape. He was, then, still the antitype of Kruger—he standing for Jingo Imperialism, as Kruger stood for Separatist Republicanism. But likewise he was only twenty-seven, and the fact that his ideas and policies were still fluid, still receptive to the impress of human and other factors, was to be of considerable significance in South African history.

One of those human factors was the third of the three men round whom the history of this period has been described as turning—Jan Hofmeyr. He was a man of a stamp quite distinct from the other two, and his influence rested on a different basis. His was not the dominating personality of Kruger or of Rhodes—he was not the man to arouse popular enthusiasm by qualities that appeal to the imagination—his power came rather from a clear knowledge of the character of his people and a perfect·control of the methods of organizing them to the fullest advantage. His training, like that of Rhodes, had been an unusual one. At seventeen, in Capetown, the town of his birth, he was editing a newspaper, which for several years brought in scarcely enough to pay the cost of production, much less an editor's salary. It was a hard school in which he served his apprenticeship, and it was only by virtue of enthusiasm and doggedness that he won through to success. But it endowed him with solidity of character and determination, the power to make up his mind as to the ideal to be aimed at, and to press on towards the attainment of that ideal, regardless of difficulties and discouragements. In 1878 he commenced his strictly political activity. In that year he created the first of the political organizations that were to carry the Afrikaans-speaking Colonists from the mute expressionless inertia into which they had lapsed to the dominant position in Cape politics. In 1879 he himself entered the House—two years later he was able to determine the fall of the Government of the day. His position was already assured in 1881 as one of the leading representatives of Dutch South Africa, and as one of the foremost men in the Cape Parliament.

What did he stand for in the political life of South Africa?

That question is far less easy to answer than is the similar
question in the case of Kruger or of Rhodes. The reason is
not that there is any need to distinguish different phases in
his career, as there is in that of Rhodes; on the contrary,
there was as striking a unity in the aims and purpose of
Hofmeyr as there was with Kruger. It is to be found rather
in the fact that his ideals and policy were determined by
laborious reflection, not by instinct and sentiment, and
represented a complex and carefully balanced whole, not
easy to describe in terms of superficial party shibboleths.
But described it must be, for it offers the key to the understanding of much in South African history.

The policy of Hofmeyr can best be understood in the light
of the emphatic approval which he gave to the declaration
made by Sir Hercules Robinson at the end of his first term of
office as Governor of the Cape Colony, that of the three conflicting influences in South Africa, Colonialism, Republicanism, Imperialism, the future lay with Colonialism. The
policy of Hofmeyr was the policy of Colonialism, and the
development of that policy was one of the significant features
of the years that followed the first Transvaal War. What,
then, was Colonialism?

Colonialism differed from Imperialism and Republicanism chiefly in respect of two questions—the question of the
association of South Africa with the British Empire, and the
question of the relations between Dutch and British in South
Africa itself. On the first of these questions Republicanism
stood for a Dutch South Africa under its own flag; the
Imperialism of those days stood for the tightening of the
bonds of Empire along the lines of some form of Imperial
Federation, and the determination of South African questions in terms of Imperial policies. Colonialism for its
part cordially accepted the British connection on the basis
of consent, not in the case of a man like Hofmeyr on any
sentimental grounds, but because its continuance appeared
to be quite definitely in the interest of South Africa. It
went further. It emphasized the importance to South Africa
and to the world of the maintenance and the strengthening
of the Empire, and was prepared to work towards that end.
But it refused to accept any policy which would mean the
impairment of Colonial autonomy, and it aimed at the

settlement of South African questions in South Africa by
South Africans with primary reference to the interests of
South Africa. Those who preached the doctrines of
Colonialism in the eighteen-eighties were, indeed, pioneers
in that movement which has resulted in the modern concep-
tion of Dominion status.

The second question was that of the basis of national
unity in South Africa. On that issue Republicanism was
frankly separatist and anti-British. Imperialism desired
unity, but it was a unity based on the absorption of Dutch by
British, with the British element in a position of assured
superiority. The ideal which Hofmeyr put forward was
that of the union of Dutch and British into one South African
nation, with a common feeling of South African nationhood,
but the union was to be based on complete and absolute
equality. It was to be a union between two national groups,
each of which had first realized and developed to the fullest
extent its own distinctive individuality, and it was to assume
the recognition and acceptance by each of the traditions,
the language, and as far as possible the sentiments of the
other. Hofmeyr's ideal, then, was an indivisible South
African feeling of nationality—an English–Dutch Afrikaner
nation, he himself phrased it. But he never forgot that the
unity rested on a duality, that it was necessary first to build
up each of the component parts to fulness of stature if the
unity was to be stable and secure. The ideal of unity was
always with him, but he also never forgot that the awakening
and the development of Dutch national feeling were indispensable pre-requisites to its adequate attainment. In this
spirit he desired national unity; in this spirit also he laboured
consistently for a political union of the South African States.
So it was that his first appearance on a political platform was
in support of the Carnarvon Confederation proposals, and
his last public service was to assist in the consummation of
the Union of South Africa as a member of the delegation
which went to London in connection with the passing of
the Act of Union through the Parliament of Westminster.

It is possible now to consider the interplay of the tendencies
embodied in the three men who have been described. First
the tendencies represented by Kruger and Hofmeyr came
into conflict. During the period of the British occupation

of the Transvaal they had co-operated wholeheartedly. It was Hofmeyr who had applied his growing influence in the organization of the protests of the Dutch Colonists against the annexation; it was he who, though he had supported the original Carnarvon scheme, secured the defeat in the Cape House in 1880 of a proposal for the summoning of a Conference to discuss Confederation, since its acceptance at that stage would have implied approval of the position in the Transvaal. But when the struggle was over, the divergence between the ideal of Republicanism and Colonialism evidenced itself. One of the results of the War of Independence was the manifestation of widespread sympathy throughout South Africa for the ideals which Kruger represented. The manner of its ending aroused the national consciousness of the older population everywhere. In the ardour of a national awakening it is natural to go to extremes, and the stream started flowing strongly in separatist and Republican channels. The new spirit found expression in an organization known as the Afrikander Bond, which professed as its aim a United South Africa under its own flag, and the upbuilding of a purely Dutch national senti-ment. The danger of such a movement for the Cape Colony at that time needs no emphasis. That danger Hofmeyr realized. He met it by joining the Bond and setting himself to modify its spirit and ideals from within. It was a severe struggle, but the broad South African ideal prevailed, and thereafter the Bond stood loyally at Hof-meyr's side in the carrying out of his policy. But the victory was won at a price. It was Kruger's ideal which had suffered defeat, and though Kruger himself had not been involved in the struggle, he never forgot Hofmeyr's opposi-tion to that ideal. That remembrance did much to deter-mine the aloofness which was to characterize his attitude towards the Cape.

In this episode Rhodes had, of course, played no part; he had as yet no established position in political life. But already his contact with peoples and problems more repre-sentative than those with whom he had dealt at Kimberley was beginning to break down the narrowness of his Im-perialism—already he was realizing, dimly indeed, that for the Colonial statesman Colonial interests must always come first. But his enthusiasm for the British Empire remained, nor was there any relaxation in his determination to find a field for British expansion in Africa. He was to find it by way of Bechuanaland, but there also he was to find a new policy and a new direction.

In 1882 there came into existence on the south-western boundary of the Transvaal, in what came to be called British Bechuanaland, two republics which received the names Stellaland and Goshen. Their founders were for the most part Transvaalers in whom the restless spirit of the Trek-boer still lived. The future of these republics soon presented an awkward problem, for they lay athwart the main trade-route northwards, and so blocked the development of which Rhodes dreamed. There is no evidence to prove that Kruger had inspired this westward movement of his burghers, but it is clear enough that he was determined to use it as a means to what he regarded as the legitimate expansion of his State, by annexing the new States to the Transvaal. This desire Hofmeyr supported, for, despite differences of flag, he regarded the Transvaal and the Free State as partners in the South African Commonwealth, and believed that the Transvaal should participate jointly with the Cape in the development of the north, to which the possession of Bechuanaland gave the key. To Rhodes, however, such a view was entirely unacceptable, and here he won his first great political victory. With the help of the Governor, Sir Hercules Robinson, he prevailed on Downing Street to bar Kruger's western advance, and the Convention of London, which in 1884 finally settled the status of the retroceded South African Republic, placed most of Stellaland and Goshen outside of its limits.

But though the incident commenced with a conflict between Rhodes and Hofmeyr, which was typical of the deeper conflict between the policies of Imperialism and Colonialism, or, let us call it, South Africanism, for which they stood, it proved in the end to be the commencement of their alliance. It happened in this wise. Ill-advisedly the Transvaal Government annexed, though subject to Britain's consent, a portion of Bechuanaland which had already been proclaimed a British Protectorate. At once there was evoked a violent outburst of that spirit of British Jingoism which, no less than Dutch Nationalism, had been stimulated by Majuba. The British Government was pressed to despatch a force which should eject the Stellalanders and Goshenites, and, if possible, pick a quarrel with the Transvaal. This demand Robinson and Rhodes supported, and as a result Sir Charles Warren, with 5,000 men, marched through Bechuanaland to expel 300 farmers, who retired peacefully before them. It was Warren who completed the conversion of Rhodes. His studied disregard of Colonial interests, his hostility even to perfectly legitimate claims of the Stellalanders, to many of whom Rhodes had deeply committed himself, his flagrant attempts to insult Kruger, and to force on a war which would ' avenge Majuba,' and his final proposals for the settlement of Bechuanaland in such manner that it should be closed to ' all Dutch Boers ' and non-teetotallers, all helped to convince Rhodes of the incompatibility of the policy of a thoroughgoing Imperialism with the dignity and interests of a self-governing Colony. ' I have been through the fire of Bechuanaland,' he said a few years later; ' I was a rabid Jingo once; I am that no longer.' Bechuanaland and Sir Charles Warren weaned him from the Imperialism of his first phase, and set his feet firmly on the path that led to what Robinson was to describe as Colonialism. Thereafter it was his voice that was loudest in the raising of the cry: ' The Imperial factor must be eliminated.'

These events served to bring Hofmeyr and Rhodes together. When the question of the inclusion of Bechuanaland in the South African Republic had been decided against Kruger, Hofmeyr had fallen back on the position that at least the introduction of Imperial troops and of Imperial government must be prevented in a matter that concerned only South Africa. On this issue Rhodes had defeated him, but at the last the defeated cause won the adhesion of the conqueror, and for the next few years Hofmeyr and Rhodes fought side by side for the principle of Colonial Home Rule. In their efforts they had the support of Robinson, whom also Warren had converted, and their combined action was not without effect. By 1890 they had united the Cape House in support of the principle, and had also secured its acceptance by the Colonial Office.

But as Rhodes approximated towards Hofmeyr, Kruger drifted away, and consolidated his policy of separatism. Hofmeyr, in a spirit characteristic of his broad South Africanism, had refused to abandon the quest of a concrete expression of South African unity. The annexation of the Transvaal had postponed the attainment of political union to a distant date; he sought, therefore, to prepare the way for future progress to that goal by the development in the meantime of economic co-operation through a South African Customs Union and the common acceptance of a broad policy of railway intercommunication. In those efforts he met with support from the Free State, but he found Kruger by no means friendly. Hofmeyr's opposition to Republicanism at the Cape had convinced the President that, to ensure his isolation from the British, he must also isolate himself from their Colony, and therefore on questions of tariff co-operation and railway extension he presented a solid wall of opposition to the Cape. Once only did he relax this attitude. In 1885 the economic difficulties of the Republic induced him to make overtures to the Cape Government of the day with a view to an understanding in tariff and railway questions. But the Transvaal had as yet no golden bait to dangle; and the suggestion was temporarily shelved. Next year gold was discovered on the Witwatersrand. Kruger's position was enormously strengthened. It was he now who held the strongest hand. He threw all his energies into the construction of his Delagoa Bay railway, and when, in 1889, the Cape and the Free State joined in a South African Customs Union, he definitely refused to co-operate, and for long placed all the obstacles he could in the way of the extension of the Colonial railways in the direction of his State. It was the attitude adopted by him in this matter, marking as it did the consolidation of his isolationist policy as against the Cape, which in 1890 finally confirmed the alliance of Hofmeyr and Rhodes.

That alliance was for the next six years the determining element in South African politics. On the basis of the ordinary conception of Rhodes it is no easy matter to understand how these two men could have continued for so long in close co-operation and alliance; that a man like Rhodes should have been Prime Minister by the gift of a man like

D

Hofmeyr, for it was he who, with the backing of the Bond, controlled the Cape Parliament, though he declined to accept office; that it was by Hofmeyr's goodwill that the execution of Rhodes's projects in the north and the establishment of the Rhodesias were made possible. Nor was the alliance a mere matter of political convenience, for with it was coupled a personal friendship which was deep and real. It can in fact only be understood, when it is remembered that the Rhodes of this alliance was the Rhodes of the second phase, the Rhodes who had been through the fire of Bechuanaland, the Rhodes who had paid wholehearted homage to the ideals of Colonialism. Colonial Home Rule was the basis of his policy, and he defined its aim as being ' the government of South Africa by the people of South Africa with the Imperial tie for defence.' To secure that aim, and to make Colonial Home Rule real and effective, he emphasized the necessity of racial co-operation, the working together of Dutch and British for the good of their common home. Of that his own co-operation with Hofmeyr and the Bond was typical. With the general outlook of his allies he had much in common. When once his early Imperialism had been modified, the alliance was, indeed, a natural one—and it was certainly in accord with the policy of Hofmeyr that he should accept Rhodes's proffered hand of friendship. Rhodes was the outstanding representative of British South Africanism, of that spirit the assimilation of which to Dutch South Africanism was in time to produce that comprehensive national spirit which Hofmeyr desired. Kruger had gone out on a different path, co-operation with him had become impossible—' Ephraim is joined unto idols; let him alone '—what more natural than that the leader of the Bond should turn to the man whose views coincided so largely with his own, and association with whom was an earnest of the policy for which he stood? So the alliance was consummated, and it was fruitful indeed in its results. Rhodes's schemes in the interior were brought to fruition; at the Cape British and Dutch worked heartily together, under the banner of South Africanism; the Free State, refusing to fall in with the Kruger policy, was drawn into effective co-operation; the ideal of national unity progressed mightily. But for the cloud as big as a man's hand on the northern horizon, all seemed to promise well for South Africa.

Then came that cataclysmic event—the Jameson Raid. In the circumstances that led up to it both Rhodes and Kruger had their part. Each made a great mistake, and together their mistakes had tragic consequences. But in the case of Kruger the mistake was a blunder—in the case of Rhodes it was a crime. Kruger made his mistake when he rejected the advice of wise old Jan Brand—to make the new Uitlander population of the Witwatersrand his friends. At the worst, he should have known that the danger from an extension of the franchise to them was small, since those from whom he had most to fear would not have surrendered their British for Transvaal citizenship; since, moreover, by deepening the economic cleavages in the Uitlander element, he could have minimized the threat which as a united body they seemed to present. And it was a mistake which, apart from the pretext that it was to give for interference from without, seemed likely to cost the President personally dear. Many of his former adherents disapproved of his policy— gradually he lost support—and indeed it is practically certain that at the time when the Raid took place he could no longer have counted on a majority among his own burghers. Therein lies the tragedy of the Raid. But for it the next Presidential election would almost certainly have seen the return to power of a President committed to a different policy.

But if Kruger erred, Rhodes's mistake was far more grave in character, and history will hold him mainly responsible for the tragic course of subsequent events. It is difficult, indeed, to discover how such an act came to be committed by the man who was the friend and ally of Hofmeyr, who had repeatedly insisted on a policy of toleration and patience towards the Transvaal, who had even rebuked the Bondsmen for their impatience when they chafed at Kruger's anti-Cape policy. It may even be that a physical cause, the form of heart complaint from which he was suffering, should be held, in part at least, to account for his sudden and calamitous lapse. Rhodes's ultimate aim may be admitted to have been a high one. What he desired was to advance the ideal of a United South Africa by sweeping out of the way

the one remaining obstacle—the Kruger policy of separatism.
But in pursuing that ideal he had recourse to a short cut,
forgetting that the end does not justify the means, that
methods which have been successful in the amalgamation of
diamond mines will not work in the unification of States.
And his action exemplified another weakness of his, to which
G. K. Chesterton once called attention. ' There is nothing
large,' he wrote, ' about painting the map red. It is an
innocent game for children. It is just as easy to think in
continents as to think in cobble-stones. The difficulty
comes in when we seek to know the substance of either of
them. Rhodes could think in continents, and yet he failed
to understand a few two-legged men.' It was just here that
Rhodes came to grief in this the most critical issue of his
career. He failed to appreciate the attitude of the Johannesburg Reformers. He failed to understand Kruger. He
misjudged Sir Hercules Robinson. Above all, his conception of Hofmeyr was at fault. He believed that his friend,
because of his sympathy with his aim, would also approve his
methods, would accept the revolution as an accomplished
fact, would even render assistance in its final phases. As
events turned out, Hofmeyr played an important part in
checkmating his designs.

The Raid changed the course of South African politics.
It deflected Rhodes from the path of co-operation and
moderation which he had been treading. So strong was his
influence with the Afrikaans-speaking people of the Cape
that he might yet have recovered some of his influence and
authority, had he been willing to acknowledge his error, and
ask for pardon. But for Rhodes, for whom the adulation
born of continued success made it impossible to sink his
pride, this was too much. He preferred to regard the Raid
as ' the beginning of my political career,' to range himself
on the side of his former opponents. So he became the
instrument of the Jingo Imperialism which once he had
fought, the presiding genius of those who saw no solution of
South Africa's problems save in a war which would establish
British ascendancy on the basis of military force. On the
other side the Raid strengthened the position of Kruger.
To him it brought renewed conviction of the rightness of his
policy. His burghers were, because of the attack on the

liberties of the State, once again united in support of him, and in the determination to resist any further efforts to seize their Naboth's vineyard. Moreover, it at last consolidated the alliance between the Free State and the Transvaal, for which Kruger had striven in vain, on the basis of the acceptance by the Southern Republic of the policy for which he stood.

Thus was the ground prepared for conflict and strife. As the bitter feelings which the Raid aroused grew in intensity, the voice of moderation could no longer find a hearing, and the forces of Republicanism and Imperialism were left to hold the field alone. There could be but one result. For two a half years South Africa was plunged in bitter warfare. At the end of it the barriers arising from differences of flag and sovereignty, which stood in the way of political union, had been removed, but feelings of bitterness had been aroused, which were not soon to be allayed, and which seemed to postpone the attainment of national union into the very far distant future.

Chapter 7

The Making of a Nation

THE Anglo-Boer War lasted much longer than anyone had dreamed. Its operations covered a wide area. Not only did it range up and down the Republics, but it penetrated the Midlands of Natal and the heart of Zululand, while great stretches of the Cape Colony were involved, Boer forces riding up to within forty miles of Capetown. It brought into the field what in those days seemed great armies, the whole man-power of the two Republics, together with 10,000 sympathizers from the Cape and Natal, some 70,000 in all, and on the British side, from first to last some 300,000 troops, men from Britain, men recruited in South Africa itself, and others who crossed all the seven seas to play their parts. And as the struggle dragged out its long and weary course, arousing hopes which by their deferment made sick the heart, and lapsing into methods of warfare which aroused angry feelings in men's minds, it stored up against the future of South Africa a legacy of bitterness, based on memories of suffering and loss, which was deeply fraught with future evil.

The outbreak of war found Britain relatively unprepared, and the Republics enjoying the advantages of interior lines of communication and proximity to their base. Up to a point they made good use of their advantages, and they had their reward in important victories won in the closing months of 1899, which made it clear that the campaign was not going to be finished by 'fifty thousand horse and foot going to Table Bay.' But the victories were not followed up as they might have been. There was a lack of initiative and enterprise in the higher command. Old General Joubert, Commandant-General of the Transvaal, when the way lay open before him to Pietermaritzburg and the sea, rejected Louis Botha's advice, and concentrated on the siege of Ladysmith. Cronje, who commanded in the west, was

painfully deficient in strategic ideas, and his dilatoriness after
the relief of Kimberley led directly to the disaster of Paarde-
berg, which opened the way for the British forces into the
heart of the Republics. In March 1900 Roberts entered
Bloemfontein; less than two months later he was in Pretoria.
But the war was far from being at an end. When Pretoria
fell, the Transvaal Government retired into the field. For
a time Kruger remained with it, until in October he was
induced to sail for Europe by way of Delagoa Bay. His
colleague, President Steyn of the Free State, a much younger
man, remained with his burghers until the end. The
Republican forces scattered over the veld in comparatively
small detachments. By virtue of their mobility, and the
genius of their leaders in guerilla warfare, notably Botha, de
Wet, and de la Rey, they were able to parry the attacks of
large British forces, again and again bringing off daring
coups which echoed round the world. As part of the
campaign Republican generals, among them Smuts and
Hertzog, invaded the Cape Colony, and drew many of the
Afrikaans-speaking Colonists to their banners. The veld
of all South Africa was ablaze. Practically throughout the
Cape there was martial law, rifles crackled in regions where
none had ever dreamed it possible, blockhouses, some of
which still stand to-day as memorials of the madness of the
past, were built to guard the railway right down to within
easy reach of Capetown, Republican and British forces
harried one another, Colonial rebels and loyalists were
plunged into bitter feud, and ruin stalked through the land.
To deal with the difficulties presented by the guerilla warfare new expedients were resorted to. For a time it rained
threats and proclamations on Republicans and rebels who
remained in the field. Burghers who had surrendered were
enrolled under the British flag as National Scouts and
Volunteers to fight their former comrades in their own way.
For the destruction of sources of supply a policy of burning
farms and devastating the countryside was embarked upon.
As a corollary the women and children were brought into
concentration camps, where, owing largely to initial
difficulties of organization and errors of administration,
which were, however, later repaired, some 20,000 died.
So the war dragged on; it ended at last when, by the

Peace of Vereeniging of 31st May, 1902, the Republican
leaders, who still had some 20,000 men under their command, signed away their independence, but for the rest
received liberal terms. It was to a devastated land that
peace came. Blockhouses, and barbed-wire entanglements,
and ruined farmsteads, which might well have made those
who returned to them exclaim: ' They make it a solitude
and call it peace,' served ever to remind men of the struggle.
The memory of women and children dead in the concentration camps, approximately equal in number to the full tale
of British soldiers killed in the war, kept fresh the sense of
suffering and of grievance. The punishment of the rebels
in the Colonies, and the feuds between ' bitter-enders '
and National Scouts in the Republics were ever-present
sources of friction and difficulty. Over most of the land there
brooded a great sullenness, the more far-reaching and of the
greater significance for the future because the vicissitudes
of war and rebellion, together with the outcome of the
struggle, had broken down most of the barriers which had in
the past divided Republicans from Colonists of the same
stock, and so given greater potential effectiveness to the
expression of their common sentiments. It was peace, but
in men's hearts there was no peace.

Yet, even on the sentimental side, there was a credit as
well as a debit side of the war's account. During the
struggle Dutch South Africa had acquired self-consciousness,
had learnt to respect itself. More important still was the
sense of mutual respect to which, despite all the bitter
feelings which it aroused, the war gave birth. The British
Tommy had shown himself a far better fighting man than
the impression formed in 1881 had led men in the Republics
to believe; on the side of the British feelings of admiration
and respect for doughty opponents, to which Kipling gave
happy expression, had come to prevail; and between
British generals like Kitchener and Methuen, and Boer
leaders like Botha and de la Rey, relations of friendliness
and good-will, based on memories of courtesy and chivalry,
remained as not least significant of the legacies of the war.
Upon the foundations of mutual respect and appreciation
so laid in the two elements of the South Africa nation of the
future, the task of securing wholehearted recognition by

each of the traditions and sentiments of the other, the fulfilment of which was an indispensable condition of nationhood, could be the more easily undertaken.

In the more strictly political sphere the war brought one obvious gain, for it removed the greatest of the technical obstacles that had stood in the way of Union. Save for the German Colony on the west, and the Portuguese territories on the east, all of South Africa was now under one flag. That the ideal of Union, which had been pursued by men of diverse characters, and with different conceptions of its significance, since the days of Sir George Grey, must now be realized, seemed certain. What was not yet certain was, which conception would prevail. Would Union be imposed upon South Africa in the manner of the Carnarvon proposals of 1877, in the spirit of that Imperialism to which Rhodes had drifted uneasily back since the Raid? Or would the ideals of South Africanism, for the furtherance of which before that ill-fated enterprise Rhodes had co-operated with Hofmeyr, even yet triumph? For the moment Imperialism was in the ascendant. It had prevailed over Republicanism on the stricken field, and in the atmosphere of war the ideals of South Africanism, its only remaining rival, seemed to have lost all their power. Was it not inevitable that Imperialism should also prevail in the peace? In this new struggle it drew its inspiration, as failing vigour, and later death, removed Rhodes from the scene, from Milner, who had as Governor of the Cape Colony played an aggressive part in the events that precipitated the war, and had since been sent to Johannesburg as High Commissioner to deal with the problems that arose from the termination of the struggle. Milner was able and he was powerful. A united South Africa, with the ascendancy of the British element definitely assured, was his aim. It had been the ideal of Imperialism since the days of Wodehouse and Carnarvon. The circumstances and the man seemed now to have combined to make it a realizable ideal. The Khaki election of October 1900 had given the necessary endorsement. In the very month of the election, though the war was far from over, Chamberlain issued Milner's commission for his new post, and therein empowered him to take the preliminary steps which should lead to Federation.

This Imperialist policy of Union was based on two projects. The one was an active policy of British land settlement in the conquered Republics, so as to reduce Dutch ascendancy in the rural areas. The other was the suspension of the constitution of the self-governing Colonies until Union had been consummated, so as to ensure for the now federal State a constitution of such a nature as to make it possible for British ideas to prevail. The Milner land-settlement schemes brought into South Africa a considerable number of useful settlers, but the settlement never attained the magnitude or the effectiveness which he had hoped. The attempt to suspend the constitution of the Cape Colony evoked vigorous opposition, not only from Afrikaans-speaking Colonists, but also from English-speaking Moderates, and, most important of all, from Canadian and Australian representatives at the 1902 Conference of Imperial Premiers. The difficulties in the way of the Milner programme impressed themselves . on Chamberlain's mind. At the end of that same year he visited South Africa, and his observations satisfied him that a different path must be followed. His association and co-operation during that visit with Hofmeyr, who was still the high-priest of the gospel of South Africanism, and his declaration on his departure that South Africa must work out its own future and not expect interference from Downing Street, sounded the death-knell of the Milner policy of Imperialism. Some steps towards Federation Milner was able to take, of which the most important was the establishment of a comprehensive South African Customs Union in 1903, but for the rest he had to confine himself to the difficult task of the material reconstruction of the devastated Republics, wherein he attained remarkable success, and to leave the achievement of Union to the steady working of political evolution.

So, then, while the war had shattered Republicanism as a political force in South Africa, Imperialism in its turn had to accept the failure of its ideal of Union. From the time of the collapse of the agitation for the suspension of the Constitution of the Cape the tide of Imperialism steadily receded in South Africa. Thus was the field left open for South Africanism. There was a long and toilsome struggle ahead of it—the past was very far from being dead—and even to-day its ideals have not yet been fully attained. Yet once the first great plank in its platform had been established beyond all future challenge—that the Union of the South African communities could only be established by the action of their own freely elected representatives, without inter-ference from without—the final issue may be said to have been determined.

It followed that a necessary preliminary to Union was the grant of self-government to the Transvaal and the Orange River Colony (as the Orange Free State had been re-named). The Cape had enjoyed Responsible Government since 1872; Natal since 1893; if Union was to be the creation of South Africa itself, it must be a Union between communities of equal status, and the two Crown Colonies must receive free Parliamentary institutions. That had been foreshadowed in the Treaty of Vereeniging; but it could not of course come immediately after the end of hostilities—it did in fact come sooner than nearly everyone had anticipated. There were other pressing tasks that first demanded attention: the restoration of normal economic life in a war-stricken country, the settlement on the land of ex-combatants and returning war prisoners, the re-starting and the expansion of the gold-mining industry of the Witwatersrand. That expansion in particular Milner was most anxious to stimu-late. On its basis he foresaw the building up of an economic structure which would make possible the strengthening of the British element, and so lessen the danger of Afrikaner ascendancy, as he conceived it, in the future self-governing Union of South Africa. It was this desire that induced him to agree to the somewhat doubtful expedient of the importa-tion of Chinese labourers for unskilled work on the gold mines.

As prosperity returned in the economic sphere, there came also renewed stirrings of political activity among the people of the old Republics. Botha and Smuts, the natural leaders in the Transvaal, had at first declined to play any part in political life, when Milner offered them seats in his first nominated Legislative Council. But in 1905 they embarked on a new movement, establishing a political organization with the name *Het Volk* (the people). In the forefront of their programme they placed the loyal acceptance of the

Vereeniging Treaty, conciliation as between British and
Dutch, and Responsible Government for the Transvaal
and the Orange River Colony. Soon after, a party on
similar lines, the *Orangia Unie*, was founded in the other
Crown Colony, while at the Cape, under the inspiration of
Hofmeyr, the Afrikander Bond party had already been
reconstituted on a broader basis as the South African Party,
in such manner as to embrace many moderate English-
speaking supporters. The leaven of South Africanism was
commencing to work powerfully.

To the High Commissioner it became clear that the grant
of self-government to the Transvaal at least could not be
long delayed. On the Witwatersrand the one-time Uitlanders were commencing to press for the grant to them of
that franchise which the war had been fought to secure;
in Britain there were signs and portents of political change,
and the Liberals were not free from what Milner held to be
dangerous commitments in South African affairs. In his
view the time was not yet ripe for Responsible Government.
The strengthening of the British element, which he viewed
as a necessary preliminary, had not yet reached what he
thought was a point of safety; the assurances of the Het Volk
leaders that they acquiesced in their status of British citizenship he was loath to accept. With a view, therefore, to the
postponement of the day of the grant of full self-government,
he persuaded the Colonial Office to concede to the Transvaal Representative Parliamentary institutions, as a half-
measure, under the so-called Lyttleton Constitution. The
elective popular members were, indeed, to have considerable powers, but they would not have complete control over
the Executive, nor would they have any authority ' where
vital Imperial interests are concerned.'

But events moved more rapidly than Milner had anticipated. The Lyttleton Constitution was attacked in the
Transvaal, not only by Het Volk, but by a considerable
English-speaking section, which banded itself together into
what it called a National party; the fall of the Balfour
Government was precipitated; the new Liberal Government
won an overwhelming victory at the polls; and in December
1906 Letters Patent were issued, granting full Responsible
Government to the Transvaal. Next year a similar grant

was made to the Orange River Colony. At the elections
Het Volk and the Unie secured absolute majorities. Botha
became Prime Minister of the Transvaal, with Smuts as his
chief lieutenant, but he invited two members of the predominantly English-speaking National party to join his
Cabinet. Of the Orange River Colony Abraham Fischer,
who had been a prominent figure in Republican days, was
the first Premier, with Generals Hertzog and de Wet as two
of his Ministers. Five years after the Peace of Vereeniging
had ended the career of the two Republics, those same
territories were ruled as British Colonies by the defeated
Generals who had signed that Peace. The Campbell-
Bannerman Government had embarked upon a magnificent
venture of faith.

Of that act of faith the attainment of the Union of South
Africa was one of the first-fruits. For not only did it ensure
that all the contracting parties had the status necessary for
the negotiation of an agreement, but it also dealt a powerful
blow at the dividing wall of suspicion and mistrust between Dutch and British. It stimulated mightily Botha's
ideal of conciliation in the Transvaal. It gave new vigour
and direction to Hofmeyr's policy of South Africanism at the
Cape. Moreover, since, as a result, British mistrust of Dutch
intentions was allayed, it prepared the way for the abandonment of the old insistence on the maintenance of British
ascendancy as a condition of Union, and enabled men like
Selborne, Milner's successor, and Jameson, once leader of
the Raid, now Premier at the Cape, to take the initiative in
a new movement towards that goal. It was at the request
of the Jameson Cabinet that Selborne, early in 1907, submitted his famous Memorandum which contained ' a
review of the present mutual relations of the British South
African Colonies,' and emphasized the dangers of continued
disunion and the importance of immediate action to bring
it to an end. And, as if to emphasize the change that had
come over South Africa, Selborne, holder of the office that
had once been Milner's, stressed the point that the Union
must be born of the soil of South Africa, and nurtured by its
own statesmen.

There was no lack of incident and of evidence to support
the High Commissioner's contentions. Troubles with

natives in Natal and Zululand illustrated the importance of
the evolution of a uniform native policy. Questions of
defence, education, judicial administration, bearing on inter-
Colonial relations, were constantly cropping up. There
were serious conflicts between coast and inland Colonies in
the matter of the customs tariff, with the denunciation of the
Customs Union seemingly imminent. The very railways,
which by their destruction of geographical barriers had
powerfully forwarded the cause of Union, were now the
source of strife and conflict, since the difficulties in the way of
apportioning the valuable traffic of the Witwatersrand
between the lines to the various Cape ports, to Durban, and
to Delagoa Bay were well-nigh insuperable.

In May 1908 an inter-Colonial railway and customs
conference met, but rather than transact the business for
which it had been summoned, it passed resolutions in favour
of Closer Union, and, to that end, the summoning of a
National Convention of representatives of the Colonies.
Before the year was out, the Convention met, first in Durban,
later at Capetown. At it were present former Republican
leaders, like Steyn, Botha, and de Wet on the one hand,
Jameson and prominent Uitlanders of the past on the other;
yet the unanimity which prevailed was remarkable, and
there was every indication that a national, as well as a
political, union was being consummated. Characteristic
of the spirit of the Convention were the unanimous acceptance of the full equality of the Dutch and English languages,
and the restoration of the appellation Orange Free State to
the Province of the Union which had once borne that name
as an independent Republic. The Convention prepared a
draft constitution which, after some amendment in the light
of discussion in the four Colonial Parliaments, was submitted
to London. As the South Africa Act it was passed by Lords
and Commons, and received the Royal Assent. On 31st
May, 1910, eight years after Vereeniging, the four Colonies
became Provinces in the Union of South Africa. General
Botha took office as first Prime Minister, with Generals
Smuts and Hertzog as well as some English-speaking
supporters in his Cabinet. Jameson was left to lead an
almost entirely English-speaking Unionist part as the official
Opposition.

The creation of the Union of South Africa was a remarkable achievement. The mere unification of the four communities, when once they had been brought under a common flag, was perhaps not a task of very great difficulty. What made it a triumph of statesmanship was that, so soon after a long and bitter struggle, with its aftermath of ill-will, the leaders of the defeated peoples, entrusted now with the government of the British Colonies which had replaced their Republics, should, along with the representatives of the British element in South Africa, have devised an instrument of government which created a united South Africa under the British flag, and in terms of which the older population was, in the recognition of their language and in other respects, to be at no disadvantage as compared with the newer and victorious stock. The spirit in which the political union of South Africa had been effected encouraged the happiest of hopes for the future.

But the high hopes with which the Union was inaugurated have not been fully realized, and in part the reason is to be found in the very rapidity of the process which led up to its consummation. The two main component parts of the South African nation were descended from peoples of powerful individuality and a proud history. On either side there was abundant ground for pride in the traditions of the past, and while those of the older population felt themselves firmly rooted in the soil of South Africa by centuries of settlement and sacrifice, their fellow South Africans of the newer stock had limitless reserves to draw upon in the resources of British civilization and culture. It would have been strange indeed if either had been willing, even in the cause of building a South African nation, to surrender its individuality, or even to see it comprehended in a larger whole, until it was assured of the place to be filled by its character and traditions in that whole. And then at the end of a century of strife came the Anglo-Boer War, and the hoisting of the British flag where once there had been Republican independence. Within eight years of its conclusion, while memories were still fresh, and wounds were still raw, the attainment of a true and complete national union was in the nature of things impossible, and those who, in the expansiveness of what was called ' the Convention

spirit,' spoke comfortable words about the end that had been
set to controversy and bitterness between Dutch and British
in South Africa failed to appreciate all the facts of the
situation, and were forgetful of the power of sentiment in
political affairs.

In particular their understanding of the nature of the
reaction to the Three Years' War was incomplete. That
reaction was of a twofold nature. There was, firstly, the
political reaction, the movement of which Botha and Smuts
and Fischer and Hertzog were the leaders, a movement to
re-establish the political position of the older population,
which was numerically superior, but, as a result of the war,
politically inferior. That reaction was an important factor
in the advance towards political union. But there was also
what might be called a cultural reaction. The one-time
Dutch Republicans had lost their liberty. For the moment
they were in a position of complete subjection. A small
people, they were confronted with the mighty power of
Britain, with its world-wide culture backed by centuries of
tradition. It seemed inevitable that they should be
swamped. Instinctively they turned to the protection of
their own distinctive culture and traditions. They advanced
the claims of their language, Afrikaans, as a language distinct from the Dutch of Holland. They developed their
own literature. They resisted desperately the Milner policy
of Anglicizing their children in the Government schools,
raising funds for their own ' Christian National Schools.'
They struggled valiantly for the promotion of their cultural
distinctiveness. And this cultural movement was not confined to men from the old Republics. With them were
caught up men from the Cape and, to a less extent, from
Natal, who were bound to them either by actual participation in the war, or by the sentimental links which the war
had forged.

For the most part the two movements remained distinct.
The one point of contact was education, for the grant of
Responsible Government to the two ex-Republics left it to
the leaders of the political reaction, whom it placed in
power, to pronounce upon the fate of the Milner policy of
Anglicization through Education. Smuts in the Transvaal
effectively checked it, and enshrined the principle of instruc-

tion through the medium of the mother tongue in his Education Act, but stopped short of the complete equalization of Dutch with English in the schools. Hertzog, in the Free State, dealing with the same problem when the passions engendered by the war had had more time to subside, adopted without reservation the principle of equality, which the leaders of the cultural reaction deemed essential, but both by its enactment and by the manner of its application, his policy aroused bitter opposition on the British side. For the rest, the political reaction pursued its course from victory to victory, paying little heed to the far less obtrusive cultural movement. And the completeness of its success was demonstrated when General Botha became the first Prime Minister of a United South Africa as leader of the predominantly Dutch South African Party. That party included Het Volk, the Orangia Unie, and the old Afrikander Bond party at the Cape, and it attracted also a considerable number of English-speaking adherents from Natal. The position of the leaders of the cultural reaction seemed to be assured.

But success had been secured in a manner wherein lay the seeds of future trouble. Botha and Smuts had won through largely because of the Liberalism of British statesmen. At the National Convention the relations between Dutch and British South Africans had been of the most friendly character. What more natural than that they should place racial conciliation in the forefront of their policy, and regard the Act of Union, with its acceptance of the principle of language equality, as representing the consummation of national as well as of political unity? But in actual practice equality between British and Dutch had not yet been attained, and in the nature of things its complete attainment could not but be a lengthy process. The higher posts in the Civil Service were held for the most part by Britishers, unable to speak Afrikaans, but with rights which had to be safeguarded. On the railways, in education, in local administration, English had hitherto held a privileged position, and the establishment of practical, as well as theoretical, equality could not be brought about in a day, or even in a year. For the evolution of Afrikaans into a language, which could stand alongside of English for all purposes, time was necessary. All this meant that, in fact, the equality of status and equality of recognition, which alone could be accepted as the basis of national unity, had not yet been attained. Whatever had been achieved on the political side, there still remained a consciousness of cultural inferiority, and its survival lent a continuing distinctiveness to Afrikaans national sentiment.

The strength of this sentiment Botha and Smuts failed entirely to appreciate. With the cultural movement they found themselves increasingly out of touch. And so it was that the policy of conciliation induced a reaction, which came to a head when, as a result of disagreement with his colleagues, General Hertzog was forced to leave the Botha Cabinet in December 1912. His part in the education struggle in the Free State gave him a natural link with the cultural movement. Once dissociated from the leaders of the political reaction, he very soon joined forces with that movement, giving to it a political bias, which had hitherto for the most part been lacking. So was born the Nationalist Party, basing itself, in the first instance at least, very definitely on an appeal to a distinctively Afrikaans national senti- ment, and emphasizing, by the very fact of its existence, that the attainment of national unity was still in the future.

Hard on the birth of the Nationalist Party followed the outbreak of the Great War, which was to be a determining factor in its growth. There were many who had foretold that a German war would disclose the youngest Dominion in the British Empire as its Achilles heel; that it would be the signal for an attempt to recover the independence lost a bare twelve years before; that a Government presided over by Britain's former foes would, if it did not itself take steps to that end, at least offer no serious resistance to those who did so. But the Liberal Imperialism of Campbell-Bannerman was justified in its results. On the outbreak of war the Botha Government undertook responsibility for the land- defences of the Union, so as to relieve the Imperial garrison for service elsewhere; it agreed also to send an expedition to German South-West Africa, so as to secure control of its ports and powerful wireless station. Botha was determined to be true to the troth plighted at Vereeniging; he was willing also to accept the responsibilities as well as the privileges of membership in the Empire which he had entered.

Not all his people were ready to follow his lead. The formation of the Nationalist Party had removed many of them from the sphere of his influence, and the hostility aroused against him by the leaders of that party on the score of lack of sympathy with the sentiments of his fellow-Afrikaans-speaking South Africans had prepared fruitful soil for disaffection. In October 1914 rebellion broke out in South Africa, of which General de Wet was the chief leader. It was Botha's painful task to take the field against the comrades of other days. The motives of those who went into rebellion were diverse. Some viewed it merely as a protest against the projected invasion of a neighbouring community, with which South Africa had no direct ground for quarrel. Others were moved to action by a vague unrest, of which the causes were economic. With others again it was simply an attempt, in the tradition of the fissiparous period of Republican history, to get rid of a Government which they no longer liked. But the prime motives were undoubtedly the desire to recover lost independence, and the wish to satisfy the feelings of resentment which survived from the still all-too-recent war. Most of the participants were avowed Nationalists, and though the party as such was not involved in the rebellion, its leaders, Hertzog and ex-President Steyn, refrained from public condemnation. And when it was over, it was the Nationalist Party that, not unnaturally, took up the cause of the participants, seeking to palliate their offence, pressing for a mitigation of their punishment, and so derived political advantage from the suffering and bitter feeling to which it led.

And as the war dragged on—beyond all men's expectation—the Nationalists, finding much ground for attack in Botha's policy of ' seeing the war through,' and exploiting his activities in support of Britain's cause in their appeal to Afrikaans sentiment, went from strength to strength, and rallied ever more and more of the Afrikaans-speaking section of the community to their side. In the mutual rancours of the war it was difficult indeed for Botha and Smuts to maintain the broad South Africanism which would hold the balance even between the two elements in the national life.

It became more so when in 1917, at the instance of some of
their leaders, the Nationalists began openly to preach
Republicanism.   The spirit which Kruger had embodied,
and which had been crushed in the Anglo-Boer War, seemed
to have been reborn.

The War ended in November 1918, but the Republican
agitation in South Africa did not cease.   Instead a delegation, headed by Hertzog, was sent to Versailles to demand
independence for the whole Union, or, failing that, independence for the two former Republics.   The mission was
fruitless, but it had its effect in keeping alive that national
sentiment which was the strength of the Nationalist Party
during the period of transition from war to peace.   And,
indeed, the star of Nationalism continued to wax, that of the
South African Party to wane.   Within a fortnight of his
return from the Peace Conference Botha died, worn out, at
Pretoria.   His successor, Smuts, was richly dowered with
intellectual gifts, but he lacked Botha's imaginative sympathy and his magnetic influence over all sorts and conditions of men.   Nationalism continued to make headway in
the rural areas.   The economic troubles of the post-war
period gave wide scope for the preaching of the doctrines of
Labour in the towns.   From the 1920 election Smuts
returned with a sadly attenuated party, and it was only with
the help of his former Unionist opponents, whom Nationalist
attacks on the Government's war-policy had driven into
increasingly close support of it, that he was able with
difficulty to hold his ground.   And so Smuts, having first
made a desperate effort to re-establish unity between his
party and the Nationalists, an attempt which broke down
because of Nationalist insistence on the right to continue
Republican propaganda, came to an agreement with the
Unionists.   The Unionist Party was absorbed in the South
African Party, three of the Unionist leaders became members
of the Smuts Cabinet, and at an election in 1921 Smuts and
his enlarged party won a substantial victory.   But the
successes gained by him were at the expense of Labour.
In the country districts the Nationalists retained the strength
which they derived from their sentimental appeal.

For the moment Smuts had triumphed, and the disappearance of the Unionist Party in the South African Party

was also a triumph for the ideal of a broad national co-operation, the policy of South Africanism for which Botha had stood. But the cause of his triumph was in large measure the cause also of his downfall. Upon the fact of Smuts's association with the Unionists, erstwhile associates of Milner and champions of the creed of Jingo Imperialism, the Nationalists were able to base a new appeal to Afrikaans national sentiment. Then in 1922 came serious industrial disturbances on the Witwatersrand, which Smuts sternly suppressed. Once again his alliance with the Unionists, formerly the party of the mine-owners, could be utilized, this time to rally the Labour cause and to unite the workers against him. Moreover, the post-war depression, with the economies and the taxation which it entailed, told heavily against the Government. A common desire to achieve its downfall brought together British Labourites and Afrikaans Nationalists in a so-called Pact. The former decently veiled their Socialist objective, the latter discreetly pushed Republicanism into the background, agreeing that votes cast at the next election, when the alliance was to operate, would not be used to promote secession from the Empire. And so, when in 1924 Smuts, nettled by the difficulties which gathered thick and fast about him, appealed to the country after a defeat in an important by-election, the Pact triumphed. The Nationalists returned from the polls as the strongest individual party, and in alliance with Labour they had a substantial majority. As a result General Hertzog formed a Government, which included two (later three) Labour Ministers.

So, then, the South African Party had been defeated after fourteen years of office, and the new Prime Minister was one who owed his elevation to persistent appeals to a distinctive Afrikaans sentiment, and whose party had fought with enthusiasm under the banner of Republicanism and Secession. It might well have seemed that a vital blow had been struck at South African national unity and the ideal of South Africanism, portending a reversion to the old conflict between Republicanism and Imperialism. In fact, however, it was not immediately so. It may be questioned whether during all the years that General Hertzog led the Nationalist Party he was ever really a Republican at heart.

In the secessionist.propaganda of his party he followed rather than led. In the appeal to Afrikaans national sentiment, where it went beyond what served the legitimate end of equipping his section of the people to make its equal contribution to a greater South African nationhood, he often obeyed the dictates of opportunism rather than of conviction. As a result, in office, he failed to advance along the path of separatism as far as both opponents and followers expected him to go. In this he was helped by circumstances. The alliance with an almost entirely British Labour Party provided a useful and, to General Hertzog, not unwelcome brake upon the enthusiasm of his extremist followers. The visit of the Prince of Wales in 1925 did much to create an atmosphere of greater friendliness and goodwill. Moreover, the formulation by the Imperial Conference of 1926 of a definition of the status of the Dominions enabled the Nationalist leader to declare that he was satisfied with the position of freedom which South Africa had attained within the Commonwealth, and that therefore the need for Republican propaganda had fallen away.

In one respect, indeed, it could be said that the change of Government facilitated the growth of national unity in South Africa. The necessary basis of that unity, equality between the two elements, was laid down in the Act of Union; but the difficulty of immediately making that theoretical equality practically operative was considerable, as has already been emphasized. Under the Botha and Smuts Governments steady advance was made in that direction. The Hertzog Government, owing allegiance, as it did, more definitely to Afrikaans sentiment, was able to quicken the pace in making the Public Service bilingual, and in appointing bilingual officers, mostly of South African birth, to the higher posts. Some of its appointments were open to criticism, though here also the alliance with Labour in some measure served as a check; but the general effect of its policy in this regard, in removing the sense of inferiority under which Afrikaans-speaking South Africans laboured in the past, undoubtedly broadened the bases of national unity.

The 1929 election left General Hertzog's Government with practically the same majority as it had had before the dissolution, but in the coalition the Nationalists had grown in strength, and their Labour allies had been very much weakened. Two Labour Ministers retained portfolios in the reconstituted Cabinet, but their position was weak. At the same time, while the Nationalist Party in Parliament was recruited exclusively from the Afrikaans-speaking section of the people, the South African Party, though it retained a large number of Afrikaans-speaking voters, had by a process of attrition come to be a predominantly English party in the House.

Chapter 8

The Development of the Native Problem

SO FAR, in describing the historical forces which have produced the South African situation of to-day, I have dealt chiefly with one of the two main elements in that situation—the relations between the European peoples which have made South Africa their home. It has been a story in which controversy and division have led to complexity and confusion. The development of the problem which arises from the inter-relations between immigrant Europeans and native Africans must now be considered.

Of one aspect of that problem, the position of the coloured folk at the Cape, which the mixing of blood brought into being, little need be said here. Diverse elements entered into its composition; yet it gradually acquired homogeneity—by the middle of the eighteenth century it had come to be most difficult to find a pure-blooded Hottentot—and by virtue partly of the strain of white blood in the blend, partly of early detribalization of the native element and generations of association with white masters, it was accepted more and more readily as a portion of the community, distinct but not hostile. The Fiftieth Ordinance of 1828 did not actually equate the Cape Coloured folk with the Europeans, for their status was still held to be matter for separate legislation; but substantially it withdrew the restrictions on their civil rights, and set the course of Cape policy definitely in the direction of identity between white and coloured. When in 1853 the Constitution Ordinance was enacted granting Parliamentary institutions to the Colony, there was no mention of colour in the franchise qualifications, and the colour-blind equality which this implied was accepted all but without demur. Nor was the question raised of difference between the Cape Coloured folk and the pure-blooded Bantu. In regard to the former the policy of the Constitution Ordinance followed logically enough on what had gone before; in regard to the latter the same could hardly be said. While the coloured folk had for some time been recognized as having a place in the community, the prevailing attitude towards the Bantu had been to regard them as an alien element which should, as far as possible, be kept beyond the frontiers of the Colony and not brought within the sphere of direct European rule. But to this distinction little attention was paid at the time—it is the more natural that it should have been so in view of the fact that in 1853 the non-European inhabitants of the Colony belonged predominantly to the Cape Coloured folk, and the number of pure-blooded natives who secured a vote at the first registration was negligible.

But the balance soon began to shift, and, indeed, it is the development of the aspect of the problem of inter-racial relationships affecting the Bantu which is by far the more complex and the more important. The nature of that development, considered historically, can perhaps best be understood by observing a threefold transition that has taken place : the transition from the native problem as a frontier problem to the native problem as a problem of internal administration, the transition from the conception of it as a problem concerning primarily the Imperial Government to the conception of it as a South African problem to be dealt with in South Africa by South Africans, and finally the transition from a policy of constructive idealism to something all too deplorably suggestive of a policy of *laissez-faire.*

At first the relations between Europeans and Bantu were the relations between two peoples on opposite sides of a not very satisfactory frontier line. They had met in the valley of the Fish River, and that river was the chief geographical feature in the boundary which Governor van Plettenberg drew in 1778. But as a frontier the Fish was entirely inadequate. It was ineffective as a barrier and unsatisfactory as a military line of defence; moreover, the rectangle of the Zuurveld, which it creates by its eastward bend as it nears the coast, could not but be a constant source of friction and conflict. So it was that Kaffir war succeeded Kaffir war in the toilsome task of settling the frontier; so it was that the necessity of holding the Zuurveld by more intensive settlement was a contributory cause of the coming of the 1820 Settlers; so it was that after further trouble the experiment was tried of declaring the lands beyond the Fish, as far as the Keiskama, neutral territory, to be kept clear both of black tribesmen and white settlers by military patrols. The one aim of native policy was to keep white man and black man apart, to protect the white man against the raids and incursions of the black man, and for the rest to accept no responsibility for the administration or the civilization of the tribes. It was a policy which, in the words of a Secretary of State for the Colonies, ' sought to set up a bar of separation between the Caffres and the Colonists.' Great Britain was hesitant in the extreme to assume the government of the native peoples, and much of the history of the old Cape Colony is taken up with her efforts to evade the acceptance of any such responsibilities.

But it became more and more difficult to maintain that policy. The effective prevention of cattle-stealing on the frontier proved to be an impossible task. The control of reprisals was hardly less difficult. The neutral block did not remain empty for long, and the entry into it of both Europeans and Bantu had to be winked at. Then, to increase the restlessness of the Xosas, came pressure in their rear from tribes dispossessed by the Zulu conquerors. The Colonial Office felt that it must find a new expedient for the bolstering up its frontier system against all these difficulties —it found it, along lines which Indian experience suggested, in a policy of treaties with the native peoples. But it overlooked entirely the difference in civilization and in standards between an Indian rajah and a Bantu chief. The course of this new policy was uneasy and of brief duration. It was, indeed, challenged right at the outset. Just as it was coming to be applied, the war of 1834 broke out. To the Governor, D'Urban, it became clear that the problem would not be solved by the conclusion of treaties. It was this conviction that led him to follow up the termination of the struggle by extending the frontier of the Colony to the Kei and creating the Province of Queen Adelaide. The D'Urban policy, especially in the form into which he was forced to modify it when he found that he could not carry out his original intention of driving hostile tribes beyond the limits of the new Province, implied the direct government of

a considerable native population; the initiation of definite
efforts in the direction of civilization and development was
also in the Governor's mind.   But the Colonial Office view,
as presented by Lord Glenelg, prevailed.   The Province
was abandoned, the frontier was brought back to the Fish,
it was laid down that the assumption of direct rule over
native tribes should be eschewed, and the negotiation of
treaties with them was vigorously pressed.   Between 1836
and 1845 a large number of such treaties became operative,
and the same policy was, as has been seen, applied also to
northward of the Orange.

But as the years passed, the new policy came ever more and
more violently into conflict with the facts.   The Trek had
brought large numbers of natives under direct European
rule.   In the Republics, it is true, no very definite principle
of action was evolved, and even in the Transvaal, where
native tribes lived interspersed among the white communities, the problem continued to be regarded as a military
problem, a problem of defence, rather than one of administration; but in Natal the Republican Volksraad did initiate
a native policy in the true sense of that word, and the British
Administration which succeeded it could not, for all Downing Street's unwillingness, escape responsibility for the
government of the native peoples established within the
borders of the new Colony.

During the *Mfecane* Natal had been all but cleared of its
Bantu population, but the attractive power of a vacuum
began to operate, and when the Zulu military power had
been crushed, tribes and fragments of tribes streamed back
into it.   The Republican Government at Maritzburg very
soon found that, though it left the Zulus to rule themselves
beyond the Tugela, it had some 25,000 natives within its
borders to deal with.   The policy which it laid down for
their government foreshadowed that which has since come
to be known as Segregation.   Portions of the country were
to be marked off for European occupation; in this area
a sufficient number of detribalized natives was to be retained
for labour purposes.   The rest of the natives were to dwell
in other portions of the country, which were to be reserved
for them.   As it happened, it was the execution of this
policy which provided the occasion for British intervention

in Natal. The Pondo chief, Faku, one of those with whom Downing Street had made treaties, complained that his interests were detrimentally affected by the demarcation of the area proposed by the Republic for its native inhabitants —and the outcome was the passing of Natal into British hands. But while the white men were fighting for Natal, and subsequently during the period of transition which preceded the establishment of British rule on a definite basis, more and more natives streamed into the country, adding gravely to the complexity of the problem. The new British Administration, with but a handful of European Colonists, found itself faced with the task of governing a Bantu population of more than 100,000.

It was no easy task. The resources of the Administration were of the scantiest—there was only a small military garrison, there was no effective police force. How were these jostling bands of natives, with no fixed places of abode, to be forced to accept the conditions necessary for stability of government? Happily the need produced the man. That man was Theophilus Shepstone, a missionary's son, who had grown up among the Xosas, and who now started upon the work which will ever lend honour to his name in the history of South Africa. Less happy—but such is the perverseness of history—was his association, when that work was almost done, with the tragic episode of the Annexation of the Transvaal.

Shepstone's first step was the demarcation of locations for Natal's native inhabitants and their settlement in those locations. It was no easy matter to place them in their new homes. With no effective force to back his decisions, he had, in reliance mainly on his own judgment and discretion and knowledge of the native mind, to establish some 80,000 people in fixed abodes in different parts of the country, and so leave the rest of it, the greater part of Natal, open to white settlement. His success gave convincing evidence of his administrative skill. But it was necessary to go further. For the people whom he so settled Shepstone had to provide the machinery of government, which would make possible their development in a stable, ordered life. Had he been able to dispose of the necessary financial resources, he would have built up a system of European superintendents in each location and provided facilities for agricultural and technical education. But the resources could not be found, and the lack of them made the control of those vast bodies of natives, for most of whom as a result of the *Mfecane* the tribal ties and the tribal restraints had disappeared, a task of the most delicate character. Shepstone met the difficulty by the re-creation of the tribal system. Skilfully he gathered together scattered members of old tribes, and found chiefs for them. Patiently he sought to restore and strengthen the structure of tribal life. He secured the adoption of the principle that native law, save in so far as it was repugnant to the dictates of humanity, should be recognized as applicable to the native peoples. That law was to be administered by the chiefs, under the supervision of specially appointed European magistrates, with a final appeal to the Supreme Chief, as the Lieutenant-Governor was proclaimed to be, which meant in effect his Secretary for Native Affairs, Theophilus Shepstone. That was the system which, by his personal interest and personal influence, Shepstone saw through to success, and thereafter by the maintenance of direct contacts, and by the confidence which he inspired in the men of ' the black house,' he as Secretary for Native Affairs ruled, virtually unaided, from 100,000 to 200,000 natives. Under that rule the natives of Natal became that kindly, faithful, orderly people which observers have ever since noted them to be.

In Natal, then, Great Britain had, by a chain of circumstances, found itself embarked upon the task, in conflict with its general policy, of ruling a large native population. Not long afterwards its policy, despite persistent efforts to maintain it, broke down at the Cape also. For all the ink spilt on treaties proved to be of no avail in bringing settled peace to the frontier. Marauding and plundering and the disgruntlement of the frontiersmen still continued, the tale of thefts and reprisals mounted steadily, the difficulty of bringing home responsibility to treaty-signing chiefs was often insuperable. In 1846 war—the War of the Axe it came to be called—broke out again. When it ended, the settlement was dictated by the vigorous and impetuous Sir Harry Smith. At last the region between the Fish River and the Keiskama was definitely linked up with the Colony under the name of the district of Victoria East; part of it was set aside for white settlement, the rest was demarcated into native locations, European superintendents under an able Civil Commissioner, the Rev. Henry Calderwood, were appointed, and an active policy of civilization and development was initiated. Further east the D'Urban Province of Queen Adelaide, between the Keiskama and the Kei, was also annexed, as the dependency of British Kaffraria. In characteristically picturesque fashion, Sir Harry Smith, before a vast assemblage of natives, sent an exploding wagon skyward, to symbolize the end of the treaty system, and in its place the policy was instituted of ruling black and white as inhabitants of one and the same country.

In the administration of British Kaffraria, Smith sought to follow the same general lines of policy as in Victoria East. But the natives did not readily accept the new order of things, and the Governor's impetuous haste caused friction and disturbance. By the end of 1850 there was war again, the Eighth Kaffir War. It lasted until 1853, it led to Sir Harry Smith's recall, and when it ended the pendulum of British policy swung yet another time. To draw back the frontier once again was, indeed, no longer possible, but though British Kaffraria remained British territory, the aim in its administration came merely to be military control, no longer colonization and development. The country was viewed as a native territory, and though the magistrates remained, they were regarded as little more than diplomatic agents at the courts of the chiefs.

But in due course Cathcart, Smith's successor, who had sponsored this policy, was himself succeeded by Grey, and under him the Smith policy was not merely reverted to, but was extended and made more fruitful in its results. And since Grey's ideas were to give direction to Cape native policy in the period that followed, and to be the cause of those features of the present-day inter-racial situation which can be viewed with most satisfaction, it will be well to quote the words in which he formulated them shortly after his assumption of office:

' The plan I propose ' (he wrote) ' to pursue . . . is to attempt to gain an influence over all the tribes between the present north-eastern boundary of the Colony and Natal by employing them upon public works which will open up their country; by establishing institutions for the education of their children and the relief of their sick; by introducing among them institutions of a civil character suited to their present conditions; and by these and other means to attempt gradually to win them to civilization and Christianity, and thus to change, by degrees, our at present unconquered and apparently unconquerable foes into friends who may have common interests with ourselves.'

Grey's policy, then, rested on a twofold basis—the extension of European rule over the native tribes of South Africa as opportunity offered, and their advancement along the path of civilization by the exercise of European influences. Among those influences he regarded as most important the institution of public works of a developmental character, the creation of agencies of social welfare, more especially schools and hospitals, the replacement of the chiefs by European magistrates, and the interpenetration of the native territories by European settlement. The last of these aims was served by an extraordinary incident. In 1856 prophets arose among the Xosas who bade them slaughter their cattle and abstain from any cultivation of the land, with the promise that if they hearkened, then, on a day in the new year, the spirits of dead heroes would come forth to drive the white man from the land, bringing with them cattle and crops beyond men's wildest dreams. They obeyed the command, and then, destitute of food supplies, waited vainly for the fulfilment of the prophecy. As a result, despite all the efforts of the Governor to save them, they died in their thousands. The Bantu population of British Kaffraria was reduced by almost two-thirds, the military power of the Xosas was broken, and there was left land and to spare for Grey's European settlers. The position of Kaffraria was stabilized at last, and in 1866 its incorporation in the Cape Colony became of force and effect.

So the pendulum of British policy in South Africa continued to swing. Smith had broken down the Colonial Office policy of maintaining a fixed frontier, and trusting to treaties with native tribes for the safeguarding of it. His recall was followed by a reaction—a partial reaction in the lands beyond the Fish, marked by the adoption of the

Cathcart policy, a complete reaction in the Trans-Orange, where the Sand River and Bloemfontein Conventions registered the acceptance of a policy of non-interference with the affairs of the emigrant farmers and the tribesmen who dwelt amongst them. In Kaffraria the reaction ended with Grey; across the Orange it was terminated by his successor, Wodehouse, who intervened in the struggle between the Free State and Moshesh, proclaimed Basutoland British territory, and secured its annexation to the Cape Colony in 1871.

In Kaffraria also the Grey policy of extending the boundaries of the Colony was steadily pursued. Wodehouse, preoccupied with financial difficulties and his relations with the Free State, marked time, and left it to the newly established Responsible Government of the Colony to take the next positive step. A steady penetration of the tribes beyond the Kei by European influences prepared the way. Then in 1877 came the Ninth Kaffir War, in which tribes on both sides of the border participated. There was fighting over a wide area. When it ended, the policy of annexation was vigorously pursued. Between 1879 and 1886 all of the considerable Transkeian area, save Pondoland, was annexed. In 1894 Pondoland also became Colonial territory, and so the borders of the Cape marched with those of Natal.

Similar had been the development in the Cape's sister Colony. There the Tugela River had played the same part in British frontier policy as the Fish at the Cape. Beyond it the Zulus were left to themselves. Gradually their military power revived, until under Cetewayo it was no less powerful than it had been in the days of Dingaan—more so indeed for many of the tribesmen now carried guns bought with money earned at the diamond fields. For many years the prestige of Shepstone was able to ensure the keeping of the peace, but the desire of Cetewayo's warriors to ' wash their spears ' made war inevitable. That war, which came in 1879, and with which are associated some of the most striking episodes in South African history, finally shattered the military system of the Zulus, and so prepared the way for a further extension of European rule over Bantu peoples. It did not, indeed, follow immediately on the termination

of the war. As at the Cape, so in the case of the lands
beyond the Tugela, there was an aversion from the assumption of direct responsibility. At first Zululand was left
under native rule, though it was divided into thirteen units
each under its own chief, while in each case a British
Resident was appointed to be ' the eyes and ears ' of the
British Government. Then, when this system broke down,
Cetewayo was brought back to rule over a reduced kingdom
with diminished authority. But trouble continued, and one
result was that the opening was given for the entry into Zululand of a band of Transvaalers, who founded the so-called
New Republic, which was soon to be absorbed in the
Transvaal. This, however, seemed to portend the establishment of a potentially hostile power on the coast, and the
fear of this contingency induced the British Government,
after recognizing the New Republic, to annex Zululand in
1887. Eight years later it advanced its rule still further up
the coast over Tongaland and the territories of some petty
princelings which stretched up to the Portuguese frontier.
At the same time the South African Republic assumed
the administration of Swaziland, and the process of extending European authority over the eastern Bantu was
complete.

In the west a similar policy had been pursued. The
discovery of diamonds had led to the annexation of Griqualand West; the Warren expedition was followed by the
creation of the territory of British Bechuanaland which
extended to the River Molopo, and of the vast Bechuanaland Protectorate to the north of it. These in their turn
were, in Rhodes's dreams, but the high road to the interior,
opening the way to the settlement of the Rhodesias, and
therewith the introduction of more masses of teeming native
peoples within the sphere of European rule. But within the
limits of the future Union of South Africa the policy of the
assumption of administrative responsibility had run its
course—and had brought the result that in every part of it
white man and black man were ruled by the same Governments, with the white man everywhere in the minority.
The frontiers have been swept away, and the problem has
become one of the living together of these two elements in a
single state.

E

Alongside of the process which transformed the native question from a frontier problem into a problem of internal administration there went its conversion from an Imperial into a South African problem. As long as native policy was merely a matter of safeguarding a military frontier, it was natural to regard it as an Imperial responsibility. But when the Bantu had come to be administered as a component part of self-governing communities, it was just as natural to expect that the Imperial factor should fall away. It did not, however, do so immediately. A complex of motives came into operation. In Great Britain there was a not unnatural unwillingness to burden the British taxpayer with the cost of wars fought in defence of the property of Colonists, who had directly or indirectly influenced the shaping of the policies which led up to those wars; but there was also the pressure of missionary societies and philanthropic bodies which feared that the grant to the Colonists of unfettered authority over their relations with the natives would mean the exploitation and oppression of the tribes. In South Africa, on the other hand, there was a growing feeling that issues which were vital to South Africa should be determined in South Africa, and not at a distance of 6,000 miles, within the range of the influence of those same bodies, hostile as they were deemed to be to Colonial interests; but coupled with this feeling went the hesitancy of a young, scattered, and none too prosperous community to face the heavy potential liabilities which, in the light of past events, the assumption of responsibility for native policy portended.

It was this latter feeling of hesitancy which for long seemed likely to prevail. When Wodehouse decided on the annexation of British Kaffraria to the Cape Colony, he had the utmost difficulty in persuading the Cape Parliament to agree. He only succeeded when he had secured the passing of a Kaffraria Annexation Act by the British Parliament, empowering him to act if the Cape legislature should continue to thwart his wishes. Similar considerations led to the holding up of the grant of Responsible Government to Natal for almost forty years after it had been accorded to the Cape. On several occasions the Natal Legislative Council petitioned for full self-government. In reply to one of these petitions, that which it submitted in 1880, Downing Street intimated that compliance with the request would mean that the Colony would have to provide for its own defence. An election was fought on the issue so raised, but although the Zulu military power had been broken, the majority decided against Responsible Government on these terms. To the Natal of 1880 the privileges of an enhanced status did not seem to compensate for the responsibilities which it entailed.

At about the same time, however, there took place a series of events which brought the two tendencies sharply into opposition, and did much to determine the issue. In 1871 the Cape Parliament had agreed to accept responsibility for the government of Basutoland. Its administration, therefore, came to be one of the tasks of the Colony's first Responsible Government. For a time all went well, and the foundations of a sound administrative system were laid. But in the introduction of reforms, sound in themselves, there was shown an undue precipitancy, and an inadequate appreciation of certain fundamental features in the structure of Bantu society. Discontent gathered. Then came the application to Basutoland of the Peace Preservation Act, requiring the surrender by the natives of their fire-arms. The Basutos rose in revolt, offering a resistance which proved to be unexpectedly effective. Full use was made by them of the difficulties which the configuration of their country offered to military operations. The war dragged on without the Colonial forces being able adequately to crush the rebellion; and a large number of the burghers, weary of the lengthening struggle, deserted. The troubles in Basutoland were part cause of the fall of one Cape Government; they compelled its successor, the Scanlen Cabinet, to proceed with steadily waning prestige from one expedient to another in order to secure a settlement. For a time ' Chinese Gordon ' appeared upon the Basutoland stage, and in due course quarrelled picturesquely with Colonial Ministers. At last, helplessly confessing failure, Scanlen appealed to Downing Street for relief, and arranged to hand over Basutoland to the Imperial authorities. It was a sad blow to Colonial prestige, and it introduced a complication of the native problem which still persists, the factor of direct Imperial rule in an important native territory in the very heart of South Africa.

Scanlen had, however, been willing to go even further. For he proposed to Her Majesty's Government that it should assume the control not only of Basutoland, but of all the purely native dependencies of the Colony, including the Transkeian territories. That proposal proved to be of far-reaching significance. Its adoption would have registered the unqualified acceptance of the conception which viewed the South African native problem as an Imperial concern. It raised the issue in such manner that it could not be brushed aside, and thus it led to the consolidation of that policy of Colonialism which was to prove so important a factor in the shaping of South Africa. It drove Hofmeyr, once a member and still a supporter of the Scanlen Cabinet, into direct opposition to it. The policy for which he stood aimed at the self-dependence of the Colony. With that ideal the re-introduction of the Imperial factor as a direct governing power in lands hitherto within the Colony was obviously in conflict. Under stress of that conflict form and substance and vitality were given to the conception of Colonialism, which, while it based itself on a ready acceptance of the Imperial connection with all its privileges and obligations, proceeded to contend that the affairs of the Colony should, as far as possible, be settled in the Colony; that having received self-government, it should assume and carry out to the full the responsibilities which were entailed; and that if it needed external aid it should seek it rather along the lines of co-operation with the other South African communities than by asking help from London. This conception appealed not only to the Afrikaans-speaking section at the Cape, but to many English-speaking Colonists as well, and when, after an election fought mainly on the issue of the cession of the Transkei, Scanlen met the new House, he soon found it impossible to remain in office. His Government was replaced by one which was pledged to the policy of Colonialism.

It was at this stage that there took place the events in Bechuanaland to which an earlier chapter has made reference. There were wider issues involved in those events than that of native policy, but one important result

was that once again direct Imperial rule was introduced for
the government of large masses of Bantu.   But, happily, it
was not the only result, for it brought Hofmeyr and Rhodes
into alliance, with a common slogan, ' the Imperial factor
must be eliminated,' which enjoyed the blessing of the
Governor, Sir Hercules Robinson, himself, and so assured the
victory of the conception which viewed the South African
native problem as a South African concern.   It was significant of that victory that British Bechuanaland was transferred from direct Imperial rule to the rule of the Cape
Colony in 1895, and Zululand became part of Natal in
1897.   For a time also the Bechuanaland Protectorate was
placed under Rhodes's Chartered Company, but in the
reaction which the Jameson Raid caused, it passed back
within the Imperial sphere.

While then the conception of native administration as
being the concern of the people of South Africa themselves
had triumphed, there remained as survivals of the older view
two territories, Basutoland and the Bechuanaland Protectorate, under direct Imperial rule.   The fact of their
existence made it possible, in the days after the Anglo-Boer
War when Imperialism had regained some of its strength, for
Swaziland to be placed in the same category, and to-day
these three ' islands ' still stand out to add complexity to the
native problem of South Africa.   To the South Africa Act
was attached an annexure dealing with their incorporation
in the Union, but to its provisions no effect has hitherto
been given.

For the rest, however, the principle, to which the existence
of these territories represents an exception, has remained
unchallenged.   Significant of its acceptance was a provision
in the Treaty of Vereeniging, which laid it down that the
question of granting the franchise to natives in the new
Colonies would not be decided until after the introduction of
self-government.   It was a question to be determined by
South Africans in South Africa.   And in the South Africa Act
the same conception received further emphasis by the transfer
of the powers which had hitherto been exercised in Natal in
relation to native affairs by the Governor in person, that is, as
a representative of Great Britain, to the Governor-General-
in-Council, that is, the Union's own responsible Ministers.

To this principle which had triumphed there was attached an important corollary. If native policy was to be determined in South Africa, it should be, as far as possible, a South African policy, in other words the policy of as wide an area of South Africa as possible. The necessity of the adoption of such a policy had been emphasized time and again since the days of Sir George Grey—it was always one of the most powerful arguments for Union—the delay in its enunciation caused by the postponement of Union has cost, and is costing, South Africa dear. It is significant that one of the first of Milner's acts when he found that Union could not be brought about *per saltum* was the appointment of a South African Native Affairs Commission, on which all the four Colonies, as well as Rhodesia and Basutoland, were represented, and the report of which retains its value until to-day. The Selborne Memorandum emphasized the dangers of disunion in the sphere of native policy as perhaps the most effective of the considerations that made action imperative. The Act of Union enshrined an almost complete realization of the ideal. The three ' islands ' still exist; but the conception that native policy should be determined in South Africa by the people of South Africa as a whole may be said to have prevailed.

It remains to follow up one more line of transition in the development of native policy, and that, perhaps, less happy than those which have so far been described. In the early days of the history of native policy in South Africa two tendencies warred for mastery—the idealism of the missionary and the pragmatism of the administrative official whom circumstances compelled to take account of the trials and difficulties of the Colonist, and more especially the frontiersman. These two tendencies may be said to have blended happily in those whose names are chiefly connected with the reversal of the Colonial Office policy of treaties without direct responsibility. Shepstone was the son of a missionary, and himself an official of rare administrative genius. Smith was the darling of the Colonists, but in his constructive work he associated with himself one of the ablest of the missionaries in Henry Calderwood. Grey was a man who combined great gifts of intellect with active philanthropic interests and a high idealism. Between them they gave to native

policy a constructive idealism which long survived them,
though unhappily it lost much of its inspiration when the
dark days came, in which the European people of South
Africa thought more of the struggles amongst themselves
than of their common problem, their common task in relation
to the natives in their midst.

The main features of Shepstone's native policy have
already been described. His understanding of, and sympathy with the natives won him their devoted confidence.
His abilities secured for him a prestige, with both the Imperial
Government and its local representatives, which resulted in
his being entrusted with almost despotic control of Natal's
native affairs.   It is, perhaps, his chief claim to greatness
that he developed a new constructive idea in native policy.
The path which he followed was not the path of equalization, with which the missionaries had been identified, nor
yet the path of repression which most of the Colonists
favoured, but the path of differentiation.   His policy was
based on the conception that it was right to promote the
development of the native peoples, but that in view of the
great difference between white man and black such development should proceed, as far as possible, on distinctively
native lines, and that, under wise guidance, it should not
conflict with European interests.   At the root of his policy
was devotion to the welfare of Europeans and Bantu alike.
For the interests of the Colonists, in so far as these were
affected by the presence of the natives in their midst, Shepstone showed the fullest possible consideration; to the
natives he gave peace and good government and an economic
basis of subsistence; moreover, by endowing them with the
orderliness of settled life he set them upon the path of
progress.

It is true that he might have gone further in this latter
direction.   It has been said of him by Professor Brookes, to
whose *History of Native Policy in South Africa* this book owes
much, that though he controlled the natives, he failed to
civilize them.   But his task, it must not be forgotten, was
one of making bricks without straw.   Shepstone had contemplated as part of his scheme of native administration the
appointment of European superintendents in the locations,
and through their agency, with the help of a policy of

education and development, the progress of the native
'towards a higher and better civilization' (the words are
his). It was only financial stringency that forced him back
on the native chief as the effective instrument of his administrative policy. Even so, he did perform civilizing work of a
useful character within the limits of his system, as for instance
by the skilful infusion of European ideas into the body of
native law. Yet he is open to criticism, in that during the
later years of his regime, when funds might have been found
for a more vigorous policy of development, his natural conservatism asserted itself, and he fell back upon an attitude of
laissez-faire. And it was that which, no less than other
features of his system, impressed itself upon his successors,
and which accounts for the fact that, though Natal native
policy started well, it lost, long since, all the advantages of
that start.

Shepstone's successors were content to follow in his foot-
steps. Where they diverged from his policy, as for instance
in the rigid codification of native law, they changed for the
worse rather than for the better. But they changed little.
Moreover, the paternalism and accessibility of Shepstone
passed away, and officialdom reigned in its stead. Like
Shepstone, later native administrators in Natal failed to
civilize the natives; unlike him, they also began to lose control of them. Tribal disintegration was permitted to proceed without the provision of an adequate substitute for
tribalism, and little was done to find either in the scientific
development of agriculture, or in the creation of a system of
local government, an outlet for the energies which had once
been applied to inter-tribal strife. So it came about that
it was possible for Mr. J. X. Merriman to say before the
South African Native Affairs Commission, in language
exaggerated indeed, but not without a measure of justification: 'You have not elevated the native in Natal; you have
not raised them; you have not educated them; they are
barbarous, and you have designedly left them in a state of
barbarism.' The final evidence of the degeneration of
Natal native policy came when in 1906 there was
rebellion on both sides of the Tugela, which did not
indeed bring large numbers into revolt—the spirit of
Shepstone still prevailed to prevent that—but which

showed how widespread was the discontent that had burst into sporadic flame.

At the Cape the impression which Grey's constructive idealism left on the Colony's native policy at a time when it had just begun to be conceived as a matter of internal native administration proved to be more enduring than in the case of Natal. The Grey system diverged from the Shepstone system in two important respects, one of a permanent character, while the other was destined in due course to be modified in the direction of Shepstonism. Following on the lines of the Smith–Calderwood plan in Victoria East, Grey initiated an aggressive policy of civilization and development through European agency, direction, and example. Not the least important feature of that policy as he conceived it was the gradual replacement of the chief by the magistrate, and it is characteristic of his statesmanship that he should have succeeded in devising a method of bringing this about in such manner as neither to antagonize the displaced chiefs, nor to destroy the communal spirit which is the most valuable feature of the Bantu social system. So Grey prepared the way for that great civilizing work which able and devoted magistrates and officials have performed in the native districts of the Cape, more especially in the Transkeian Territories.

In another important respect Grey diverged from Natal policy—he did not take over the Shepstone concept of differentiation. Cape ideals of native policy could not but be influenced by the development of the relations between Europeans and Cape Coloured folk, from which had resulted the adoption of the principle of civil and political equality as between the two racial elements. That same conception came to prevail at the Cape, and subject to certain limitations still prevails to-day, in respect of the relations between European and Bantu. It is significant that in newly annexed British Kaffraria the laws of the Colony were regarded as having applicability to natives both in civil and in criminal cases. In many instances, indeed, magistrates allowed themselves to be guided by native law and custom, but they did so without any legal authority for their action. So too in the Cape franchise no colour bar was recognized, and when British Kaffraria was incorporated, it was extended automatically to those of its natives who had the qualification.

But as the area of annexation was extended to include Basutoland and the Transkei, there did come about in time a considerable modification of Cape policy in respect of this second divergence from the Shepstone system. Unlike British Kaffraria, Basutoland did not on annexation become a corporate part of the Colony, and although the Grey policy was vigorously pursued in respect of the positive encourage-ment of civilization through the magisterial system, it was for administrative purposes regarded as a distinct unit. In the Transkei, nearly all of which was restricted to native occupation, the same line of policy was followed, but with a wise gradualness born of the unhappy experience acquired in Basutoland. As the territories were annexed, they were not absorbed within the Colony's administrative system. The Governor-in-Council became the normal legislative authority, which meant that legislation was by proclama-tion, though Parliament retained the right of veto. Unless it was expressly so stated, Acts of Parliament were to have no validity in these areas. For the rest, the chiefs were gradu-ally superseded in their authority by European magistrates, native civil law was recognized and administered without being codified, and a special Transkeian Penal Code was compiled. Agricultural development was fostered, and the practice of constant public consultation with the natives was instituted. The policy of differential native development was well launched in the Transkei—in so far it was the Natal policy, but with a broader basis and greater vigour in the pursuit of its aims.

In one important respect, however, it became necessary to reconcile the Transkeian policy of differentiation with the older Cape conception of equality—that was in the matter of the Franchise. The question came up first in 1886, when the extension of the franchise to the recently annexed Transkeian Territories fell to be considered. Enfranchisement in terms of the Cape Constitution Ordi-nance would have brought masses of barbarian natives on to the rolls. To obviate this a clause was inserted in the Parliamentary Registration Act of 1887, prescribing that both in the Transkeian areas to which the franchise was to

be extended and in the rest of the Colony a share in communal occupation of property, which was the normal Bantu
land tenure, would not be deemed to be a qualification for
registration. The policy of Equality was, therefore, maintained in the matter of the franchise—there was still the
same qualification for black man as for white—but the
amendment of the law did imply a recognition of the
difference between European and Bantu conditions of life.

Gradually, however, the feeling grew that it was dangerous
to have native voters not approximating to European
standards on a common roll with European voters; and so,
five years later, the Hofmeyr–Rhodes alliance led to a
further amendment in the franchise law. The property
qualification for white and black alike was trebled, being
raised from the original figure of £25 to £75, and the would-
be voter was required to give evidence of his ability to sign
his name. The policy of Equality was, therefore, still maintained, but again a concession was made in so far as there
was to be a substantial reduction in the number of potential
native voters.

These various developments in Cape native policy prepared the way for the Glen Grey Act of 1894, which was one
of the most valuable fruits of the co-operation between
Rhodes and Hofmeyr. The Act drew its name from a
region west of the Kei, the settlement of the affairs of which
was its primary purpose, but it was conceived with a view to
its application by proclamation to other districts, and
Rhodes, indeed, described it as ' a Bill for Africa.' Under-
lying it were two main constructive ideas. The one was
that means must be found to avert the danger, which was
beginning to be realized, of the breaking down of the
authority of the chiefs, and the consequent disappearance of
the traditional machinery of native local government, with
nothing to come in its place. To that end Rhodes devised a
system which would, as far as possible, restore to the natives
control over their local tribal affairs, inaugurating a scheme
of local councils, delegates from which were to meet in
larger district councils, under the presidency in each case of
the magistrate of the area. The second main aim of this
legislation was the encouragement of native agricultural
development by the improvement of the system of land

tenure. For the gradual replacement of communal tenure, with its inadequate inducement to measures of permanent improvement, there was devised a system which was based on perpetual quitrent and gave individual ownership, but provided safeguards against the possibility of alienation to Europeans. Again it was a differential policy which was being applied to the natives, and, logically enough, it was enacted that this special form of tenure would not qualify for the exercise of the franchise.

The Glen Grey Act, then, marked an important forward step in native policy. The taking of that step must be ascribed in the first instance to the sagacity and the imagination of Cecil Rhodes, but it is not without significance that this one great piece of constructive native legislation was enacted at a time when strife between Dutch and British had been all but allayed, that, indeed, it was devised as a result of the co-operation of leading representatives of British and Dutch South Africa. And it has led to important developments in native administration in the large and almost exclusively native Transkeian region. Within a year of its proclamation the Act was applied to four Transkeian districts—next year there was instituted a General Council consisting of representatives from the District Councils. By degrees the Council part of the Act was made to apply to the whole of the Transkei, with the result that the Transkeian General Council, or Bunga, has come to be a body of real importance. It initiates and directs valuable developmental work, and exercises its not inconsiderable powers of self-government with wisdom and discretion. It is the happiest expression of the policy of differential native advancement, and perhaps the brightest feature in the complex of relations between European and Bantu in South Africa.

It is because of the significance of these Transkeian developments that emphasis has been laid upon them here, but that emphasis has also been necessary since the Transkei is the one part of South Africa in which the constructive idealism of the mid-nineteenth century had not degenerated into stagnation at its close. Certainly in the Kaffrarian districts west of the Kei, where European and native interests are much more intermingled than in the Transkei (the

Ciskei this region is sometimes called), the opportunity to proceed on similar lines was not taken.   Instead, the situation was allowed to develop without regard to definite principles; in general, the policy of equality, of identity, as between European and Bantu prevailed, without adequate regard for the facts of difference; and a crop of problems, in respect of the administration of justice, of land-tenure, of competition in industry, was allowed to spring up, which could not but accentuate subsequent conflict between white man and black.

But nowhere did the policy of *laissez-faire* prevail so completely and with such serious results for the future as in the Republics.   In the Free State the problem was relatively simple.   Its main native problem fell away when Basuto-land was annexed by Sir Philip Wodehouse.   For the rest, it had to deal merely with a native population which was really an overflow from adjacent territories, and nearly the whole of which was in European employment.   To these natives it applied the principle of paternalism—just and kindly treatment, coupled with complete subordination, social, religious, economic, and political.   But the question of setting aside areas for native habitation and of providing for the administration of such areas hardly arose.   Yet, simple as the situation was, lack of application to it here also created difficulties for the future.   The failure of the Republican Government to control the settlement of natives on European farms produced some of the most difficult questions on which the Parliament of the Union has had to legislate.

In the Transvaal the position was different, for there the Republican Government was faced from the outset with the task of administering a considerable native population. Yet, apart from the enunciation of the principle of subordination, and the provision of the necessary machinery for defence, it can hardly be said to have devised a policy prior to the Presidency of Burgers.   That ill-fated, though able, President did not fail to give his attention to the native question, but little came of it, as was the case with so much that he undertook.   Then came the Annexation, with Shepstone for a time in control of the Transvaal.   But it was Shepstone at a period when he seemed to have all but lost his powers of initiative, and the progress which might have been anticipated was not made. A Department of Native Affairs was, however, for the first time created, which was retained after the Retrocession, and the appointment by Shepstone of his son Henrique to be its head helped to give Natal ideas considerable influence in shaping the subsequent native policy of the restored Republic. Preliminary work done by him served, indeed, as the basis of subsequent Republican legislation. Of that legislation the most important was Law 4 of 1885. That law, which accepted in its preamble the principle of differentiation, gave recognition to native law, appointed the President as Paramount Chief, created the office of Superintendent of Natives, and provided for the stationing in areas with large native populations of specially qualified officials as Native Commissioners. All this, however, implied the demarcation of land for native occupation, as had been done by Shepstone in Natal. But in the South African Republic the opportunity to carry through a similar policy was never fully taken; and though a Locations Commission was constituted in terms of the Pretoria Convention of 1881 and did useful work, it did not complete its task, leaving many tribes unprovided for. A large number of Transvaal natives was left to find the means of subsistence on State- and privately-owned farms.

The Transvaal system, then, was based on that of Natal, but, though it showed most of the weaknesses of that system, not least the lack of encouragement of native development in agricultural methods or in local government, it failed even to so carry out the Natal policy logically, as for instance when it stopped short of the provision of adequate locations. That failure, at a time when the task of finding the necessary land was far simpler than it subsequently became, was destined gravely to complicate the solution of South Africa's native problem. It has made it far more difficult than it need have been to provide for reasonable native requirements in the matter of land for occupation, in view of European expansion, and, coupled with the neglect of native agricultural development, it has stimulated the detribalization of the native and his migration to the towns, there to become a permanent competitor with the poorer and less well-equipped among the whites. The Hilton-Young Commission very rightly pointed out the relief that South Africa would secure in its native problem, ' if there were adequate areas of native lands to which the natives could return as an alternative to competing in both the economic and political fields with the white man.' 'We found,' the Report continues, ' an almost unanimous opinion among the public men whom we interviewed during our visit to Capetown, that if the wheel of time could be reversed, and South Africa could start the process of its development again from the beginning, they would reserve far larger areas for native occupation on the lines actually adopted for the Transkei.' These words, which were echoed by General Smuts in his Rhodes Memorial Lectures, have special applicability to the Transvaal and to a less extent to the Ciskei.   And it was at the end of the nineteenth and the beginning of the twentieth centuries that the opportunity was lost.   It would have been well indeed for South Africa, if at that time its statesmen, and especially those in the Transvaal, had been free to give more attention to its native problem.   Instead, neglect and *laissez-faire* allowed that problem to increase steadily in complexity and in difficulty.

Nor has it been easy to exorcise the spell of the spirit of *laissez-faire*.   In the new century men waited first for the report of the South African Native Affairs Commission, and then for the establishment of Union.   The South Africa Act itself embodied no new policy, for the most part merely enshrining the *status quo*.   The first important legislation enacted was the Natives Land Act of 1913, but it was professedly provisional in character.   The occasion for the passing of that Act was presented by the complaints of European farmers that predominantly European areas were being penetrated by natives who were free to acquire land anywhere, while they were protected in their own reserves and locations.   But its real aim went further; it was nothing less than to bring about a final settlement of the land question on the basis of possessory segregation, as recommended by the South African Native Affairs Commission.   Native and European were alike forbidden to acquire land in each other's areas, and the ' squatting ' of natives on European-owned farms was severely restricted.   To provide, however, for the natives so displaced, and at the same time to check their drift into the towns where they would compete with the white man in industry, it was proposed to set aside additional areas for native possession.

But while the curtailment of native rights took place immediately, the provision of land to meet their needs was to await the report of a Commission. Commission succeeded Commission, but European interests detrimentally affected by the proposed demarcation of areas presented powerful opposition, and areas once deemed unsuitable to European occupation were later found to be productive and reasonably healthy. The needs of the natives for land on which they might advance along the lines of distinctive development remained to be met. There has been a weakening of the confidence of the Bantu in the good intentions of their European rulers, and as a corollary the stream of detribalized natives into the towns has continued unchecked.

In 1920 an Act was passed which provided for the gradual extension of the Transkeian system of local government to all native areas, set up a permanent Native Affairs Commission to advise the Minister, and created machinery for the summoning of periodical Conferences of chiefs and representative natives from all over the Union. Three years later the problems created by the drift of the native to the towns were taken in hand, and a Natives Urban Areas Act passed to regulate their residence there. In the main this and other similar legislation was sound and progressive, but the vital problem of the land remained unsolved. While that was so, while there was no adequate alternative outlet provided for the native's energies, the problems arising from his entry into the white man's industry became increasingly difficult. And, indeed, the resultant competition between white and black in the economic sphere came to bulk ever more largely in men's minds.

Chapter 9

The Coming of the Asiatic

'THE Asiatics,' so wrote Milner once, ' are strangers forcing themselves upon a community reluctant to receive them.' That expresses a sentiment held by the vast majority of white South Africans in Milner's day, as it still is to-day. Yet it was during Milner's term of office as High Commissioner that Chinese coolies were brought to work on the mines of the Witwatersrand, after the effort to secure the importation of Indian labourers had been wrecked on the rock of the Indian Government's unwillingness. That may be taken as characteristic of an inconsistency of attitude which runs through the story of the relations between Europeans and Asiatics, an inconsistency which was caused in no small measure by men's preoccupation with other issues, and their consequent failure to think out logically the problems which these relations brought with them.

Asiatics came to South Africa because it was deemed to be in the white man's interest that they should come. So it was in the days of the Dutch East India Company, when the immigration was limited in extent, and the Asiatics who came were almost completely absorbed in the Cape Coloured folk; so it was again in the nineteenth century, when their numbers were, absolutely and relatively, very much larger. It was the desire to exploit the potential wealth of the coast-belt of Natal which led to their coming in this later period.

The Indian coolie was brought to Natal for the cultivation of sugar. The natives, so the planters declared, could not be induced to come out to work in sufficient numbers from the reserves which Shepstone had set aside for them, and when they did come, their labour was inefficient. The nascent sugar industry, for which the coast-belt seemed to be so admirably fitted, was denied the hope of expansion, if it could not get the labour that it required. But not far off in Mauritius indentured Indian labour had set sugar-plant-ing upon its feet. Why should not Natal follow suit? So the request was sped to India, and though at first the Indian Government was unwilling, it gave way in the end. In November 1860 the first shipload of Indian labourers, together with a statutory proportion of women, was landed in Natal. They came at the expense of the Natal Government, which proceeded to allocate them on arrival to approved masters under a three years' indenture. The employer had to reimburse the Government for its expenditure, and pay the coolie in addition to his keep a wage which started at ten shillings a month in the first year, and rose to twelve shillings a month in the third. After the three years the labourer was required to re-indenture for a fourth year, or, if he wished, for two additional years. Thereafter he was free to live and work as he willed. After a further five years he had the right to either a free return passage, or the equivalent of its cost in Crown land. The ultimate end of this policy was clear from the outset. The Indian was to be welcomed as a permanent settler in the Colony, and as a contributor to its prosperity. A few voices were raised in opposition—but they were only few. The conception of the Indian as ' a stranger forcing himself upon a reluctant community ' was not to emerge until later.

The new policy did not fail to yield the results which men had hoped. The Indians came, many of them remained readily enough when their term had expired, they spread over the coast-lands, they increased and multiplied—and the sugar-industry prospered mightily. Sugar dominated the coast-belt, and the word of the planter began to prevail in the councils of the land. The decision of the Government of India to forbid further importation in 1866 was held to portend ruin to the Colony; the withdrawal of the prohibi-tion in 1874 inaugurated a new era of prosperity. An Indian Immigration Trust Board was established, to which the Natal Government contributed £10,000 annually, and on all sides the coming of the coolie was hailed as an un-qualified boon to the Colony. The maintenance of a steady stream of Indian immigration and an atmosphere of buoy-ancy and optimism were regarded as complementary, the one to the other.

Then, in the 'eighties, the voice of criticism began to be heard. The number of indenture-expired Indians was increasing steadily. More and more Indians were coming to the Colony on their own account. And these two classes of so-called ' free ' Indians were, so men observed, entering into and threatening to secure the monopoly of certain occupations, which had previously been in the hands of Europeans. The Indian had the advantage in competition of a lower standard of living. At last the European began to realize the danger which that implied to himself and his children.

As a first sign of the new-born ' reluctance ' a Commission was appointed in 1885 to investigate the position created by Indian immigration. It revealed a preponderance of European opinion in the Colony against the ' presence of the free Indian as a rival or competitor, either in agricultural or commercial pursuits.' But Indian immigration had built up the prosperity and the power of the sugar-planter; the sugar-planter was determined that Indian immigration should continue—and his wishes were not lightly overridden. It was not until 1894 that the annual grant to the Immigration Trust Board was abolished, and that the policy of inducing the indenture-expired Indian to remain in Natal was replaced by one which put pressure on him to return to the land of his origin. To that end an annual tax of £3 was imposed on each ' free ' Indian, but the stream of immigration continued to flow unchecked. Public feeling was, however, now roused, and it grew in intensity, until in 1897 an attempt was made to prevent forcibly the landing of 500 new arrivals. The result was the enactment of legislation which in effect prohibited the entry of ' free ' Indians, and at the same time sought to check the trading activities of those already in Natal. It marked the definite adoption of a policy of differentiation against the Indian. It was not, however, pursued to its logical conclusion, for the importation of indentured labour was allowed to continue. That fact and the considerable natural increase of the stranger within the gates, as he was now viewed, meant a rapid growth of the Indian population, and soon it exceeded the European. At length in 1911 the Government of India forbade any further recruiting, and the rate of increase consequently declined; but even so it was not until 1923 that the European population of Natal overtook the Asiatic.

It was the Indian coolie who was brought to Natal—it was the Indian trader, nearly always a Mahommedan, and in most cases from Bombay, who followed in his wake, and spread himself over other parts of South Africa. The Free State early passed a law which prohibited ' Asiatics and other coloured persons from trading or carrying on any business whatsoever '; that law is still in force to-day, and the number of Asiatics in the Free State is negligible. The Cape Colony until 1902 imposed no restrictions on Asiatic immigration, but it lay off the beaten track, and comparatively few Asiatics crossed its borders. It was the Transvaal which naturally received the overspill from Natal. To the Transvaal in the later 'seventies the Indian trader began to make his way. By 1884 his presence began to be felt, and those whose interests were affected by his presence, especially the commercial communities in the towns, raised their voices. The Republican Government would willingly have given ear to their representations, and have acted as its sister-Republic had done, but its hands were not entirely free. In terms of the Convention of Pretoria ' any person other than a native ' had to be allowed full rights of residence and trade within the limits of the Republic. With some difficulty the British Government was prevailed upon to regard as not in conflict with this provision the terms of Law 3 of 1885, which excluded all Asiatics from the franchise, made registration compulsory, empowered the Government to demarcate areas for Asiatic habitation, and forbade the acquisition by them of fixed property outside of such areas. Subsequently, by a decision of the Courts, this was interpreted as also permitting the Government to confine Asiatic trading to the demarcated areas, or bazaars, and though Great Britain, in the interests of its Indian subjects, contested the legality of this, the Republican view prevailed on submission of the issue to arbitration.

But in practice these legal restrictions were not enforced in other than half-hearted fashion. The Republican Government had much else wherewith to occupy itself, as the danger to the independence of the State became more and more imminent; moreover, it was loath to give new grounds for complaint to the British Government. Bazaars were in fact only demarcated in a few towns; even there no serious attempt was made to enforce the segregation of those for whom they were intended; the Asiatic population increased steadily, numbering several thousands, when the war of 1899 broke out, and seriously threatening the European small trader. Under cover of the disunion which prevailed in South Africa, yet another problem was being allowed to develop.

The restrictive laws which affected Great Britain's Asiatic subjects had been one of the grievances which the Uitlanders enumerated against the Government of the South African Republic. But the change of regime produced no change in the policy of restriction. On the outbreak of the war most of the Asiatic inhabitants left the Transvaal. When it ended they returned—and many others came with them. The attempt was made to confine the right of entry to those who had resided there under the Republican Government, but the records of registration were defective, and Milner soon found himself with more Asiatics to govern than ever Kruger had had. The threat to the European, whom the Asiatic could under-live and under-sell, grew in seriousness, the voice of remonstrance was heard more and more insistently, and the outbreak of plague in the Indian quarter of Johannesburg gave matter for even louder outcry. Great Britain's Asiatic subjects, in the result, got no more consideration from Milner than they had received from Kruger. Republican restrictions were not relaxed, and but for the veto of the Colonial Office, they would have been increased in severity. Kruger had chastised them with whips; Milner was fain to chastise them with scorpions.

Yet it was the same Milner who allowed himself to be prevailed upon to take the risks contingent on the introduction of still more Asiatics into the Transvaal, in the form of Chinese coolies for the gold mines. It was in June 1904 that the first Chinese labourers came to the Witwatersrand. Their coming was the result of a skilfully organized campaign set on foot by the mine-owners, who were suffering severely from the shortage of native labour. Opposition there was— in South Africa the results of Natal's importation of Asiatic

labour were held up as a warning—in Britain the principle
of indentured labour was vigorously assailed—'white'
Australia and New Zealand, which had helped to bring the
Transvaal within the Empire, raised questioning eyebrows.
But the opposition was overborne. Milner was convinced
against his better judgment, and some 50,000 Chinese came.

They brought a peck of troubles with them, troubles for
the Conservative Government in Britain, in the determining
of whose downfall the cry of 'Chinese slavery' was destined
to have perhaps more than its due weight, troubles for their
employers, troubles for the public of the Transvaal. The
Chinese 'slaves' were none too docile labourers, nor were
they kept under such restraint as to prevent them from in-
dulging in robbery and, in some cases, even murder. In
outlying parts of the Witwatersrand a mild terrorism prevailed, arms had to be issued to farmers for their protection
against Chinese marauders, and the clamour for repatriation
increased in volume. Campbell-Bannerman forbade any
further importation, and left the fate of those already in the
country to the Responsible Government which should be
formed as a result of the Transvaal's first elections. The
state of feeling in the Colony on this issue undoubtedly did
much to win the elections for Botha; and, having won it,
he declared that on the expiry of their contracts all the
coolies must return home. They had played their part in
the re-establishment of the gold-mining industry. The
output had soared, profits had risen, money had been put
into circulation, and the European population of the
Transvaal had increased considerably. Moreover, South
African natives were again coming forward to work in such
numbers as made it possible to dispense with the Chinese.
The gold-mining industry had been enabled to set its house
in order. There were those who thought that the same
results might have been achieved without the risks which the
importation had involved. At least South Africa could
congratulate itself that it had been spared the permanent
complication of its problems which the venture might have
entailed. Its Asiatic problem remained almost entirely an
Indian problem.

To Botha and Smuts, Campbell-Bannerman had also left
the handling of the question of the Indians in the Transvaal.

The expiring Legislative Council of the Transvaal Crown Colony had in 1906 unanimously adopted an Ordinance dealing with the registration of Asiatics. The Colonial Office held it up in view of the impending change in the Colony's form of government. The Botha Cabinet, for whose policy in these matters Smuts, as Colonial Secretary, was responsible, promptly secured its re-enactment, and, in addition, imposed restrictions on immigration, including an education test and the registration of finger-prints. There was a storm of protest, and the leader of the opposition was Mohamdas Karamchand Gandhi, who was finding in South Africa nurture and inspiration for the indomitable spiritual qualities which were in days to come to make him an outstanding figure on the world stage. There were many who confidently expected that the Imperial Government would prevent this legislation from becoming of force and effect; but the Royal Assent was not withheld.

So ended—in Smuts's favour—the first round in the contest between Gandhi and himself. The Mahatma had come to South Africa, a well-born, cultured, Indian gentleman, a member of the English Bar, to fight a case in the Courts. But to the generality of men in Natal and the Transvaal in those days the fact of his colour equated him with the Indian coolie whom they knew so well, and by bitter experience the meaning of colour prejudice was borne in upon him. But also there came home to him the status of his fellow-Indians in South Africa as a cause worth fighting for, and to that cause he gave a great part of his life. So it came about that it was with Gandhi, as spokesman of the Indians, that Smuts had to deal, and when protestations and appeals against the stigma of discrimination failed, it was Gandhi who had recourse to the weapon of Passive Resistance with which India was in time to become acquainted. Often there is justice in the working of history. India had given to South Africa one of the most difficult of its problems; South Africa in its turn gave to India the idea of civil disobedience.

For years the struggle continued. At times Gandhi argued, and protested, and appealed for an improvement in the position of his countrymen, linking up their cause wherever he could with the national movement in India. At other times he and his followers defied the law, crossed the border without registering finger-prints, went to gaol and out of it, perfecting the while the creed of self-abnegation, and learning its power and effectiveness as a weapon. When Union came, the scope of the problem was widened, for Natal had in 1908 passed new legislation making it more difficult for Indians to get trading licences, and the Cape Immigration Act of 1906 had prohibited the entry of male Asiatics over sixteen years of age from oversea, and seriously hampered their admission from other parts of South Africa. On the wider stage of the Union the Smuts–Gandhi struggle continued to be waged. It was Smuts's aim to secure the passage of legislation which would close the door finally to the admission of the Asiatic to South Africa; Gandhi fought in effect for free entry and for the grant of full citizen rights to Indians in South Africa on a basis of equality with Europeans. His plea commended itself to the idealism of many outside observers, but it would have been strange if South Africa had been willing at that stage to concede the privileges of British citizenship in South Africa to those who would, for the most part, have been ' untouchables ' in their own land, and whose standard of living made men view them as a serious economic menace.

At length a spectacular climax was reached when in 1913 Gandhi led a band of 2,700 Indians on foot from Natal into the Transvaal in defiance of the law which controlled the crossing of provincial boundaries. There followed riots and disturbances in Natal, Gandhi's arrest, investigations and inquiries, until finally a temporary settlement was arrived at. Smuts's Immigration Act was passed without specific reference to Indians, but in such manner that it can be used, and has been used, to prevent their entrance into South Africa; and at the same time an Indian Relief Act was enacted, which conceded some of Gandhi's points, including the abolition of Natal's special £3 tax on ' free ' Asiatics. For the rest, Gandhi, having received from Smuts an assurance that ' existing laws ' would be administered ' in a just manner with due regard to vested rights,' accepted it, in conjunction with the Relief Act, as ' a complete and final settlement of the controversy,' and returned to India.

It was the end of the Smuts–Gandhi controversy, but not the end of South Africa's Indian problem. The immigration question had been settled by the cessation of the importation of indentured labour and the virtual prohibition of the entry of the 'free' Asiatic, but there remained those already in the country, more than one in ten of the whole European population of the Union, actually at that time in the majority in the province of Natal. There remained, also, on the one side the limitation of the Indian's civic rights, in matters such as the franchise, trading licences, the ownership of land, freedom of movement from province to province, and on the other side the pressure of Indian competition in the economic sphere. On that economic issue the battle continued to be waged. The Indian trader made steady headway in the Transvaal—not so rapidly, indeed, as his opponents alleged, but rapidly enough to provide the occasion for agitation against him—and he was finding the means of evading the restrictions upon his ownership of land. So again the cry of the Asiatic menace went rioting through the land. Compulsory repatriation of Indians, well over two-thirds of whom, be it remembered, are of South African birth, was a popular slogan at elections —anti-Asiatic leagues were formed—there was further restrictive legislation dealing with Asiatic landholding and trading—protests poured in from India and from Anglo-India—and controversy raged over the nature of the 'vested rights' which, in terms of the Smuts–Gandhi agreement, were entitled to protection.

At length—in 1924—the Smuts Government, after having inaugurated a policy of aided voluntary repatriation of Indians with some success, introduced a Class Areas Bill, which aimed at the compulsory segregation of Asiatics. It fell before the Bill could be proceeded with, but the Hertzog Government which followed re-introduced it in a more drastic form. Then at last the protests of the Government of India were heeded. There was consultation and discussion, and an amicable arrangement was in 1927 arrived at. As a result the proposed legislation was dropped. The Indian Government undertook to assist in making the policy of voluntary repatriation more effective. The South African Government offered assurances which implied a more sympathetic attitude towards the upliftment of the Indians who remained in South Africa, and gave its blessing to the principle of their advancement in the scale of education and civilization. Mr. Srinivasa Sastri spent two years in South Africa as Agent-General for India, and by his gifts of personality and intellect did much to break down settled prejudices. But the economic essentials of the problem, arising from the presence of the Asiatic in the South African racial complex, remained, and still remains, fundamentally unaltered.

Chapter 10

The Union and its Neighbours

WHEN men speak of South Africa there is often need to ask whether it is the geographical or the political unit to which they make reference—the difference is considerable, and in certain aspects of very wide significance. The natural boundary of South Africa, considered geographically, is the Zambesi and its extension westwards. But within that boundary there are, in addition to the Union itself, a mandated territory three-fourths its size, a self-governing British Colony, the most important part of Portugal's oldest African dependency, and three Protectorates directly under the administration of the British Government. For the understanding of the Union's political position and the appreciation of its opportunities and problems in relation to the continent of Africa, some consideration must be given to the manner in which the relations between itself and its neighbours have developed.

Stretching northwards along the west coast from the Orange River through almost twelve degrees of latitude lies the territory of South-West Africa. Its seaboard is for the most part harbourless, and its coast lands are a sandy waste; moreover, the districts of the Union which adjoin it are, despite mineral wealth, a desolate and unattractive region. It is not to be wondered at that it should for so long have remained outside of the main current of South Africa's life. As far back as 1814 the Cape Government despatched a German, von Schmelen by name, to carry on mission work among the Hottentot tribes beyond the Orange, but there the Colony's interest in the area ended. Von Schmelen, however, made progress with his work, and in due course the Rhenish Missionary Society sent out from Germany reinforcements to his aid. As often, trade followed the missionary, and Germany's interest began to grow in this new land. But expanding trade also attracted the attention of Cape merchants, and the prospect of annexation was canvassed. The British flag was indeed the first to be hoisted, but the area annexed was limited to the harbour of Walvis Bay and the Guano Islands off the coast. Further expansion was checked by the doubts and vacillation, first of Downing Street, and then of the Colonial Government in Capetown, and so the field was left open just long enough for Bismarck to be able to proclaim a German Protectorate in 1884. Thus Germany acquired a foothold in South Africa, and was in fact one of the Union's neighbours when the explosion at Serajevo fired the train in 1914.

At first the European element had grown but slowly in South-West Africa. The desert coast-belt checked development, and there was much trouble with the native inhabitants, especially the Hereros, who had come southwards as the western wing of the Bantu migration. Indirectly, however, the native wars made for progress; they stimulated the homeland's interest in its new Colony, and, since many of the soldiers elected to remain there, they fostered the increase of its population; as a result, the possibilities of the grassland interior for stock-raising began to be appreciated, and considerable mineral resources, of which diamonds were the most important, were discovered. When the Great War broke out, German South-West Africa had entered upon a period of marked progress, and its German population had grown to 15,000.

Its conquest by the troops of the Union under Generals Botha and Smuts was one of the best executed operations of the war. True, they had the benefit of a considerable numerical superiority in the forces under their command, but nature had interposed many serious difficulties, and the rapidity, the completeness, and the smallness of loss with which the victory was won constituted a considerable achievement. As a result the Government of the Union assumed the administration of the country, at first under martial law. Later there was issued to it a mandate of the C class in pursuance of the treaty of Versailles. The mandate empowered the Union to administer South-West Africa as an integral part of its territory, but it imposed upon it various limitations, the main intention of which was to protect the interests of the native peoples. In its form the

South-West African mandate was similar to others issued by the League, but the difficulties of the mandatory power were considerably increased by the fact that, here alone among the African mandated territories, was there a large European population of ex-enemy stock firmly rooted in the country. Under Union administration the territory, despite troubles with the natives, advanced steadily. The post-war German population showed, it is true, a reduction by emigration of more than forty per cent., but this loss was made good several times over by immigration from the Union. In 1923 the Union Government came to an agreement with Berlin, as a result of which German nationals in the territory, save those who contracted out before a fixed date, became British subjects; among other concessions made by the Union, the German language was recognized for certain official purposes, and as a medium of instruction in the schools. On the basis of this agreement the territory was given a measure of self-government in 1925. It received a Legislative Council, partly nominated, but with an elective majority, conceived on similar lines to the Provincial Councils in the Union; it had a wider range of subjects to deal with, but the supremacy of the Union Government was adequately secured.

Corresponding to South-West Africa on the west lies the Portuguese Colony or ' Province ' of Mozambique on the east, roughly equal to it in size, but less compact in shape, and occupying a position of far greater strategic importance in South Africa's economic life. For while South-West Africa and its excellent harbour of Walvis are separated from the most productive parts of South Africa by great stretches of arid and semi-arid country, Portuguese East Africa is not sundered by any such obstacles, and Delagoa Bay is the natural port for practically the whole of the Transvaal.

The Colony of Mozambique goes back to the days when Portugal was mistress of the Indian Ocean. Upon it was squandered much blood and treasure, for in those days the exploitation of a fever-sodden coast-belt with an undeveloped hinterland offered all too scanty compensation. When its maritime supremacy declined, Portugal maintained but a precarious foothold on the seaboard, until, in the fulness of time, the development of the interior from the healthier south provided an economic basis for the welfare of the coastal region. It was then that the importance of the harbour of Delagoa came home to men. For the opening up of the road which gave access to it early Voortrekkers gave their lives; the question of its ownership was matter for anxious thought and scheming in Pretoria, Lisbon, and London, until the MacMahon Award settled it; about the building of the railway to the interior, and the fierce competition that ensued with the Cape and Natal harbours and railways, much of South Africa's history has turned; and in the latter days of the Republic there was constant coming and going of warships in the waters hard by the Bay, while Rhodes sought eagerly to ' do a deal ' with the Portuguese, and Britain, Germany, and France manœuvred ceaselessly for position.

The establishment of British rule in the Transvaal led to simplification in the complexities of international relations which had their origin in Delagoa Bay. But it did little to simplify the difficulty, now inherited by a British Government, of adjusting the competing claims for the rich traffic to the Witwatersrand. For the Province of Mozambique had come to acquire a new importance for the Transvaal, quite apart from the opportunities which it offered for the importation of goods at cheaper rates than would have ruled if the interior had been dependent solely on the more distant British Colonial ports. It was now recognized as a most important reservoir of labour for the gold mines, and even before the Anglo-Boer War ended, Milner concluded the so-called *modus vivendi* with the Portuguese Government, in terms of which, in exchange for facilities for the recruitment of Mozambique natives, the Delagoa Bay railway was guaranteed the continuance of the proportion of the traffic which it had enjoyed in Republican days. In the same spirit the Responsible Government of the Transvaal concluded the Mozambique Convention in April 1909, to ensure the safeguarding under Union of the Transvaal's interests in the adjacent Portuguese territory.

With the years, then, the town of Lourenço Marques, which is built on the shores of Delagoa Bay, has, by virtue of its close relationship with the Transvaal, grown in prosperity; to the northward Beira, which is as much the natural harbour of Rhodesia and Nyasaland as Delagoa Bay is of the Transvaal, has grown similarly with the opening up of those northern lands; and on the foundations of commercial prosperity thus laid the Province of Mozambique has, more especially in recent years, taken active steps to exploit its own natural resources.

But the relations between the Union and Mozambique have not been uninterruptedly cordial. Union interests in the harbour of Delagoa Bay are, of course, considerable. Much of the trade of the port is in British and South African hands. Portuguese officialdom has not always been easy to work with, and for a time the vagaries of the Portuguese currency caused grave inconvenience and loss. Moreover, there was growing dissatisfaction with the facilities available for the handling of the Union's growing export trade. All this led to a demand by General Smuts's Government for a measure of Union control over the railway and the harbour, which was strenuously resisted. On its side the Mozambique Government, finding that the works of development which it had initiated increased the local demand on its native labour force, became less and less compliant in the provision of facilities for recruiting. For several years negotiations ran a troubled course; for a time the Convention, or most of it, was allowed to lapse, and a new Convention was only negotiated in 1928, with great difficulty and at the cost of considerable concessions on the side of the Union. On the basis of that agreement friendly relations prevail to-day, but Portuguese ownership of South Africa's most convenient natural harbour continues to represent a deficiency in the geographical completeness of the Union.

The Province of Mozambique outflanks the Union on the east—it also outflanks the colony of Southern Rhodesia, with the difference, however, that the latter has no independent means of direct access to the sea. As a self-governing Colony, Southern Rhodesia is still of fairly recent birth. The greatest monument to the memory of Cecil Rhodes, it is the creation of his dominating idealism and his restless energy. The north was his passion and his dream. Under its inspiration he worked to keep Bechuanaland, ' the Suez Canal of the Interior,' out of Kruger's hands; under its inspiration he won control of the diamond mines of Kim-

berley, so that the profits might be available, as he himself
phrased it, ' to acquire a country and form an Empire ';
under its inspiration he built up his political influence and
power in the Cape Colony, conceiving it as the base for his
northward advance. In 1888, when Germany, Portugal,
and the Transvaal were all showing interest in his ' North,'
Rhodes took the first steps towards the foundation of
Rhodesia. Backed by him and by Sir Hercules Robinson,
the missionary Moffat secured in that year from Lobengula,
chief of the Matabele, and ruler of the lands between the
Limpopo and the Zambesi, a binding undertaking to cede
no part of his territory without the Governor's leave. Upon
that followed a concession by the chief to Rhodes's representative, Rudd, granting a monopoly of the minerals in
his domains, and upon that again the foundation of the British
South Africa Company. The day of the Chartered Company had come once more in the last part of the nineteenth
century, and Rhodes also secured a Royal Charter for his
Company in 1889. Next year he sent his pioneer column,
which established itself firmly in Mashonaland, the eastern
portion of the area in which Lobengula was paramount, and
in its wake he despatched settlers, most of whom he recruited
in the Cape Colony. There followed collisions with the
Portuguese, and Rhodes, who had learnt the lesson of
Delagoa Bay, struggled hard to secure the port of Beira, but
an Anglo-Portuguese Convention in 1891 demarcated
Portugal's sphere in such manner as to leave all of the coast-
belt in its hands.

It is on the interior plateau, then, that the Colony of
Rhodesia has developed. Of difficulties and disappoint-
ments it has had its share. There were two wars with the
Matabele, the latter of which, that of 1896, was especially
severe, and did not end until Rhodes himself entered the
camp of the Matabele unarmed, and won their submission
by his courage and the power of his personality. The
Anglo-Boer War seriously retarded Rhodesia's development,
and it shared fully in the depression which followed. The
prospects of great mineral wealth which were for many years
dangled before expectant shareholders were destined to be
very incompletely realized. But steadily the country
established itself as a region fit for European settlement, and

Rhodes's dream of 'homes, more homes' has in large measure been realized in the land that bears his name.

The direct administration of the Chartered Company prevailed for a much longer period than Rhodes had ever contemplated. With the increase in the European population and the establishment of settled conditions, the introduction of some form of self-government seemed a natural development, and, indeed, already in 1898 the settlers were given an elective minority on the Legislative Council. Soon too, as might have been expected, they began to chafe under Company rule, the more so because, when once the personal touch and the broad humanity of Rhodes had been withdrawn, it became, in their minds, the government of a corporation without a body to kick or a soul to save. But before a change could be made there were some difficult questions to settle. The Company claimed the ownership of all unalienated land; it asked also for the refund to it of the amounts which it had expended to meet deficits in the administration of the territory. Had Rhodesia been established as a self-governing Colony with the burdens which the concession of these claims would have imposed upon it, its position would have been precarious indeed, the more so as the Company would still have been functioning in its midst as a powerful commercial corporation, controlling the railways, and wielding other important interests. For many a long year the dispute dragged on. In its course the question of incorporation in the Union was raised more than once. At the National Convention Rhodesia was represented, and in the South Africa Act provision was made for its facultative admission to the Union after presentation of an address by the Union Parliament. But nothing came of it. The war and other difficulties delayed the settlement of the question of the Company's rights, which was held to be fundamental to any substantial change in Rhodesia's constitutional position. Then at last in 1918 the Judicial Committee of the Privy Council gave its decision, that the unalienated lands were the property of the Crown, but that the Company had the right to be reimbursed in respect of the administrative deficits. Three years later the amount due to the Company was fixed by the Cave Commission.

In the light of the position thus disclosed the choice

F

between Responsible Government and incorporation in the Union was keenly canvassed. The Smuts Government submitted attractive terms of incorporation, but in the now predominantly British Rhodesia there was fear of the potentially Republican and secessionist Union, and on a referendum the advocates of incorporation were defeated. Responsible Government followed almost as a matter of course. The British Government agreed to pay the amount due to the Company, and to hand over the Crown lands to the Rhodesians on easy terms. In September 1923 the Colony of Southern Rhodesia was formally annexed, and its new constitution was at once granted to it.

To complete the account of the Union's neighbours it is necessary to refer to the three Protectorates, Basutoland, Swaziland, and Bechuanaland. Geographically their connection with the Union is close. Basutoland is an island within the Union, Swaziland is almost entirely surrounded by Union territory, the frontier of Bechuanaland is for more than three-fourths of its length a common frontier, either with the Union or with South-West Africa. But the course of historical development has set them upon a path of their own, and although they are for Customs purposes regarded as virtually part of the Union, they still remain distinct elements in the South African community.

Of the three, Basutoland was the first to pass under the control of the Imperial Government. In 1884, as we have seen, the Cape Colony, which had failed so signally in its efforts to enforce order and obedience, transferred it to the direct authority of the Crown to be exercised by the High Commissioner. The Bechuanaland Protectorate followed in 1885, and after various experiments in its government, one of which—its transfer to the control of the British South Africa Company—gave Jameson a jumping-off place for his Raid, it also was brought under the High Commissioner's authority. Finally there was Swaziland. There the prodigality of the Swazi rulers in the granting of concessions and the conflicting interests of concessionaires, British and Dutch, caused much friction between Great Britain and the South African Republic, which ended at last in the recognition of the latter's right to administer Swaziland, though not as an integral part of its territory. Then after the Anglo-Boer

War it passed under the control, first of the Governor of the Transvaal, and later of the High Commissioner for South Africa.

All three Protectorates are predominantly native territories. In Basutoland no land is held otherwise than by natives, and the European population consists almost entirely of officials, missionaries, traders, and labour agents. In Bechuanaland relatively small areas have been allotted to European owners for agricultural and pastoral purposes, and though the European population is not much larger than in Basutoland, a European Advisory Council has been constituted, as well as a Native Advisory Council, to assist the Resident Commissioner. A similar statement would apply to Swaziland, save that there, as a result of the concessions, a much larger proportion of the land is available for European occupation. But in all three cases the British Government regards itself as primarily in the position of a trustee for the native peoples, and the doctrine of the paramountcy of their interests prevails.

Chapter 11

The Union's Constitution

THE constitution of South Africa is set forth directly in an Act of the British Parliament, but it was an instrument drafted by the National Convention in South Africa which that Act made effective, practically without amendment, and it gave to the South African Parliament which it created the right to amend the Union's flexible constitution. Selborne's principle that Union must be born of the soil of South Africa, and nurtured by its own statesmen, had therefore prevailed. It was the will of the people of South Africa which became of force and effect at Westminster.

The ascertainment of the common measure of that popular will had not been easy. The communities which were to be united had been left for all too long to tread divergent paths. There had come into being clashing interests, opposing policies, and conflicting political conceptions. The task of reconciliation was beset with many difficulties—the result is to be seen in the extent to which compromise is writ large over the constitution of the Union.

Compromise there was even in determining the fundamental principles on which the constitution was to be based. At first when men spoke of Union in South Africa they thought in terms of Federation. The precedents of other countries which seemed applicable pointed in that direction, and certainly in the nineteenth century nothing else would have been possible. Federation, and Federation alone, was what Grey, Carnarvon, and others who had worked for Union contemplated. But gradually the tide began to set towards a closer form of Union; Milner himself asked the question, ' Why stop at Federation? ' And in the minds of those who carried through the groundwork for the National Convention the conception of a unitary constitution took shape. The Convention, when it met, found that most of the preparatory work which had been done rested on such a basis. There were, however, also powerful influences which made for a Federal system. The smaller Colonies, Natal and the Free State, tended to be particularistic, and were acutely apprehensive of being swamped by their larger neighbours. At the Cape, too, Federation found powerful support. Some saw in it the most effective method of safeguarding the equal political rights which non-Europeans enjoyed in the Mother Colony alone; others, like Hofmeyr, believed that political union should keep pace with national union, and felt that until more fruit had been borne by the work of reconciliation which had been initiated after the Anglo-Boer War, it would be a mistake to draw too close the constitutional bonds which were to unite the former Republics and the older Colonies.

But at the Convention itself those who championed the unitary principle won a speedy triumph. They stressed the difficulties which a Federal constitution had brought with it in other Dominions, and the dangers which might arise in South Africa from the absence of a strong central Government; the atmosphere was charged with a sense of weariness with the divisions of the past; and so, naturally enough, Federalism was dismissed as an unnecessary concession to human weakness, and the alternative was preferred which seemed to offer the greater measure of logical completeness. But even so the position of those who were either more cautious or more particularistic could not entirely be ignored. As fundamental to the new constitution was accepted the idea of a sovereign Parliament legislating for an essentially unitary State, but despite that, significant concessions to Federalism were made. Had it not been for such concessions, it is probable that Natal would have withheld its adhesion to Union.

Of great importance, then, in the Union's constitution is the fact that it is divided into four Provinces which are co-terminous with the pre-existing Colonies. In each of these Provinces there is a Provincial Council, and there can be no alteration of boundaries save on the petition of the Councils of the Provinces affected. In some measure the Provincial Councils are lineal successors of the former Colonial Parliaments, but they are in no sense sovereign bodies. Their activities are limited to certain specifically defined spheres, and even within those spheres their enactments are only valid in so far as they are not repugnant to any Act of the Union Parliament. The power of Parliament remains supreme, no less within than outside of the sphere of the Provincial Councils' competence. Professor Dicey has singled out as the main characteristics of a Federation the supremacy of the constitution rather than of Parliament, the distribution of the powers of government among bodies with limited and co-ordinated authority, and the wide discretion of the Courts in the interpretation of the constitution. No one of these characteristics is to be found in the case of the South African Union.

Parliament consists in South Africa of the Queen (represented normally by a Governor-General), a Senate, and a House of Assembly. The principle of a bi-cameral legislature was adopted by the National Convention, and though it has since been subjected to sporadic attack, it still prevails. In the constitution of the Senate we find another concession to Federalism. In federal constitutions the upper house is usually conceived as the representative of State rights. In South Africa the principle of equal representation of the Provinces, despite great differences in size and population—a principle which is suggestive of that conception—has been adopted. Each Province is represented by eight Senators, who are elected by the members of the House of Assembly from that Province and of its Provincial Council sitting together for that purpose, while eight others are nominated by the Governor-General-in-Council. In regard to the nominated Senators the principle of equal representation of the Provinces has also come in practice to prevail.

The Senate's normal term is ten years, but it may be dissolved either along with the Assembly, or by itself within 120 days of the Assembly's dissolution. The Assembly, in its turn, has a maximum life of five years, but it may, of course, be dissolved at any time. Its membership was in the first instance fixed at 121; later, under the provisions of the Constitution, it was increased to 150. There are, in addition, six members to represent South-West Africa and three members elected by the natives on a communal roll.

For the event of deadlock between the two Houses the South Africa Act makes adequate provision. The supremacy of the Lower House is set beyond all doubt, and an adverse vote in the Senate is by implication deprived of any influence on the Government's continuance in office. While the Senate has the power to amend or reject all Bills, save money Bills, which it may only reject, provision is made for a joint session of the two Houses in the event of the Assembly not accepting the Senate's decision. In the case of a money Bill such a joint session may be held immediately; in the case of other measures only after the lower house has reaffirmed its original proposal at a second session, and the Senate has again failed to concur. Since the Assembly is considerably the larger of the two bodies, its views would normally prevail. As a result of these provisions the Senate has in effect come to be mainly a house of review, and ' a place,' so it has been described, ' where Ministers may make graceful concessions which they have refused elsewhere.' But it has also rendered service of greater importance than such a description would suggest. In one of the gravest political crises in South Africa—that which arose over the question of the determination of a national flag—the exercise of the Senate's power of delaying that decision into a second session was an important factor in securing a settlement by consent.

The equal representation of the Provinces in the Senate marks, as has been pointed out, a concession to Federalism; a more significant concession, and one which is, perhaps, the most interesting feature in the Union's constitution, is to be found in the arrangements made for the administration of the Provinces. In each there are three organs of government. There is a popularly elected Provincial Council with powers of law-making in respect of a specified list of subjects, of which the chief are Education, Hospitals, Roads, Local Government, and Taxation within a carefully demarcated field. There is an Administrator appointed by the Union Government with a five-year term of office, and a salary which is voted not by the Provincial Council, but by Parliament. There is an Executive Committee which consists of the Administrator and four members elected by the Council on the basis of proportional representation.

In the inter-relation of these organs there are several peculiar features. While up to a point the conception of the Administrator's position as set forth in the South Africa Act is in relation to the Province similar to that of the Governor-General in relation to the Union, he is certainly not to be regarded as merely the Lieutenant-Governor of a province or State in a Federation. He is the regular chair-man of the Executive Committee, and participates, personally and directly, in the administration of the Province; he sits in the Provincial Council with all the privileges of membership save that of voting, occupying in it virtually the same position as the Prime Minister does in the House of Assembly; and he has considerable powers of control in financial affairs which he may exercise without reference to the Executive Committee. But with all this, since he is an official of the Union Government, the Provincial Council can exercise no control over him. There is a similar absence of responsibility in the case of the Executive Committee. The Provincial Council sits for three years, and is not subject to dissolution save by effluxion of time; the Executive Committee is chosen after each general election of the Council, and it holds office until the next Executive Committee is similarly chosen. In the intervening period there is no authority which can dismiss it or enforce its resignation. On the one occasion when a Provincial Council sought to withhold supplies, the Union Government stepped in to rescue the Executive Committee. Moreover, the fact that the Executive Committee is elected by proportional representation tends in the direction of its not being ordinarily a homogeneous body. The provisions of its constitution certainly do not make for effective collective responsibility.

For the understanding of a constitution which departs so markedly from the traditions of Parliamentary Government one must remember that it had its origin in compromise. That compromise was of a twofold character. In the old Cape Colony there were in existence at Union well-developed organs both of urban and rural local self-government; in the three northern Colonies there was no local self-government outside the towns. It was felt that in this deficiency in administrative machinery there was a powerful argument against the unqualified centralization of a strictly unitary constitution; at the same time there was such powerful opposition in the rural areas of those northern Colonies to anything savouring of taxation of the land as to make the creation of small rural councils with rating powers impracticable; as a result the Provincial Councils were established as a compromise between the idea of a purely rural local authority and the idea of a body suitable for the administration of a considerable region embracing urban as well as rural areas. Alongside of the difficulty met in this way there presented itself the necessity of finding a compromise which would make some concession to the principle of Federalism. To that end it seemed good that the former Colonies, which were to become Provinces, should be allowed to retain something like the local Parliaments to which they were accustomed, but shorn of the Parliamentary trappings, and with their constitution so defined that they could not be regarded as sovereign bodies. For that reason it was considered necessary, not merely to subordinate their legislative powers to Parliament, but also to give them in each case an Executive not responsible to the Council and an Administrator whom, as an official of the Union Government, it could not control.

Such a constitution, despite its departures from tradition, might have provided a satisfactory system of local government for compact areas administered with reasonable freedom from party spirit. Where, indeed, those conditions have been approximated to, as in the smaller provinces of the Union, in which the overwhelming strength of one or other party has tempered the acuteness of political strife, it has worked reasonably well. But in the Cape and Transvaal Provinces, where the parties have been more evenly divided, party spirit has at times run high in the Councils, and the constitutional difficulties have, on occasion, been very serious. Alongside of the constitutional difficulties there have also been experienced financial difficulties, arising both from the complexities of financial relations between Union and Provinces and from the obstacles to the imposition of taxation which the composition of some of the Councils has presented, and administrative difficulties, which spring from the manner in which functions are divided between Union Government Departments and the Provincial

Administrations. There is a very large measure of agreement in South Africa that the provincial experiment has not
been a success.

There is less agreement as to the manner in which this
weakness in the constitution should be repaired. It follows
from the fact that it is a result of a compromise between the
principle of Federalism and the principle of Unification,
that the remedy must be found by advancing towards the
more logical application of one or other of those principles.
There are those, especially in Natal, who would seek to
magnify the powers of the Councils, and to go as far towards
the restoration to them of the status of the former Colonial
Parliaments as is compatible with the maintenance of the
Union. But public opinion is in general against such a
tendency, and, indeed, a reversion to Federalism, where
once the constitution has given so much authority to the
central Government, would seem to be contrary to all
political experience. The absorption by Parliament of the
functions of the Provincial Councils would appear to be the
more natural line of development. It will not, however, be
as easy to pursue as it might be, for the northern provinces
are still without effective organs of rural local self-government, and men's aversion from the grant of rating powers to
such bodies continues to be difficult to overcome. In their
absence the objections to undue centralization remain
considerable.

There are other aspects of the Union's constitution where
the effects of compromise are similarly apparent. One of
the most difficult questions with which the National Convention had to deal was that of the franchise, more especially
in regard to native representation. For the institution of a
uniform franchise for the Union it was necessary to reconcile
the systems in operation in the four Colonies, based as they
were on conflicting ideas. Under the Cape franchise law,
there was required of the voter the possession of a property or
salary qualification and the ability to sign his name, but
there was no distinction of colour or race. In the Transvaal
and the Orange River Colony there was manhood suffrage,
specifically limited to Europeans. Natal had in principle
followed the Cape system, but with such limitations as in
effect practically to exclude native and coloured voters.

The Cape was loath to abandon the principle of political equality; the Transvaal and the Orange River Colony were even more loath to accept it. For a time the Convention toyed with the idea of a civilization test which would have been more exclusive than the Cape franchise qualification, but the acceptance of which would have meant a Union-wide colour-blind franchise. But it was not acceptable to the Convention, and so recourse was had to the expedient of leaving the existing franchise laws unchanged in each of the Provinces, until such time as Parliament should have devised a uniform franchise for the Union. That Parliament did not do. The pre-Union laws remained in force, modified only to the extent of granting the franchise to women. So the compromise was effected on the basis of the *status quo*, and it was confirmed by mutual concession. On the one side it was agreed that the non-Europeans at the Cape should lose the right of candidature for Parliament which they had until then enjoyed. At the same time it was laid down that of the eight Senators to be nominated by the Governor-General-in-Council, four should be chosen on the ground ' of their thorough acquaintance by reason of their official experience or otherwise, with the reasonable wants and wishes of the coloured races of South Africa.'

Compromise prevailed also at the National Convention in questions arising out of the basis of representation and the allocation of seats in Parliament. There were two main issues. First there was the question of the representation in Parliament of the areas of the four Colonies. The Cape Colony at the time of Union had a European population almost as large as those of the other three Colonies taken together. They, however, and especially the Transvaal, were determined to prevent Cape predominance in the Union, and they were favoured by the fact that the Cape's numerical strength was at the time balanced by financial weakness. In the constitution of the Senate they prevailed to the extent of securing equal representation of the four Provinces. In the case of the Assembly the original Transvaal proposal was that seats should be allocated on the basis of the number of European voters in each Province, which would have favoured the Transvaal and the Orange River Colony with their unqualified manhood suffrage.

The Cape contested this proposal, and emphasized in particular that it made no allowance for its non-European voters. Eventually a compromise was accepted which took as basis the number of European male adults in each of the Provinces. But in the application of that basis special treatment was accorded to the smaller Provinces, each of which was given a minimum representation of seventeen, and this was done mainly at the expense of the Cape, which not only received no consideration in respect of its coloured and native voters, but was also handicapped in other ways. At the same time provision was made for a system of automatic redistribution by a judicial delimitation commission, which was to be determined by the increase or decrease of the Union's white population as revealed by a quinquennial census. The increase in the number of members was, however, to be checked at 150, and thereafter the principle of distribution between the provinces on the basis of the number of European male adults in each was to apply without restriction.

The other issue was that of the method of allocating within the provinces the membership allocated to each. Here the National Convention had to lay down principles for the guidance of the delimitation commission. At the Cape it had been customary to take account of the special circumstances of rural districts by giving the country population more seats in proportion to its numbers than the urban population. The Transvaal members of the Convention were, however, committed to the principle of ' equal rights,' or ' one vote, one value '; they worked also to ensure the representation of minorities, and they therefore proposed a system of proportional representation with three-member constituencies as nearly as possible equal in the number of voters. This issue came nearer than any other to the wrecking of Union. In the end proportional representation was abandoned, save in the elections for the Senate and for Provincial Executive Committees, and single-member constituencies were instituted, but the principle of ' equal rights ' was accepted, save in so far as it was provided that the Commission might in its work of delimitation take account of sparsity and density of population to the extent of fifteen per cent. either way.

It cannot be said that these compromises have been entirely satisfactory in their operation. Considerable minorities have, over large areas of the Union, been left entirely or almost entirely unrepresented, and in the country as a whole there has at more than one election been a large discrepancy between the distribution of the votes cast and the resultant distribution of parties in Parliament. It is not easy to find a remedy for defects such as these under a system of party government, but the time will almost certainly come when Parliament will find itself compelled to face the position.

Two other points in the Union's constitution, both like those already mentioned based on compromise, remain to be noticed. The first is the question of the Union's capital. The choice lay in the first instance between Capetown and Pretoria. The former was the birthplace of South African civilization, but it was placed eccentrically, and in its coast-belt surroundings it was in large measure isolated from the wider South Africa of the interior plateau; the latter was younger, smaller, less favoured in its natural amenities, but geographically and in spirit a better centre of the nation's life. The deadlock between the two towns opened up the possibility that one of the other claimants—and there were many—most probably Bloemfontein, might be chosen. At the last a Solomon's judgment was given. Pretoria was declared to be the seat of government of the Union, with Capetown as the seat of the legislature, while to Bloemfontein, as a consolation prize, fell the honour of providing the home of South Africa's Court of Appeal. A dual capital, with its members 1,000 miles apart, has obvious disadvantages. It is costly, it is inimical to efficiency, and it is the source of many a grievance. But so far the compromise has been loyally adhered to, although its essential impermanence is coming to be more and more widely recognized.

To all the aspects of the Union's constitution so far mentioned the fact that they are based on compromise lends a measure of instability, and at some date, earlier or later, a change would seem to be inevitable. In regard to that which has still to be mentioned, the prospect of amendment is much more remote. The language question was one which the Commission found it could not avoid. It was framing a constitution for a country, most of the inhabitants of which were Afrikaans-speaking, but which had a very large English-speaking minority, and in which the English language had until then held pride of place in official recognition. Dutch had steadily won its way in the old Cape Colony, and the privileges thus secured had been accorded also in the Transvaal and in the Orange River Colony, but there was as yet no absolute equality of language rights. And such equality was an essential corner-stone in the temple of South African unity. That fact the National Convention recognized, and it enshrined in the constitution which it framed the principle of the complete equality of English and Dutch; it was left for Parliament at a later date to make specific mention of Afrikaans. So it is that South Africa has two official languages, and though that also is a compromise which involves inconvenience and expense, no one who really understands the spirit of South Africa would urge to-day that in this matter any change should be made. Of all the compromises on which the Union's constitution is based this is the happiest, and it promises to be the most permanent.

Chapter 12

South Africa and its Place in Africa

I N THE Public Gardens at Capetown there stands that
city's tribute to the memory of Cecil Rhodes—a statue
with northward-pointing finger, and the inscription,
'Your hinterland is there.' That statue gives expression
to what was the main inspiration of Rhodes's political
activity, the development, as the hinterland of South
Africa, of what he loved to call 'the interior.' Back in
1883, in the old Cape House, he spoke 'as one tired of the
mapping-out of Africa at Berlin,' of the ' enormous expansion that lies before us in the dark interior,' and of his faith
that ' remote as our starting-point is, the development of
Africa will occur through the Cape Colony.' When, in
those days, he used more specific language about the Africa
the opening up of which he foreshadowed, he limited it by
the Zambesi, but his thoughts even then, and later also his
public expressions, embraced a far wider area. In 1894,
at a public meeting in Capetown, he told how even in the
days of the speech just quoted, he had indicated to Sir
Hercules Robinson, that he would stop ' only where the
country is not claimed,' and on that same occasion he
anticipated the possibility that ' five and twenty years hence
you might find a gentleman called your Prime Minister
sitting in Capetown, and controlling the whole, not only to
the Zambesi, but to Lake Tanganyika.' Had it not been
for the intervening German territory Rhodes would, doubtless, have forecast even wider expansion for the united
South Africa of his dreams, for already he was thinking in
terms of, as he phrased it, ' keeping the continent together.'
But though the twenty-five years have been lengthened by
several decades, the Union is still bounded by the Limpopo;
it has not even reached out to the Zambesi over the lands
which Rhodes declared that he was taking ' in trust for the
Cape Colony.'

The Rhodes policy, as thus conceived, was a two-fold policy—European settlement in the undeveloped spaces to the north of the Cape Colony and the Transvaal, and administrative continuity in respect of the areas so settled. For that policy he could find powerful backing in geography. That interior plateau which has, in an earlier chapter, been described as the chief feature of South Africa's structure, stretches almost uninterruptedly through the Rhodesias into East Africa up to Abyssinia. At an elevation of over 3,000 feet throughout, it has considerable areas which are more than 5,000 feet above sea level, and where, despite proximity to the Equator, the climate is pleasant and agreeable to the European resident. Moreover, this geographical continuity provides one of the bases of community of interests and ideas, and has thus played its part in creating conditions that make for administrative continuity. It is, however, only the first part of the Rhodes policy that has hitherto been effectively followed up. Rhodes himself spared no effort in the colonization of Rhodesia. To the north-east the British and German Governments, neither of them entirely uninfluenced by his ideas, pursued a similar policy. At the end of the nineteenth century the Uganda Railway was built, and the settlement of what are now known as the highlands of Kenya was actively encouraged, some of the settlers being men of Afrikaans speech from South Africa. Germany took similar action in the Kilimanjaro area and in other parts of her East African Colony. There followed World War I. The manner of its ending, the passing of Tanganyika Territory under mandate to Great Britain, the launching of schemes for the settlement of ex-combatants, quickened the pace, and the phrase ' the East African Dominion of the future ' began to fall from men's lips.

There is much in the African scene that would bring satisfaction to Cecil Rhodes. The writ of Queen Elizabeth runs from a united South Africa, through the Rhodesias that bear his name, into Nyasaland, Tanganyika, Kenya, and Uganda, right up to the borders of Abyssinia; on the other side of Uganda there lie the Anglo-Egyptian Soudan, where a somewhat shadowy *condominium* tempers the reality of British power. And in these lands of ' the interior ' there has been steady progress in European settlement. Rhodes's dream of a European State in tropical Africa has been shown to have been no mere imagining.

But the other part of his policy is still substantially un-fulfilled. True, South Africa has been united as far as the Limpopo, but it has no administrative continuity with the lands of the British Empire that lie to the north of it, and they, in their turn, constitute six distinct units, or seven if Zanzibar is included, representing very diverse stages of constitutional development. To that extent the Rhodes policy has ended in what he would have described as failure, but for that failure much of the responsibility must be placed on his own shoulders. The short cut to political union, which he was fain to take when he became a party of the Jameson Raid, set back the clock of national union for more than a generation—it effectively prevented the north-ward advance of a united British–Dutch South African nation; it released strong currents of feeling within South Africa itself; it set Rhodesia, not without encouragement, indeed, from the post-Raid Rhodes, upon a course of senti-mental development, which makes it glory in the intensity of its British patriotism, in what one of its interpreters has described as 'its super-British Imperialism, a loyalty to Flag and Empire which appears to be old-fashioned in Great Britain to-day.' Between Southern Rhodesia and the Union of South Africa there is at present a barrier which is more than geographical—that barrier stands effectively in the way of the realization of the second part of the Rhodes ideal as it was originally conceived.

The opening up of the region between the Limpopo and the Zambesi was one of the first-fruits of the Hofmeyr–Rhodes alliance in the Cape Colony—in its conception, therefore, it was regarded primarily as an expansion of the already existing South African settlement, and as a joint British–Dutch enterprise. Rhodes himself talked of the wisdom of taking ' the balance of the North for the Cape Colony ' with a view of the creation of new homes for its expanding families; he did all in his power to encourage the young Afrikaans-speaking South African to participate in the enterprise; he emphasized the worth of the Boer as a pioneer of a new land. And, indeed, there were those who characterized his policy of northern development in the phrase, ' Dutch colonization under the British flag.' It was in this sense that he spoke at the Congress of the Afrikander Bond, held at Kimberley in 1891, declaring that ' the development of the North is Cape Colony development,' emphasizing the unity of ideals between himself and the Bond, and foreshadowing the day when there would be a self-governing white community up to the Zambesi in connection with a united South Africa. That was the spirit in which Rhodesia was founded; but the Raid changed many things, and one of the last messages of the founder to the land which bore his name was couched in the form of a warning against the acceptance of advances that might be made from the South. Rhodesia, he said, ' must remember the rock from which she was hewn, and the Empire of which she is an outpost.' It is to Rhodes's later, rather than to his earlier utterances, that Rhodesia has been true.

Yet there has been no lack of effort to direct her course towards union with the South. Lord Selborne, in the Memorandum which prepared the ground for South African Union, uttered a grave warning as to the ' unwisdom of allowing the political organization of the Northern countries to take place in utter independence of the community already established in the South,' and cited the parallel case of the incorporation by the newly established Dominion of Canada of the North-West Territories, where the Hudson Bay Company had till then controlled its hinterland. In the National Convention Rhodesia participated, though its representatives held only a watching brief, and from it he who was later as Sir Charles Coghlan to be its first Prime Minister returned as a strong ' Unionist,' or supporter of its entry into the Union. But though the spirit of the Convention had engendered enthusiasm for the ' new nation ' to north as well as to south of the Limpopo, that enthusiasm was subjected to many a shock during the years that followed, and in Rhodesia it soon waned and disappeared. In its stead there grew up a strong sense of Rhodesia's own individuality, and a consciousness of the difference between itself and its southern neighbour. The emotions stirred by World War I, Rhodesia's own unquestioning enthusiasm in Britain's cause, the opposition of many in the Union to

effective participation in the struggle, all helped to strengthen
that feeling of distinctiveness.   Rhodesia was, it is true, not
one hundred per cent. British.   Because of the original
policy of its founder, it had a considerable Afrikaans-speaking population, and a large proportion of the English-
speaking balance was of South African birth.   Yet in its
spirit Rhodesia came to be ' more English than the King of
England,' determined that its British character should be
maintained, shrinking from bilingualism, apprehensive of
Dominion status with all its possible implications.   And
therein is to be found the reason why, in 1922, Rhodesia,
under the inspiration of the slogan ' Rhodesia for the
Rhodesians and for the Empire,' voted down ' Union,' for
all the attractiveness of General Smuts's proposals, in favour
of ' Responsible Government,' in the conviction that so
there would be assured to it a closer and more living relation
with what it thought of as the Mother Country.

Southern Rhodesia then has definitely elected to strike
out on a path of its own making, and that not, so it readily
admits, because of any weakness in the Union's desire for
its partnership, nor yet because of any lack of liberality in
the terms of association offered.   Feeling in Southern
Rhodesia has in recent years perceptibly hardened against
any idea of entering the Union, and to that hardening events
such as the accession to office of a Nationalist Government,
and the flag controversy, have made substantial contributions.   The overwhelming majority of the people is united
in steadfast support of the policy of Rhodesia working out its
own salvation in its own way and in accordance with its
own ideals, ideals which quite definitely do not include any
thought of submerging its individuality in the Union, either
now or in the future.

What, on the other side, has been the Union's attitude
towards Rhodesia?   In the past the matter has been one of
party political controversy.   When General Smuts made his
offer in 1922, his political opponents declared that its chief
motive was the strengthening of the ' British ' element in the
Union, with a resultant access of strength to the South
African Party.   Their attitude towards the project therefore was characterized by suspicion and hostility.   Again
at the 1929 election a speech by General Smuts in which he

envisaged the extension of the Union's interest and influence northwards was made an issue of the contest; what was represented as a revival of the Rhodes policy was bitterly attacked, and the impression was left in many minds that General Hertzog and his followers were irrevocably committed to a policy of little South Africanism.

The section of Lord Selborne's Memorandum in which he referred to the unwisdom of allowing the political organization of the northern countries to proceed in utter independence of the southern community, concluded, after a reference to the British territory which stretches northwards from the Zambesi, with this pregnant sentence: ' In whatever degree this great region is a country where white men can work and thrive and multiply, by so much will the opportunity of expansion inherited by South Africans throughout the British Empire be increased.' That is an appropriate text for a discussion of the part which the Union is to play in these trans-Zambesian lands. First in the consideration of that text must needs come the question of their probable future as the homes of settled European communities. Reference has been made to the fact of their geographical continuity with the Union. That fact must not, however, be allowed to blind our eyes to two important points of distinction. The first is climatic. It is true that the great African plateau runs through these territories, that the conditions which prevail on it are vastly different from those that are found in the coast-belt, that there are considerable areas with sufficient elevation for the climate to be agreeable and healthy for the white man—yet it remains true that over large areas conditions are inimical if not to the white man's health, then at least to his capacity to perform sustained manual work. The second point of distinction is to be found in the relative proportions of the races. In the Union the black man outnumbers the white man by nearly four to one; in the Central and East African territories the proportion is rather more than four hundred to one. It is a fact which weighs very heavily against the possibility of that region ever being a white man's country in the sense even in which South Africa is a white man's country to-day.

That at once brings us face to face with a conflict of

ideals in regard to the future of these lands. On the one side there are those who accept the ideal, in relation to tropical Africa at least, of ' Africa for the Africans,' who believe that Africa is the home of the black man, just as Europe and America are homes of the white man, and that the European, therefore, can claim no justification for his intrusion into ' this natural and predestined home of the blacks and of an indigenous native culture.' They point to the sufferings which the African has endured at the hands of Europeans in the past; they press for the recognition of the paramountcy of his interests in the future; they declare that, while the keynote of the continent's history has, hitherto, been ' the exploitation of Africa by Europeans in the interests of Europe,' the time has come for the adoption of a new slogan, ' the development of Africa by Africans in the interests of Africa.' On the other side there are those who, in the tradition of Rhodes, champion the cause of white settlement, representing it as not necessarily harmful to the African, but, when rightly directed, the best method of fostering his development. That view can suitably be presented in the words of General Smuts :

' From all this it follows that the easiest, most natural, and obvious way to civilize the African native is to give him decent white employment. White employment is his best school; the gospel of labour is the most salutary gospel for him. The civilization of the African continent will be a vain dream, apart from white employment, without the leading hand of the settler and the employer, away from the continuous living contact with the actual example and the actual practice of European industry and agriculture. The civilization of Africa therefore calls for a definite policy, the policy of European settlement, the establishment of a white community inside Africa which will form the steel framework of the whole ambitious structure of African civilization. Without a large European population as a continuous support and guarantee of that civilization, and as an ever-present practical example and stimulus for the natives, I fear that civilization will not go far, and will not endure for long. From the native point of view, therefore, just as much as from the white or European point of view, nay, even more from the native point of view, the policy of African settlement is imperatively necessary.'

Those are the two conflicting ideals, and the future must be left to decide which will prevail; the decision will be determined in large measure by the natural and economic forces from which they cannot be dissociated. That considerable progress has been made in the realization of the ideal of white settlement, in the establishment of European civilization in the trans-Zambesian territories, will be clear from what has already been said—and white South Africa naturally enough views that progress with satisfaction— but it would be foolish to ignore the strength of the forces which limit the extent and the permanence of such settlement. First it is necessary to guard against a facile overestimate of the areas which may be deemed to be available for European occupation, when regard is paid both to physical conditions and to the present requirements of the native peoples. In Uganda the climate is in general unfavourable to the white man, and the native population is dense; there is certainly little room for European colonization on any considerable scale. To most of Nyasaland the same applies. In Kenya, apart from the areas occupied by Europeans, the Colony is either forest, waste land, semi-arid country, or native reserve. The suitability of Tanganyika to European agriculture is doubtful. In all these cases, save that of Nyasaland, the total area at present alienated to nonnatives, or under present conditions, possibly admitting of European settlement, is less than ten per cent. of the whole. It is only in the case of Northern Rhodesia, where the native population is sparse, that the proportion is in any way considerable. Speaking in general terms, one may say that the area in which white settlement is likely to take place is small in proportion to the whole, and that its carrying capacity in terms of European population cannot, on the basis of our present knowledge of agricultural possibilities, be estimated at a very high figure.

There are also the climatic considerations already hinted at. Are the highlands of Central and East Africa a white man's country in the sense that the white man can not only live there, but found a family? What will be the ultimate effect of residence at a high altitude, with exposure to the direct rays of the sun, on the maintenance of the vigour of the stock? These are questions on which doctors—and laymen—differ. Even in Kenya, with its relatively long period of settlement, parents are only now beginning to take the risk of keeping their children with them during the school-going period. But if on this point there is uncertainty, there can be none in regard to the economic effect of the dependence of the European community on non-European labour, for which climatic conditions are partly responsible. That community is to-day not a self-sufficing community. As in South Africa, it is dependent on the labour of the coloured man—only more so. For while in South Africa most of the unskilled work is done by non-Europeans, in Central and East Africa the same applies also to most of the semi-skilled and skilled work, to nearly all the retail trading, and to much even of the clerical work, certainly in the lower grades. Therein lies a grave threat to the permanence of the European community, which finds the sphere of its activity limited to agriculture, the professions, and positions of management and oversight. The first generation of settlers in these lands is mostly of high quality, and capable of maintaining itself within this limited sphere. But that quality cannot be maintained uniformly. In the second generation there will be many Europeans not suited to agriculture, nor fitted for the higher posts in commerce and industry. For them there will be no openings as unskilled labourers or as skilled artizans. The problems which arise from the coming into economic competition of races with widely different standards of living will present themselves in a far more acute form than that in which we have seen them in South Africa. And a European civilization established on such a foundation may well be found to have been built on nothing more permanent than shifting sand.

There are, however, two possibilities of which account has so far not been taken. The first arises from the steady progress which man has made and is still making in the conquest of nature. Secondly, there is always the chance of mining developments which may produce revolutionary results. Let it not be forgotten that the discovery of gold raised the Transvaal in less than a generation from the most backward to the foremost state in South Africa. And what has happened once may well happen again. Southern Africa is one of the most richly mineralized regions of the earth's surface, and the mineral deposits do not cease at the Limpopo. Southern Rhodesia may have disappointed the soaring anticipations of its founders, but Northern Rhodesia has been revealed as the possessor of vast copper deposits, and already men of sober judgment have spoken of its mining field as likely to prove a second Witwatersrand. That may, in view of the limit to the world's demand for copper, turn out to be an exaggerated forecast; but at least it would seem to be assured that there will be a considerable increase of population, that the resultant creation of a market will stimulate the exploitation of the territory's extensive agricultural resources. Such developments cannot but produce far-reaching changes in Central Africa. To quote General Smuts again: ' A large European community settled on the healthy uplands in the heart of Africa, and forming not only a new centre, but a fresh support and stimulus for western civilization throughout vast surrounding areas, may revolutionize the whole outlook for the future.' The Transvaal yesterday, Northern Rhodesia to-day, perhaps Kenya or Tanganyika to-morrow—who shall, in the light of the possibilities of mineral discoveries, venture to prophesy as to the future of European settlement in the trans-Zambesian lands? And we must admit, however regretfully it be, that possibilities such as those here adumbrated rather than the respective merits on idealistic grounds of the two policies to which reference was made will determine the future of Africa.

It is with due regard to such contingencies that South Africa's relations with Central and Eastern Africa must be considered. There is no present lack of bonds of union. The very name of Northern Rhodesia is one such bond, but apart from that the present development of that area is largely a matter of South African concern. The South African financier, the South African engineer, the South African artizan, are playing important parts in the establishing of the new copper-mining industry, which has in large measure been directed from Johannesburg. To that industry South Africa's young men have been making their way in a constant stream. Nyasaland in its turn owes a great debt to a noble band of South African missionaries— it is still the most important foreign field in the missionary enterprise of the great Dutch Reformed Church of South Africa. Both in Kenya and in Tanganyika there are considerable bodies of Afrikaans-speaking South Africans among the settlers, men who for the most part sought new homes in the north after the Anglo-Boer War. The wresting of Tanganyika from Germany was an enterprise in which South Africa played a considerable part. Kenya has drawn heavily on South Africa for aid in dealing with its administrative problems. Again and again men with South African experience have been invited to fill responsible posts on the railways and in the public service, or to lend their advice on specific problems. They are also being appointed in increasing numbers to the routine posts in the state's employ, and in commercial and professional circles many of them are to be found.

These are all present links—to them must be added the bonds of future opportunity. Certainly, quite apart from any consideration of a possible extension of boundaries, South Africa may quite naturally regard the trans-Zambesian regions as her hinterland. To the enterprising South African the North will always present an opportunity and a challenge. It is not only for South Africa, but for a large part of the African continent that the secondary schools and the universities of the Union are training her sons. They should be conceived as existing to meet more than the Union's demand. No less important are the opportunities which the North presents in the economic sphere. Two points were seen to be of special importance in the consideration of South Africa's prospective advancement as a secondary producer—the barrier imposed by the restricted nature of its home market to successful competition with countries where industries operate under conditions of mass-production for the markets of the world, and the tremendous economic importance of the native as consumer. In both these respects the development by the Union of its relations with the British Colonies and De-

pendencies to the north-east of it, and the exploitation of
their vast native markets cannot but be of great importance
for the growth of its industries. It is true that the terms of
the Congo Basin Treaties limit the special concessions which
may be made to South African exporters, but even so the
field of opportunity is a large one.

Along these and other lines it may be anticipated that the
bonds between South Africa and the North will be drawn
increasingly close. But it must not be inferred either that
administrative continuity will necessarily follow as a fact,
or that it should be accepted as an ideal for the guidance of
action. To any such administrative continuity Southern
Rhodesia at present bars the way, and as has already
been said it is a matter for the people of Southern Rhodesia
to determine whether and when that barrier shall be lifted.
But even if we assume it to be lifted, the question does not
yet become a simple one. Lord Selborne when he spoke of
the possibility of South Africa's expansion beyond the
Zambesi, was careful to limit it to the degree to which ' this
great region is a country where white men can work and
thrive and multiply.' That must needs continue to be the
determining factor. Let us not forget that point of distinction which has already been noted between South Africa
on the one hand and Eastern and Central Africa on the
other, in the matter of the respective proportions of white and
black. South Africa definitely conceives itself as a white
man's country, a land, that is, in which the white man ' can
work and thrive and multiply,' founding a family, engaging
in all manner of occupations, deriving his prosperity from
the country itself, regarding it as his only home. But no
one of the trans-Zambesian territories is at present a white
man's country in this sense, and it remains doubtful if they
ever will become so. While that doubt remains, South
Africa, the more so since the white man even within its
present borders is in a minority, and his position cannot be
regarded as established with absolute security, cannot speak
or think in terms of administrative continuity or fusion
with those lands, although it must always be deeply interested in what happens in them, and in the possible
repercussions of such happenings on its own problems.
While that doubt remains, the fulfilment of the ideal which

has sometimes been set forth—the ideal of the United States of British Africa—remains a remote possibility and nothing more.

But the ruling out of any form of organic union from the sphere of practical politics does not remove the opportunity or weaken the challenge presented by the great field of co-operative endeavour which opens out to-day. ' South Africa and Eastern Africa,' wrote the Hilton-Young Commission, ' have closely connected interests. They can learn much from each other, and do much to help each other. . . . Among those whose lives are rooted in the soil of Africa there exists a bond of common experience and of mutual understanding which is lacking in those whose contacts with the continent are more superficial and transient.'

African co-operation is no mere matter of the machinery of government and administration. No less important are the contributions which the relatively well-established European community of the south can make to the day-to-day advancement of the European communities of the north. South Africa has already trodden the none too easy path of African development upon which their feet are now set, and in its journey it has garnered for itself experience, which no less than its accumulated resources, material, scientific, technical, are of great value to those that must follow after. In that connection one thinks chiefly of the gifts that Science is called upon to bring to the progress of civilization in Africa, and of South Africa's part as the transmitter of those gifts.

There is, indeed, no part of the earth's surface which to-day presents so insistent a challenge to Science as does the continent of Africa. It is Science which, more than any other single factor, can define, determine, and guide the future of Africa. Perhaps previous failure helps to make the challenge even more pressing. European culture has sought before now to bring Africa within its sphere. In the Mediterranean lands of Africa the Greco-Roman civilization won some of its greatest triumphs, and the evidences of these triumphs are even now being uncovered from the sands of what has been allowed to become North African desert. But in the end Rome failed to conquer Africa for civilization —failed because of the solid mass of African barbarism, and the defiant resistance of African nature. Those who in the nineteenth and twentieth centuries have taken the place of Rome in the response to the challenge of Africa are still faced by the same enemies, but in taking up that challenge they are not alone. Partner with them in the enterprise is Science, vigorous, resourceful, purposeful, able to confront those foes with weapons of which Rome never dreamed.

Africa then challenges Science to bring its contributions to bear upon the solution of the problems presented by African barbarism, those contributions that are derived from an understanding of the character and mentality of primitive peoples, and from the exploration of those regions of social life where are to be found the factors that determine their reaction to diverse methods of administration. It challenges it also to forge the weapons that must be used in the conquest of African nature. In that regard there are three great tasks confronting Science. It must make Africa safe for the white man to live in; it must combat those insect and other foes to cattle and to crops in the production of which Africa is so prodigal; it must harness the great natural resources of Africa, ' directing,' to use the phraseology of the Institution of Civil Engineers, ' the great sources of power in nature for the use and convenience of man.' In large measure Africa will be what its scientists and technical men make of it—it is in the laboratory of the research-worker and at the desk of the engineer that many of the problems which presently challenge African statesmanship will find solution.

In the rendering of the gifts of Science to Africa South Africa may well cast itself for the rôle of transmitter. The twentieth century has been marked by great progress in South African science. It has created universities, established research institutes which have won world-wide recognition, built up active and extensive state scientific departments. In many fields of investigation important work has been done, and South African science has shown its capacity for the exploitation of that rich field of scientific labour with which nature has endowed it. Science is becoming conscious of the challenge which comes to it from the wider Africa, the challenge to apply the technique and the practice suitable to African requirements, which it has itself built up in the conditions of an undeveloped land, to the great areas to the northward which await the gifts that Science can bestow. Of its willingness to accept that challenge, to become consciously and deliberately African in its outlook, its ideals, and the tasks to which it applies itself, it is already giving evidence. Its eyes have been opened to behold the new field of opportunity and achievement which stretches mightily outwards from its borders, and into that field it will not fail to enter.

Therein, it may well be, is to be found South Africa's greatest task in relation to the North. Cecil Rhodes dreamed his dreams of geographical expansion, of painting the map red, of conquest and dominion, but there is also a dominion of the spirit; and the ideal of a South Africa which, while it aspires to leadership on the African continent, conceives that aim not in terms of the exercise of political authority, but rather of unfailing readiness to bring its intellectual and material resources to the aid of all who are engaged in the development of the greatest undeveloped area of the earth's surface, with all its mighty potentialities for human welfare—that surely is no unworthy ideal for any nation.

Chapter 13

South Africa and the British Commonwealth of Nations

IN ONE of the striking speeches made by Mr. Amery when he visited South Africa in 1927 as Secretary of State for Dominion Affairs, he passed on from a reference to the ' leading, guiding, inspiring part ' which South Africa, ' as the one part of Africa in which European civilization is no mere exotic thing, but lives at home,' should take in the development of its continent to an anticipation of the important rôle it would play ' in the future evolution of the Empire, contributing by the development of its resources in a policy of Imperial co-operation to the life and prosperity of the whole.' It is, indeed, no unnatural transition to advance from the consideration of South Africa's place in Africa to the consideration of its relations with the Commonwealth and the Empire.

The question of these relations was for long a determinative factor in the politics of the Union. Secession, Republicanism, loyalty to Flag and Empire—these were party cries for more than a decade. Then came the Imperial Conference of 1926, and its report on inter-Imperial relations gave a new direction to political thinking. The acceptance of that report and the exposition of it which the Dominions Secretary gave during his visit to South Africa buried those issues, it was hoped for all time.

It will be well then to see what that acceptance implies. It is natural to commence with the central sentence of the Report—its definition of the status and mutual relations of the group of self-governing communities composed of Great Britain and the Dominions.

" They are autonomous communities within the British Empire, equal in status, in no way subordinate one to another in any aspect of their domestic or external affairs, though united by a common allegiance to the Crown, and freely associated as members of the British Commonwealth of Nations.'

That is a formula of carefully adjusted checks and balances, reflecting the juxtaposition of two principles, two ideals, at first sight mutually exclusive, and their synthesis, in a spirit of philosophic detachment, in a single conception. The Dominions are autonomous, but they are within the Empire. They are equal in status and free from all subordination, but they are united by a common allegiance to the Crown. They are associated as members of the Commonwealth, but their association is based on freedom. And it was in the light of this synthesized duality that Mr. Amery expounded to South Africa its Dominion status.

On the one side of the duality there is the concept of freedom and equality. That concept, as Mr. Amery pointed out, meant that there could be no subordination of any one nation in the Commonwealth to any other, no claim on the part of any of them, even the oldest, to a prerogative or privilege which was denied to any other, no power or function of national life of the exercise of which any could be deprived. The acceptance of all this registered the abandonment of the conception of Imperialism as embodying, even in a minor degree, the superiority of one nation in relation to others—the realization, in Lord Balfour's phrase, that ' Law without loyalty cannot strengthen the bonds of Empire, nor can we co-operate in handcuffs.' No longer would the Empire be something outside, an external power imposed upon its constituent parts. If it was to continue to exist, it could only do so because there applied to it a truth similar to that contained in the dictum that the kingdom of heaven is within us.

But alongside of the concept of freedom, equivalent and equipollent with it, is the concept of co-operation. That is implicit not merely in the use of the word ' associated ' in the Balfour formula; it is implicit also in the fact that the nations of the Commonwealth are united in a common allegiance to a common Crown. It is the unity of the Crown and all that it stands for—common loyalty, common traditions, a common political faith, common ideals—which pervades, infuses, and vivifies the world-wide mass; by virtue of their loyalty to a common Crown the constituent nations are under an obligation of helpfulness, of support, of friendship, of co-operation, each to the other.

These are the two concepts which the Balfour formula brought together. It recognized that, while co-operation must be based on freedom, freedom in its turn must express itself in co-operation, that, in Mr. Amery's telling phrase, ' if freedom is our birthright, unity is the moral law by which that freedom is directed,' that the acceptance of and compliance with the obligations of co-operation may well be seen ultimately to be the highest freedom.

The reconciliation of these two concepts is, when viewed not just as a philosopher's formula, but as the registration of the outcome of a process of historic evolution, one of the supreme achievements of the human spirit. For throughout history we can trace the conflict between the principles of Imperialism and Nationalism, of freedom and co-operation. That age-old problem—the problem of harmonizing the ideal of Empire with the idea of the free state—has in our generation at last been solved. It is true that the Roman Empire approximated towards a solution, but the reconciliation of the two ideals which it found was in the creation of one great world-state, in which all men should be equal; in our day it has been found in the establishment, as an effective organ of co-operation, of a partnership of self-dependent nations. And as a result Imperialism and freedom have, indeed, become one. In the process each has, to some extent, changed its character. Imperialism has lost the idea of domination, but the notion of co-operation, the most fruitful part of it, has been retained and strengthened. Liberty has kept the note of freedom, but there has been divorced from it the conception which would see it expressed in a nation that lives only unto itself. It has been realized on the one side that Nationalism, as Mr. A. G. Gardiner pointed out more then twenty years ago, is the root of the only Imperialism that can endure. It has been realized on the other side that liberty is only true freedom in so far and for so long as it is guarded by co-operation from degenerating into a narrow self-sufficiency.

To South Africa the definition of the new Imperialism

which was thus set forth meant the presentation of the Commonwealth as a partnership, the privileges and obligations of membership in which it was asked to accept on the basis of free choice. It meant that it was recognized as a free people indeed, but a free people which could find no better expression for its freedom than in co-operation and fellowship with the sister-nations to which it would in the Commonwealth be linked by a free association, and with whom it would be united by a community of ideals and a community of interests. And just as a man does not limit his liberty but rather enlarges it, when he abandons the licence of savagery, and by entering into association with an organized society accepts the obligations of co-operation, so its entrance into this partnership of nations would mean, not the surrender of its liberty, but rather the enlargement and the enrichment of its South Africanism.

And so South Africa, through the leaders of all its political parties, accepted this new conception of Empire, and there was historic fitness in the acceptance. For was it not in the old Cape Parliament, and by none other than Cecil Rhodes, away back in 1883, that there was first adumbrated the principle of the reconciliation which was to be recorded formally in 1926? ' I believe,' he said, ' that confederated states in a Colony under Responsible Government would each be practically an independent republic, but I think we should also have all the privileges of the tie with the Empire.' That statement was made with reference to the federation of the South African communities as they then were, but at the root of it there is the conception of complete Colonial or Dominion independence, inside of an Empire which is united by a strong moral tie. South Africa in 1926 was, however, thinking not of what Rhodes had said forty-three years before, but of its own conflict between those who stood for South Africa's freedom and those who would have her remain within the Empire. It was the virtue of the Balfour formula that it gave a definition of freedom within the Empire. The fact that it was given at a time when most people in the Union had become a little weary of the controversy, helped to make it generally welcome and acceptable.

At this stage it is well to emphasize the point that the majority of the people of South Africa have not in the past

G

looked upon, and could not be expected to look upon, the British Empire from the same angle as do the people of Great Britain or those of British stock in the other Dominions. To the man of British birth or ancestry the Empire and Commonwealth represent the supreme historic achievement of his own people. It is in the nature of things that the Afrikaans-speaking South African could never regard them in this way. In the minds of many of them the events of the past had engendered feelings towards Great Britain which were not feelings of friendship. To many the Empire stood as a symbol of conquest, of subordination. The thought of it prompted a consciousness of subjection—the sentiment which it evoked was one not of pride, but of estrangement. It was to such as these that the Balfour formula was presented, recording, it may be, merely a stage of evolution which had been reached—' rather epoch-marking than epoch-making,' it has been well said—but no less important on that account, because it set forth in definite and authoritative language a new conception in relation to the Empire. It was a conception of an institution based not on subordination, but on association, a conception in terms of which South Africa's relationship to Great Britain was conceived as one of free and equal partnership, and the British Commonwealth of Nations was represented as a free association of autonomous peoples, each determining its own policy in accordance with its own popular will.

It is upon the concept of freedom in the Balfour definition that emphasis has in South Africa chiefly been laid. There has been a tendency to represent that freedom as a full, sovereign independence, devoid of restrictions or limitations of any kind. Such a claim was in fact made by General Hertzog, when he asked the Union House of Assembly to record its approval of the 1926 Conference Report. ' A Dominion,' he declared, ' is a sovereign independent State, internationally recognized,' and again, ' the words " British Empire " and " Commonwealth," when used in the Report, have no other object to serve than that of indicating collectively certain territorial or State entities standing in certain relations to one another, without the least intention of assigning to these terms any *persona* or functional existence— they are mere names, and nothing more.'

There are constitutional authorities who dispute this view. It is held, firstly, that within the scope of the wide international rights and duties which they are now entitled to exercise, the Dominions have become separate persons of International Law. Secondly, it is impossible to hold that they are persons of International Law of identically the same character as those which are called fully 'independent sovereign States,' although it must not be forgotten that those sovereign States have themselves in recent years in fact limited their own independence by the new rules of International Law to which they have agreed. Thirdly, while they are persons of International Law, they are persons who are, in the phrase of the 1926 Report, in a 'special relationship' to each other, a relationship not known by other international persons; a relationship which makes of them when they act together as a group, as they sometimes do, a single entity in the Society of States; and that entity, the British Commonwealth, is therefore not only a political unity, but also for certain purposes a single unified person of International Law.

These are conclusions to the acceptance of which one appears to be forced, and, indeed, even on General Hertzog's own showing it would be difficult to take any other view. At the Imperial Conference of 1926 he spoke repeatedly of the ' will to live in the Empire '; in the final message to His Majesty the King, to which he was a party, the Crown was described as the abiding symbol and emblem of the unity of the British Commonwealth of Nations; the Balfour formula itself, to which he gave unquestioning acceptance, lays an emphasis on the words ' within the British Empire,' which is entirely inconsistent with the view that the Empire is a ' mere name, and nothing more.'

South Africa then in common with the other members of the Commonwealth, including Great Britain itself, falls short of full theoretical sovereign independence, and to its freedom there attach certain limitations and restrictions. The language of Professor Noel Baker may be used to enumerate those features which, after the acceptance of the 1926 Report, constituted the relationship between the sister-nations of the Commonwealth a ' special relationship,' and made them individually still different from wholly independent sovereign states like Belgium or France:

> ' the existence of a common Crown; the common duty of allegiance; common nationality; the universal validity of the royal prerogative; the exercise of the executive functions of the royal prerogative through the institution of the Governor-General; its exercise in respect of foreign relations through the formal intervention of the King and a British Secretary of State; the common jurisdiction of the Privy Council; the fact that if the King is at war in respect of one part of his Dominions, all the rest are automatically involved; the surviving " legislative supremacy " of the Imperial Parliament; the right of each member of the Commonwealth to be consulted about foreign policy, and to take part in any international negotiations if it should so desire.'

It is true that some of these may be viewed as minor restrictions, that the removal of others awaits merely the completed action of machinery which has been set in motion. Yet in the last resort, for so long as the obligation of common allegiance to the Crown endures, it is difficult to see how all limitations on Dominion freedom can disappear. In that connection it is of particular importance to note that the Committee which was set up in terms of the Conference Report to consider the operation of Dominion legislation and of the Merchant Shipping Code, submitted a report aiming not merely at the withdrawal of the present ' legislative supremacy ' of the Parliament at Westminster, but also at the removal of any shade of uncertainty about the position of the Crown. It was laid down clearly that no alteration might be made in the law touching the succession to the Throne, save by the act of all the Parliaments of the Commonwealth. Acceptance of this principle at once removed any possibility of the union between the partner-States being regarded as merely a personal union. There have been those, both in South Africa and elsewhere, who have held that Great Britain and the Dominions are in International Law as separate as were England and Hanover in the days when the Georges ruled over both, as kings in two different capacities, and the wearers of two different crowns each with its own law of succession. If that conception of the Monarchy were correct, it would involve acceptance of the view that the Commonwealth has no personality in International Law. But, as Mr. Amery has pointed out, it is not correct. ' There is no such division within the British Empire (as there was between England and Hanover). The King is not King of Great Britain in one capacity, King of Australia in another. He is King in the same sense, and as wearer of the same Crown, of the whole Empire.'

In its consideration, then, of the concept of freedom in the Balfour formula, South Africa has concerned itself to a considerable extent with the question of the existence of limitations upon that freedom. In the speech to which reference has already been made General Hertzog raised also the question of the position of a Dominion in the event of war. Starting out from the conception of the members of the Commonwealth as internationally recognized independent states, he proceeded to declare that ' the Union, as every other Dominion, has, in case of war between Great Britain and any other state, the right to remain neutral, and to have her neutrality respected by the belligerents.' This declaration of General Hertzog was not allowed to pass unchallenged in the Union Parliament. Prior to the making of it, Mr. Amery had stated that ' in war no subject of the King can be a friend of the King's enemies, or, in other words, neutral in the strict sense of the word '—and this view won the general acceptance of constitutional authorities. In the words of Mr. McNair, which Professor Baker quotes with approval:

' Unless and until there is some definite constitutional act dissolving the Empire, whether as a consequence the constituent parts come to form a true Personal Union under the Crown . . . or become entirely separate states, it is legally impossible for Great Britain to be at war without the whole of the Empire, self-governing or not, being at war too, and equally impossible for any Dominion to be at war without Great Britain being at war. It is only the King that can legally make a declaration of war, and the King, unless and until the British

Empire becomes a Personal Union of States acknowledging him as their sovereign, cannot be partly at war and partly at peace.'

The substantial correctness of this reasoning it is, indeed, difficult to challenge. Certainly it is for a Dominion itself to determine the extent of its active participation in any war—and its belligerency may, in fact, be a ' passive belligerency '—but that is very far from being the equivalent of neutrality. Certainly also it follows from the 1926 Report that the exercise of the initiative leading to war by any one member of the Commonwealth has been made dependent on prior consultation with all the other members —but it is no less clear on that account that no member can actually be at war without involving all the rest. That is one of the restrictions upon their freedom, which, by the acknowledgment of their common allegiance, the Dominions have accepted.

On another issue which has been raised in South Africa there is considerable disagreement among the constitutional lawyers. That is the question of a Dominion's right of secession. On this question, as on the question of neutrality in war, neither the Conference of 1926 nor that of 1930 made any pronouncement, though General Hertzog stated that the latter of these Conferences ' noted ' his own view that such a right of secession exists. Would it be possible, to put the issue concretely, for the South African Government, having secured the consent of both Houses of Parliament to a Bill reconstituting South Africa as an independent Republic, to advise the King to give his assent to it, and to receive that assent with no more question than would be raised in the case of a Bill amending the constitution in respect of the exercise of the franchise by women? On that point the lawyers differ. There are those who hold that such a right follows inevitably from the Dominions' equality of status, and that the King would have no constitutional right to veto a Bill involving the secession of any one part of the Commonwealth, to which his responsible Ministers in that part advised him to assent. There are others who contend that he has not only a constitutional right, but also a constitutional duty, to veto such a proposal, or who urge that it is in accord with the implications of the 1926 Report that it should be held not to appertain merely to the affairs of the Dominion which raises it, but to be a group question which cannot be disposed of by unilateral action. At the least there seems to be solid ground for the contention that no proposal for the abolition of the King as part of the Parliament of any one of the member-states and the consequent renunciation of its common allegiance can be given effect to without a constitutional revolution, even though it may be a peaceful revolution, and that to that extent it is impossible to hold that a Dominion possesses any legal right of secession.

These are some of the questions which have arisen in South Africa in regard to the nature of Dominion freedom. Whether or not present legal obscurities are cleared away, and present restrictions removed, South Africa is in fact ' the master of its destiny.' In the matter of secession it is generally admitted that if, in the free exercise of its discretion, it determines that, for the realization of its genius as a nation and for the rendering to the world of such contributions as it is best able to render, it is well that it should stand aside from the Commonwealth, there is no power outside of itself that would wish to say it Nay.

Chapter 14

South Africa and the Problems of Colour

IT HAS been said by Dr. J. H. Oldham, in writing of the manner in which the position hitherto held by the white race is at present being challenged, that ' the ultimate political problem of the world is how the different races which inhabit it may live together in peace and harmony.' That is likewise the ultimate political problem of South Africa—and its significance is the greater because it is also a problem of the world. We have considered the tasks with which South Africa is confronted in relation to its own future, to the continent of Africa, and to the British Commonwealth of Nations. Now we must place it in a wider setting, and regard it in relation to the world-problem of inter-racial relationships.

A white South Africa! That is the potent cry in South African politics, the cry which, for all that most of those who use it would be hard put to it to define its implications, is the one which, more effectively than any other, turns votes and wins elections. The appeal which used to be made to a narrowly national sentiment—Vote British, Vote Dutch—has lost much of its force—it has in large measure been super-seded by the slogan: Vote for a White South Africa. And that is the result of a correct appreciation of the great fear which gnaws at the heart of the European in South Africa. Anthony Trollope, as Sarah Gertrude Millin has reminded us, once wrote: ' South Africa is a country of black men—and not of white men. It has been so; it is so; and it will be so.' Is this prophecy true?—so in growing anxiety men ask themselves. ' And if it is true, what of our children? ' The reaction is natural—' We will make this country safe for Europeans; we will ensure the white man's dominance; for us, who know no other home than South Africa, the issues are issues of life and death; essentially it is a South African question, a question for ourselves alone.' And yet, whether

South Africans like it or not, their problem is not so easily isolable from that ' ultimate political problem of the world,' of which it is but an aspect.   In this rapidly contracting twentieth-century world more than ever before, no nation liveth unto itself, and a policy laid down in one land may unleash forces which will encircle the globe, and perhaps come back upon that land with added momentum.   The Indian in South Africa is part of that complex of peoples whose home is in the Indian Peninsula; the Bantu is part of black Africa—in the case of both, though at different stages of development, there is growing rapidly an all-embracing national consciousness; behind both there stand ultimately all the coloured races of the world.   So it is as aspects of the world problem of colour that these South African questions have to be considered, not as questions for South Africa alone.

In earlier chapters the past development of the relations between the white man and the native and coloured man, and again between the white man and the Asiatic, has been traced.   These relations in their bearing on the present and the future have now to be considered.   And first there falls to be discussed the place of the Asiatic in the South African community.

It is natural to commence with the figures of population. In the Free State, where the old restrictive Republican law is still in force, there are 29 Asiatics; at the Cape there are 10,500; in the Transvaal 26,000; in Natal 184,000.   The problem is, therefore, almost entirely a problem of the Transvaal and Natal.   That problem is, in the first instance, an economic one—it is also, though to a less extent, a social one.   The Asiatic maintains a lower standard of living than the European.   That gives him a considerable advantage when he enters the competitive field, as he does, in the Transvaal almost entirely in trade, in Natal in other walks of life as well.   Trade-union organization and wage regula-tion may neutralize his advantage in industrial occupations; but commercial competition is relatively unaffected by these factors, and in that competition the European trader, especially the small trader, who must needs work on a higher basis of profit, tends to be crushed out of existence. There has been no lack of effort to check the activities of the

Asiatic storekeeper, but, with his back to the wall, he has shown boundless ingenuity in the evasion and circumvention of the law. Moreover, his low standard of living tends to be reflected in the appearance of the premises which he occupies, and his coming to a particular area causes the depreciation of property and the decline of the neighbourhood. The European may find it difficult to resist the temptation of buying cheap at an Asiatic store—but he will not welcome the establishment of such a store next to his own property; he will become acutely conscious of maladjustment when he sees the business of the Asiatic growing until he is able to attract European salesmen and European girl assistants into his employment; and his anger will rise within him when he sees European children playing in the street with Asiatic children. So there is constant friction, and a growing feeling of hostility, and the perfectly natural determination of the European to defend his economic standards against insidious attack from within. The segregation of the Asiatic in special areas or ' bazaars,' and the restriction of his freedom of competition to the greatest possible extent, appear to the European to be the only solution—to the Asiatic, to whom, as in the Transvaal, nearly all avenues of employment, other than trading, are in effect closed by law or by convention, such a policy seems to spell ruin and starvation.

It is still customary for men in South Africa to think of the Asiatics as constituting an alien element, ' strangers,' in Lord Milner's phrase, ' forcing themselves upon a community reluctant to receive them,' and in that spirit to speak lightly either of enforced repatriation to India, or at least of segregation in such manner as to make effective competition with the white man virtually impossible, regardless of the destitution and pauperization which may possibly result. But it must not be forgotten that the charge of alienage is becoming increasingly difficult to maintain. Well over two-thirds of the Indians at present in South Africa were born in the Union—many are already in the fourth generation— they know no other homeland, and India is to them but a mere name. As a result of the effective stoppage of Asiatic immigration, this will within a measurable period of time be true of practically the whole of the Union's Asiatic population. They are the Union's own people, and the Government of India can fairly claim that it was in order to ensure their treatment as such that it agreed to acquiesce in and even further the policy of preventing immigration and assisting repatriation. These Asiatics, then, who elect to remain in South Africa, despite all the inducements held out to them to leave it on a voluntary basis, are a permanent part of the people of South Africa, and in relation to them it becomes reasonable to argue that their continued backwardness, still more their retrogression in the scale of civilization and welfare, would constitute a menace to the white community. An Indian witness before a Parliamentary Select Committee, arguing against a policy of segregation, made this point forcibly, if somewhat confusedly, in these words: ' Ghetto prisoners sooner or later burst their bonds, and Ghettos give up not only their dead, but their living also; and while dead pasts may bury their dead, the ghosts of the bad pasts have been observed to haunt the posterity of those who saw no further than their own day.'

It was in the recognition of the force of considerations such as these that in the 1927 Agreement with the Government of India, the Union Government declared its firm belief in and adherence to ' the principle that it is the duty of every civilized government to devise ways and means, and to take all possible steps for the uplifting of every section of their permanent population to the full extent of their capacity and opportunities,' and its acceptance of ' the view that in the provision of educational and other facilities the considerable number of Indians who remain part of the permanent population shall not be allowed to lag behind other sections of the people.' Raise the standard of the Asiatic and so, rather than by attempts at repression, seek to remove the menace which at present he seems to present to white civilization—that was in effect the policy which South Africa undertook to put to the test.

But there is another consideration of a different kind which points in the same direction. It may, perhaps, be suggested in words used before the Committee already referred to by a representative of the Chinese community, in itself but a small body, a few thousand in all, an almost negligible part of the Union's Asiatic population. 'The mistake is often made in this country,' he declared, 'that the Government in dealing with a few thousand of Chinese here thinks it is just dealing with a handful of them, but in reality it is dealing with the great number of four hundred millions of people living in China and also scattered throughout every corner of the earth.' Not less, but rather more significant are the dealings of South Africa with these other hundreds of millions whose home is in the Indian peninsula. And when regard is paid to the manner in which the self-respect of the Asiatic peoples has been slighted by the exclusion of their nationals from other lands controlled by Europeans, and by the discriminating treatment meted out to those who had previously gained admission, the responsibility of South Africa appears to be the heavier in respect of the possible effect of its dealings with the stranger within its gates upon the already strained relations between East and West.

To many the effect of these considerations will appear to be clear and precise; yet the path which any South African Government must tread remains a rough and difficult one. The Indian signatories of the 1927 Agreement frankly recognized that a popularly elected Government cannot in its actions go very far in advance of public opinion. In the shaping of policy present exigencies as well as future contingencies must receive consideration. It is as natural for a country to defend itself against the lowering of its economic standards from within, as it is to seek to ward off aggression from without, and South Africa is not the only country which has found it necessary to protect its European inhabitants against Asiatic competition. It will be no easy matter to lay down the terms on which European and Asiatic will be enabled 'to live together in peace and harmony' in the Union. But by its success in grappling with that task South Africa is destined in no small measure to be judged.

From the Asiatic we pass to the native. Viewed in the light of history it is no easy transition from the inheritor of age-old civilizations and religions to the savage of the kraal. Yet the essentials of the two problems are the same. There is the European's consciousness of his superiority in relation to both Asiatic and African; there is his fear of that superiority being weakened and destroyed. It is the Asiatic's standard of living that he fears, and the menace which it directs to the integrity of his life and institutions; it is the native's numerical preponderance. Does not the native outnumber him four to one?—and nearly always when he speaks of it, he exaggerates the ratio. Is not the native's rate of natural increase higher than his own?—and usually he forgets the factors which to-day tend to limit that rate of increase. He has asserted his mastery over the native in the past; to-day he has all the material resources necessary for the enforcement of his will—but what of the subtler, deadlier struggle of the future? To whom in that day will the battle be?

Certainly there is reason for apprehension. In many lands white and coloured races have met, but nowhere are the circumstances the same as those that prevail in South Africa. In some of those lands, as for instance India, climatic conditions have determined that the white man shall dwell merely as an official or as a trader, not as a settler and the founder of a family. It is not so in South Africa. It is a ' white man's country,' and the white man who dwells there, for the most part, knows no other home. In some lands again, as for instance Kenya, climatic conditions are more favourable, but there are other circumstances which make it probable that the number of Europeans permanently settled there will always be small—in South Africa the white population is smaller than, but still of the same order of magnitude as, the native. In some lands the coming of the white man has led to the extermination of the coloured races, or at least to the establishment by him of an assured numerical superiority—in South Africa the effect has rather been the stimulation of the growth of the native population, as a result of the cessation of inter-tribal warfare and the lowering of the natural death rate. In some lands racial intermixture has been allowed to run its course—in South Africa a vigorous public opinion demands race purity. So then, in the Union to-day European and Bantu face one another as distinct elements in a land which each, with an equal measure of historical justification, can claim as its homeland, the European superior in political power, in the instruments of defence, in the arts of civilization, the Bantu four times as numerous (and when comparisons are made between South Africa and the United States, let this not be forogtten), his rate of increase as yet substantially unchecked, his lower standards a grave menace to the white man's economic position, his feet firmly planted upon the ladder of progress.

And when the white man considers the advancement of the native, and observes his educational progress, his rising social standards, his attempts to organize on trade-union lines, his thoughts, not unnaturally, are thoughts of fear, fear not of being overwhelmed physically, but fear lest his position should be undermined in far more subtle ways. He fears the encroachment of the low-paid native further and further upon his economic preserve. He fears the growth of native political rights, and the possibility that some day numbers will tell in the government of South Africa. Chiefly he fears that native development along these lines will lead to social equality, to race mixture, to the drowning of the white man in a black ocean. And he is determined that these things shall not be.

But where fear is at the root of public opinion, it is no easy matter to build up a native policy on the foundations of justice and fair dealing. In that same public opinion the desire to act justly, to do the best for the native, is also an important factor, but that desire fights a difficult battle for expression against the power of fear. This is how Sarah Gertrude Millin put it in conversation with an American negro: ' You know the relative numbers of black and white in South Africa. Well, consider the black people as a big man struggling in a swamp, and the white man as a little man standing on the edge of the swamp. The little man wants to help the big man. But how far dare he? Isn't it more possible that the big man will pull in the little man, than that the little man will pull out the big man? That is the question we are always asking ourselves in South Africa.'

How, then, shall South Africa shape its native policy? Let us consider the possible lines of action. That means the clear recognition at the outset of two things. The one is that the black man lives in among white men, that in fact it is upon the foundation of the black man's labour that, for

better or for worse, the economic structure of South Africa
has been built.   The other is that, whether the white man
likes it or not, he must accept it as a fact that he has awakened
the native, he has ended his savage life, he has set his feet
upon the long road that leads to the white man's civilization.   He has bidden the native to follow in his wake,
carrying his goods, relieving him of his burden, and now
there is no going back.

The two extreme policies can, perhaps, easily be ruled out.
There is the policy which would use the black man's labour
to promote the wealth and comfort of the white man, but
having done so, would regard him as a mere chattel, created
to serve the white man and for no other end, would keep him
' in his place,' with physical force, and that alone, as sanction,
would repress every effort on his part to rise, lest so he might
add to the gravity of the ' black menace.'   There is pathos
in that policy, from the black man's viewpoint.   Said one
of them not so long ago : ' The white man came to us, and
he told us that we must throw off our barbarism, we must be
educated, we must advance.   We have obeyed his words,
and now because we have done so, because we have
advanced, he tells us that we are a menace and a danger.'
It was one of those statements to which it is not possible to
find an answer.   And from the white man's viewpoint, that
policy is dangerous, if not impossible.   For he has changed
the world of the native, he has in large measure destroyed
the sanctions of the kraal, he has given to the native the
opportunity of developing a self-consciousness, a race-
consciousness, an industrial consciousness, he has aroused in
him new wants, new desires for material satisfactions, for
spiritual satisfactions, he has led him on to the point from
which he can look below the surface of things, he has
awakened his soul with the stirrings of a divine discontent.
And having done all that, he cannot, save at great peril to
himself and to those who will come after him, seek to block
the stream in the channel into which he himself led it, while
he provides for it no other outlet.   It is natural, and proper,
and right, that the white man should seek to lay the foundations of a permanent European civilization in South Africa,
but he can never lay those foundations securely upon the
basis of a repressed, discontented, hostile native population.

But while this policy cannot be entertained, the other extreme policy which aims at the complete equality, the identity of black man with white, social no less than political and economic, is no more possible of acceptance. The ideal of racial equality has appealed to men of all nations—its attractiveness as an ideal should not be permitted to make us close our eyes to differences which really exist, not merely differences between individuals, but differences in social tradition and in attitude towards life. It is a challenging fact that when in 1919 Japan pressed for the acknowledgement in the Covenant of the League of Nations of the principle of racial equality, the request was resisted by the President of that very Republic which had been founded with the declaration of the ' self-evident truth ' that all men are created equal. It is rendered no less challenging by the fact that those who drew up that declaration were themselves slave-owners. And although there exists a fundamental equality in principle of men as men alongside of the existent facts of inequality, more cannot be claimed for that fundamental equality than is done by Mr. J. H. Oldham, who states it in these words: ' Men are not equal in their capacity to serve the community, nor are they equal in their needs. But they are equal in the possession of a personality that is worthy of reverence. They are equal in the right to the development of that personality, so far as may be compatible with the common good.' *So far as may be compatible with the common good.* It would be difficult to establish that the adoption in South Africa of a policy of complete equalization of black man with white would be for the common good, or, indeed, for the good of either element in the community. Certainly it would magnify, rather than minimize, racial antipathy. And though it may be argued that racial antagonism is not innate or instinctive, that it is communicated by social suggestion, as for instance when an Englishmen who comes to South Africa from an environment in which he would, without scruple, have received a black man in his house, assumes within the briefest of periods the prevailing tone and sentiments of his new homeland, yet all this does not really reduce its significance as a fact which must be taken account of, which cannot just be brushed aside, in the South African complex. Certainly also social equality, with its corollary of intermarriage and miscegenation, is not lightly to be embraced. These are considerations which, in South Africa at least, cannot be overlooked. In those parts of Africa where Latin peoples rule, a different outlook prevails, but to the South African the attitude of mind which is implied in the declaration, ' France is not a nation of thirty-nine million inhabitants, but one of a hundred million subjects,' is repugnant, and for the ' common good ' of peoples such as those who dwell in the Union it is well that it should be so.

We have dismissed as inapplicable to the conditions which prevail in South Africa to-day policies which are based either on the repression of the native or on his identification with the white man—the two conceptions, be it noted, from which the traditional policies of the Republics and the Cape respectively proceeded, though in neither case without substantial modification as time went on. We have ruled out equality, we have ruled out subjection; where then, short of superiority, shall we find the right basis of policy? The answer is that we must seek it along the lines of a different category. The important thing is not the native's inferiority, or his equality, or his superiority; what is important is just the fact that he is different from the white man. The recognition of this fact of difference should be the starting-point in South Africa's native policy.

In that recognition Theophilus Shepstone took the lead, when he set forth as his aim the development of the native peoples on distinctively native lines, and in such manner as not to conflict with European interests. That policy of Shepstone's has come to be known as the policy of Segregation. It is a policy which, proceeding logically from a sound conception of inter-racial relationships, commands a very large measure of support in South Africa to-day. But it should be pointed out at the outset that while a policy of segregation in the sense of territorial separation of black men from white was not only possible, but easy in the Natal of Shepstone's time, the conditions are very different in the South Africa of to-day. It is well also to urge that, as will indeed have been suggested by the account of the development of the Shepstone policy in an earlier chapter, there is a considerable difference between a constructive and a repressive, even a negative, policy of segregation. It is the more necessary to make these points since Segregation has in South Africa become somewhat of a 'blessed word,' with the same soothing quality for the minds of many as Mesopotamia had for the old lady.

What in its crudest form does Segregation mean? No more than the extrusion of the native from the white man's life, save in so far as he is necessary for ministration to the white man's needs, the setting aside for his occupation of land so inadequate that dire necessity will drive him out to labour for the white man, the refusal to regard him as other than a means to an end, or effectively to encourage his development as an end in itself. But for many Segregation means much more than that. Let us take the definition of what might be described as constructive Segregation, given by General Smuts with reference to the wider Africa in his Rhodes Lecture: 'A policy which will not force her (Africa's) institutions into an alien European mould, but which will preserve her unity with her own past, conserve what is precious in her past, and build her future on specifically African foundations.' Such a policy would detach the black man from permanent association with the white man's life; it would at the same time give him the facilities and the encouragement to develop along his own lines, and to make a distinctive contribution to the good of the whole. The end which it envisages is a white nation and a black nation dwelling side by side in the same land.

The policy of constructive segregation has, as far as South Africa is concerned, received its most effective and successful expression in the administration of the Transkeian Territories of the Cape Province on the principles adumbrated by Cecil Rhodes in his Glen Grey Act. That Act had, as we have seen, two main purposes, to check the wastefulness of the native's rural economy with its basis in communal tenure by the substitution of a form of individual ownership, and to provide him with the machinery of self-government in respect of his own specifically local concerns. It has not been found possible to achieve the first of these ends over as wide an area as was once hoped, but in regard to the second the Act has worked most successfully. The system of local government has been extended throughout the Transkeian

Territories, which cover an area of 16,000 square miles, all but a thousand of which is reserved for native ownership, and carry a population of a million and a half natives; the native has been encouraged to determine the lines of his own progress; under the sympathetic guidance of European magistrates he has learnt something of the art of self-government; there has been developed in him a feeling of pride in his own institutions, a sense of responsibility, a growing experience in administrative affairs. The principle of differentiation has been given successful practical application.

In how far can the solution of the wider South African problem be found along Transkeian lines? Let it be said at once, to avoid a possible misunderstanding, that anything in the way of the complete separation of white and black in South Africa is not practical politics. White and black are still economically necessary to one another—it is difficult to see how they can cease to be so. It is inconceivable that the white man should be able completely to dispense with the black man's labour on his farms, in his mines, in his factories; it is just as inconceivable that there should be set aside for the black man's occupation land sufficient to provide for all his needs independently of the white man's wages. Even the Transkeian native, with a marginal subsistence secured to him in the land of his reserve, goes out to work to-day in order to find the means of satisfying his expanding wants and desires—but his home remains in the Transkei, and to it he returns. And that, indeed, is as far as even the constructive segregationist will normally go—the reservation to the native peoples of sufficient land to make possible the maintenance of their family and tribal life, no restriction of their going out to work for the white man for definite periods, but the retention of the reserve as their home and the centre of their life and of their distinctive advancement. It is in the reserves alone that an indigenous native culture can be fostered, and the natives be given the means of really developing along their own lines.

The Transkeian system, thus conceived, has become the acknowledged ideal of South African native policy. There are other native areas in the Union, smaller than the Transkei, but otherwise similar to it, where that system can be extended, and is being extended. The Natives Land Act of 1913, for all its provisional character, definitely enshrined the principle of the demarcation of reserved areas for natives. The Native Affairs Act of 1920 set in motion machinery for the extension of the Council system in such areas. But the realization of the ideal is still far from complete.

For the root idea of the policy of constructive segregation is native homes in distinctively native areas, and South Africa has already advanced very far in the opposite direction, so far, indeed, that it can no longer readily retrace its steps. That has happened because of its failure in the past to make adequate provision for the native as an independent agriculturist; it has happened because of its desire to enjoy the full advantage of cheap native labour.

It must not be forgotten that the standard of living of the native is very much lower than that of the white man, and also that on the average the agricultural value of the reserve lands is high relatively to South African land in general; but even so the distribution reflected in the figures quoted could have but one result, the breaking up of native family and tribal life in native areas. The native has gone, to an ever-increasing extent, *with his family*, to make his home in the towns; he has gone, *with his family*, to make his home on the farms, and it has been in the interest of the European farmer to encourage him to do so. ' The whites,' said General Smuts at Oxford, ' like to have the families of their native servants with them. It means more continuous and less broken periods of labour, and it means more satisfied labourers. It means, moreover, the use of the women and children for such work as they are fit for.' Well over a half of the native population of the Union is to-day living outside of the reserves—of these about one-fourth, close on three-quarters of a million, are in the towns, and over two millions live in rural areas. Not all these of course represent native families, but even so the process of migration to the white man's farm and the white man's town, away from tribal influences, to become the raw material of the agitator and the soap-box orator has gone very far, and when the tribal bond has been snapped, then, unless it can be pieced together again, Segregation breaks down.

Can it be pieced together again? On that question, raising as it does the further question of the provision of adequate reserves for native occupation and the return, voluntary or enforced, of native families to the reserves, the issue depends for the segregationist, if he would carry out his policy logically. What, in the light of the conditions which prevail in the Union, must be the answer?

Let us consider it first from the white man's viewpoint. And there the natural question to ask is, will he pay the price? For a price there is to be paid—a considerable price. There is a price in respect of labour: less continuous, as the native family is moved to the reserve; less abundant, as native development proceeds and absorbs more of its own labour; less cheap, as the native in the building up of his own life becomes more independent of the white man's wages. There is a price also in respect of land, for it means setting aside as native reserves areas which are open to the European to-day, and which are deemed to be eminently suitable to European exploitation and settlement. Let it not be thought, be it said again, that it will be necessary to provide sufficient land for the adequate maintenance of all the native people of the Union—labour for the white man will still have to be regarded as a necessary element in the economic structure of Bantu life. Let allowance also be made for the fact that the native to-day does not always use his land to the best advantage, that with the improvements in native agriculture now taking place under the fostering care and encouragement of the Union Government and of the natives' own Councils, the reserves as a whole can carry a larger population than inhabits them to-day. Yet, if the ideal of the application of the Transkeian policy to the whole of South Africa is to be carried out, then enough land must be set aside for the building up of native homes for all the native people of South Africa, enough land to provide them at once with a safeguard against economic exploitation, an inducement to retain their domicile, and the facilities for effective development. And that is a price which the European inhabitants of South Africa, taken as a whole, have so far given little indication of their willingness to pay. It may be doubted whether much more is really feasible along these lines than the conservation and the adequate development of such land as is already the native's portion.

But there is also the native's viewpoint. Speaking generally, the ideal which has been stated in the preceding paragraphs is one which, if it is to be adequately realized, the great majority of the natives might reasonably be expected to accept. But there is one class of native which it would be wrong to leave out of account—the educated native. There are to-day many among the natives who have risen to a European standard. They have been educated on European lines, they have been trained to think and feel like Europeans. To-day they claim the privileges of Europeans, and very largely the resistance to that claim is at the root of present native discontents. What is to be the place of such men in the scheme of the segregationist? It is easy to reply, their place is with the rest of their people, as their natural leaders, from them they should not be dissociated. That would be reasonable enough if the policy of differential development had been followed, logically and completely, from the outset. It has not been followed, and in the meantime the native has been encouraged to break away from his African traditions, to become a European. Is it natural to expect him, having responded to that encouragement, now to direct the development of his people on African lines? Is it right to deprive him of the enjoyment of the place in the sun into which he was urged to enter, to throw him back into the loneliness and the frustration of his outworn tribal associations? Is it not already too late?

Too late. And therein is South Africa's tragedy. It has waited too long, it has busied itself too much with other things, no longer can it give thoroughgoing application to the policy which seems to it to be natural, and logical, and right. It must be content to compromise, to take account of obdurate facts, and as a result to face the dangers of an uncertain future. Despite all the energy with which it sets out to promote and encourage the distinctive development of the tribal native where yet it is possible, it must take account also of the Europeanized, detribalized native in its midst— and admit that he has come to stay. And having made that admission, it must make the best of it, and of him, accepting him as a co-worker in the building up of South Africa's economic life.

If the European is to admit the native to a permanent place in his industrial system, then in his own interest he cannot allow him to remain an inefficient, jog-trot worker, without any stimulus to his ambition to raise himself in the scale, and by the lowness of his standards depriving the poorer white man of an economic basis of subsistence. Rather should the European exploit the native's productive powers by giving him encouragement to advance, in the recognition that his advancement in its turn will stimulate industry, will widen rather than restrict the white man's competitive area of employment, will by opening up the field of unskilled labour to the white man, extend the inducement to immigration from oversea.   Dr. Aggrey once used the simile of the white notes and the black notes on the piano to emphasize the point that each of the two races has its contribution to make to the world's harmony.   That is certainly true also in respect of South Africa's economic progress.   Distinctive development in the reserves as far as may be possible, and for those for whom there is no room in the reserves unrestricted encouragement as co-workers in the white man's industry—that would appear to be the only policy which is now left for South Africa to follow.

But, it will be asked, does not this necessarily bring us back to the ideal of complete equality which was rejected at the outset?   Does it not mean the abandonment of our starting-point, the recognition of the differences between white man and black?   Will not the development of the native in this way, the extension to him of virtual economic equality, lead inevitably to social equality with all its attendant evils?   It need not necessarily be so.   Racial and social segregation, based on the acceptance of the facts of difference, alongside of equality of economic opportunity, is no impossible ideal—the economic development of a coloured race living in amongst a white race does not necessarily involve the breaking down of its racial distinctiveness, and the abandonment of its social segregation.   It is possible for unity in the aim of an operation to co-exist with a very great deal of diversity in those who are engaged upon it—in function and in other things.   If it is asked further whether the adoption of such a policy would ensure the future ascendancy and leadership of the white man in South Africa, it is not, it is true, possible categorically to give an affirmative answer—but it is no more possible to do so in the case of any other policy which can at present be adopted, and it would seem, indeed, that South Africa must be content to regard its native problem as one in which finality is not yet possible, one towards the solution of which it can but advance, one step at a time, as the light may lead it. Certainly there is to this policy but one effective alternative—the policy of repression, and the dangers which attach to that will almost certainly be found in the long run to be the greater.

There is, however, one condition which it will be essential to observe if the course of action here suggested is to be pursued. If the white man is, in the peculiarly difficult position in which he finds himself, to hold his own in South Africa, he on his part must be ready, in consonance with his ancestry and his traditions, to bring out the best that is in him, to prove his superiority, physical, intellectual, and moral, in the stern struggle in which he is engaged, and the State on its part must make every effort to strengthen him for his task. He must be strengthened qualitatively, by education and by social legislation; he must be strengthened quantitatively, by the encouragement of immigration. The problem of the maintenance by the white race of its position in South Africa cannot, as Mr. Amery pointed out in Johannesburg, ' be solved by South Africa alone within her own resources; it can only be solved, if she brings to her aid in abundance fresh blood from overseas.' It is along the lines of strengthening the white man rather than of holding down the black man that it should be approached.

The main features of South Africa's most pressing problem have been presented, and the path indicated along which a solution should be sought. Will South Africa succeed in finding it? Will it create conditions under which the white man and the black man who inhabit it ' may live together in peace and harmony '? That is, indeed, its greatest task. For it is dealing with a phase of the dominant issue of the twentieth century in world politics, an issue which, it may well be, is heralding one of the great upheavals of history, and it is asked to find a solution under conditions more difficult than those that prevail in any other land. To-day, not unnaturally, it regards its task from the viewpoint of making South Africa safe for the white man. But, perhaps, it may yet be, that to it there applies the supreme paradox of the New Testament: ' Whosoever will save his life, shall lose it, but whosoever shall lose his life for My sake and the Gospel's, the same shall save it '; and, perhaps, also the better way for the white man to save himself in South Africa will be seen to be along the line of approach which keeps in view the world-aspects of the problem and his country's possible contributions to a larger whole, rather than along that where the vision is limited to the selfish pursuit of individual salvation.

BOOK TWO

Chapter 1

Disruptive Forces

JAN HENDRIK HOFMEYR first entered the Union
Parliament by winning a by-election in 1931. At that
time the minds of leading statesmen in South Africa
were under the influence of the Statute of Westminster,
which had given the Dominions full sovereign independence
within the family of British nations. The founder of the
republican Nationalist Party, General Hertzog, was able to
declare that South Africa's independence and equality were
complete. 'There is no single reason now,' he added, ' why
South Africans should not meet in statesmanship and
politics in a spirit of one consolidated South African nation.'

And yet even as General Hertzog was uttering these
words, a small group among his followers was busy forming a
Republican League whose aim was secession from the
Commonwealth. General Hertzog was a man of strong and
decisive views who brooked no opposition from within his
own party, and he put down the movement with a firm hand.
At the time it seemed that little more would be heard of
republicanism in its extreme form.

What most people failed to realize was that republicanism
was something more than a political demand for separation
from the British Commonwealth. It was an ideology—a
movement towards a new and different philosophy of government. It bore many of the characteristics of the National
Socialist movement in Germany, by which it was deeply
influenced.

The movement was based on racial domination or
' baasskap,' to use the Afrikaans word. The aim was to
create an Afrikaans Volk with a distinctive Afrikaans
culture and an indigenous Afrikaans way of life. In its
narrowest form this conception opposed any dilution of
Afrikanerdom through intermarriage between the Afrikaans
and English sections of the population. It fiercely resisted

the infiltration of English or other 'foreign' ideas. It sought to establish the Afrikaner as a patriarch, God-fearing and obedient to his Church. The Sabbath would be observed with piety and reverence; dancing and other forms of frivolity would be declared 'un-Afrikaans.' As the oldest and largest group in the European population, the Afrikaans people would rule South Africa. The attitude towards other European groups—the English, the Jews, and other 'foreign' elements—would be tolerant provided they did not challenge Afrikaans baasskap, or domination. The English would be permitted a share in the government, and their language and culture would be acknowledged, always in the hope that they would one day be absorbed into the larger Afrikaans nation, much as the Huguenots had been absorbed into the early Dutch colony in the Cape.

A secret society was formed to further the ideals of the Afrikaans nation in its narrowest concept. This movement was known as the Broederbond, and it was confined to avowed republicans, mainly intellectuals. Its aims were to promote Afrikaans culture; to secure the appointment of its members to key positions in the State, provincial and municipal services; and to encourage specifically Afrikaans commercial and industrial undertakings. Its supporters have declared that the Broederbond is purely a cultural movement, and that it does not meddle in politics. Yet there is a widespread belief in South Africa that its influence in politics has been considerable and that it was to a great extent instrumental in maintaining a hard core of uncompromising Republicans when General Smuts and General Hertzog led their two great parties into a coalition in 1934. General Hertzog himself denounced the Broederbond, but, unlike the Republican League, it proved too strong for him. From time to time the movement was attacked by non-Republicans in Parliament, on public platforms, and in the Press, and as late as 1951 it formed the subject of an acrimonious exchange between Dr. Malan, the Prime Minister, and Mr. J. G. N. Strauss, the Leader of the Opposition.

Another influence in Nationalist republican thought was the tie of friendship that existed between a great many Afrikaners and Germany. Not only were a number of Afrikaans families of mixed German–Dutch descent, but the sympathy shown by Germany towards the South African Dutch in the Anglo-Boer War had never been forgotten. The rise of Hitler in Europe was observed by a great number of Nationalists in the Union with unconcealed admiration. The Nazi Herrenvolk concept was not so very different from the general idea of Afrikaans baasskap advocated by the Broederbond and its allied movements in South Africa. This is not to say that extreme republicans approved of the more brutal aspects of Nazism—the concentration camps, the gas-chambers, and the terrorism of the Gestapo. Reports of these atrocities were disbelieved or dismissed as anti-German propaganda. It is possible, too, that the real nature of the Nazi weltanschauung was not fully understood in South Africa.

Nevertheless the apparent progress of Germany under the leadership of Hitler evoked an emotional response among many Nationalist Afrikaners, and much study was given to Nazi institutions. An Afrikaans broadcast service from Zeesen materially assisted this process.

Perhaps the greatest influence of all, working almost unconsciously on men's minds, was the presence in South Africa of the native people. The Afrikaans outlook towards the natives was traditionally that of the patriarch towards the members of a lesser and subservient tribe. It was essentially a master–servant relationship. It was not necessarily oppressive—the Afrikaner was anxious to be a kindly master; to ensure that his black servant was happy and well-fed. Many Dutch Reformed Church missions did, and are still doing magnificent work among the native people. It was only when the Afrikaner (and many an English South African, for that matter) felt that the master–servant relationship was being challenged, that he was inclined to react strongly and to seek to fix the relationship by legislative and other means.

Behind this attitude was a great fear: a fear of being submerged beneath the overwhelming mass of primitive native Africans. The white worker was haunted by the nightmare of being displaced by lower-paid natives. The white parent, whether Afrikaans or English, had his dreams disturbed by the vision of a half-caste nation of the future. The crude election-cry of 'Are you willing to see your daughter married to a Kaffir?' was capable of swaying almost any white electorate. In this emotional atmosphere the idea of baasskap—of a white group permanently ruling a more primitive, more numerous black group—seemed to be the only way to prevent the ultimate submergence of Western civilization in South Africa. And white South Africa did not pause to think that when the principle of baasskap was once accepted, there was no logical reason why it should not be extended to groups within the white group itself.

The latent strength of all these influences was not realized in the early thirties, when General Hertzog was denouncing the Republican League. The Nationalist Government was running into economic difficulties that were aggravated when Britain abandoned the gold standard and the Union decided to remain on gold. A serious depression set in, and among the institutions affected were the Provincial Councils, who were forced to seek a higher basis of subsidization from the Central Government. In the discussions that followed, the Government indicated that it was contemplating abolishing the Provincial System, and this provoked violent opposition from the Province of Natal. A movement arose there in favour of seceding from the Union, and though it is doubtful whether such a step would actually have been attempted, the Government was sufficiently impressed to withdraw its threat to abolish the Provincial System.

Towards the end of 1932 a former Nationalist leader who had been appointed to the Bench, Mr. Justice Tielman Roos, suddenly resigned from the Supreme Court to re-enter politics. This step threw the political situation into a state of flux. Mr. Roos demanded the abandonment of the gold standard and called for the formation of a national government. Negotiations were opened between Mr. Roos and General Smuts for a coalition, but the talks broke down. General Smuts had a larger goal: coalition with the Nationalists and the formation of a broadly based national government. He saw an opportunity of following up the Statute of Westminster with a merging of those political forces that had been based on racial distinctions. The next phase, he hoped, would be the rise of new political forces divided by economic rather than racial considerations. Early in 1933 he called upon the Nationalist Government to resign, and he offered to serve under General Hertzog in a national government.

It was a great act of statesmanship on the part of General Smuts. He knew that in the event of an election his own South African Party would almost certainly be returned to power. But he also realized that the margin would most likely be small, and that the return to power of a South African Party Government would intensify the agitation for a republic. Above all, he wanted unity between the two white races. General Hertzog rejected his appeal, but he repeated it two months later. By then public opinion in favour of a coalition had gathered considerable strength. Defections were occurring within the Nationalist Party itself, and General Hertzog began to realize that the position of his Nationalist Government was in serious danger.

Then occurred one of those seemingly insignificant incidents that sometimes change the whole course of history. A popular Nationalist Minister, Mr. Charlie Malan, died, and both General Hertzog and General Smuts attended the funeral. They stood near each other at the graveside, and General Hertzog invited General Smuts to return from the cemetery with him in his car. General Hertzog had been particularly fond of Mr. Malan and he was deeply moved by the funeral service. In the car, General Smuts paid a tribute to Mr. Malan, and added that it was a tragedy that they had worked in different political camps when the divisions were really so artificial. In a sudden impulse, General Hertzog seized the hand of General Smuts. A few days later he sent a letter to General Smuts accepting his offer to negotiate a coalition. The talks were spread over several weeks, and there were moments when they appeared likely to fail. However, in the end an agreement was reached. This was unanimously endorsed by the caucus of the South African Party, but in the Nationalist caucus it was opposed by twenty-eight out of a total of seventy.

These twenty-eight Nationalist opponents of coalition with the South African Party represented the hard core of Afrikaans baasskap—the dour, unrelenting section of republicans led by the Broederbond and its associated cultural movements. In the general public satisfaction over the coalition and the abandonment of the gold standard,

H

the twenty-eight uncompromising republicans were forgotten. During the following year their ranks in Parliament actually dwindled to nineteen, and it seemed that the era of full Afrikaans–English collaboration had at last dawned. And yet, only thirteen years later, the unrelenting nineteen swept into power, and South Africa was plunged into the greatest racial turmoil she had suffered since the Anglo-Boer War.

Part of the compact between General Smuts and General Hertzog was an agreement to bring a series of important bills before Parliament ' to settle the native problem in South Africa.' The Bills required a two-thirds majority of both Houses of Parliament in order to become law, and they had hung fire for Session after Session while a Select Committee tried to reconcile differences on native policy between the various parties. Now, with the backing of General Smuts, the Bills were assured of the necessary majority, and they were brought before Parliament in 1936. Their effect on white–black relationships will be described in greater detail in a later chapter. Sufficient to record here that natives enjoying the vote on the common roll in the Cape Province lost this vote. Instead, machinery was created for the election by natives throughout the Union of four white Senators, and three white Members of the Assembly to compensate for the loss of the franchise in the Cape.

During the debate on these measures, Jan Hofmeyr emerged as a strong champion of the Liberal point of view in South Africa. Though a prominent member of the Coalition Cabinet, he refused to support the native Bills. In a speech that was prophetic he declared that the so-called ' settlement of the native problem ' would prove to be no settlement at all; that the machinery then being set up would break down, and that the foundations were being laid for severe racial conflict in the future. Jan Hofmeyr stood almost alone, yet before his death he saw his forebodings begin to come true.

A year later, in 1937, he made another strong stand—this time successfully—on behalf of the South African Indian community. There had been agitation in Natal and the Transvaal in favour of imposing further restrictions on trading and the ownership of property by Indians, and a Bill was drafted by one of the Nationalists in the Cabinet, Mr. Oswald Pirow. The measure was referred to a Select Committee, and when Jan Hofmeyr threatened to resign from the Cabinet and to fight the measure on the floor of the House, it was tactfully dropped.

The Indian question was not again raised until the end of World War II. Anti-Asiatic sentiment had continued to smoulder in Natal, and a clamour arose for the removal of Indians from predominantly white residential areas. Under the pressure of public opinion, a Residential Property Regulation Ordinance was passed by the Natal Provincial Council. This provided that if a white person wished to sell property to an Indian, the National Housing Board would have the first option of purchase. There were strong protests from the Indian community in South Africa, and from the Government of India. Jan Hofmeyr used his influence inside the Cabinet against the measure, and the Government advised the Governor-General to withhold his consent to the Natal Ordinance.

Meanwhile white opinion in Natal continued to demand the imposition of further restrictions against Indians, and a commission to consider the whole question was appointed under the chairmanship of Mr. Justice F. N. Broome. Among its recommendations, this Commission advised the Union Government to invite the Government of India to send delegates to a round-table conference, but the suggestion was ignored.

A compromise was attempted in 1946. In exchange for accepting residential restrictions, Indians were to receive a measure of political representation. They would be directly represented in the Natal Provinical Council by two persons, who could be Indians. In the Natal and the Transvaal they would elect two Senators who would have to be whites. Voting on a communal roll, the Indian community would elect three white Members of the Assembly. But the Indians were not prepared to accept the compromise. An Act embodying these provisions was passed by Parliament in the face of strong disapproval from the Government of India. In Natal, Indians organized a passive-resistence movement, and a number of persons were sent to gaol. The Government of India recalled its High Commissioner in South

Africa, imposed a trade embargo on the Union, and referred the dispute to the United Nations Organization. General Smuts suggested that the question should be referred to the International Court at the Hague, but the proposal was rejected by the General Assembly of the United Nations. Instead, a motion was adopted that the treatment of Indians in the Union should be in conformity with international agreements concluded between India and South Africa together with the provisions of the United Nations Charter. India and South Africa were requested to report at the following session of the General Assembly on the measures that had been adopted to give effect to the resolution.

Thus began the clash between India and South Africa in the councils of the United Nations which imposed so heavy a strain on Commonwealth relations, and had not been resolved at the time these words were written. India led the opposition in the United Nations to South Africa's policy in regard to the territory of South-West Africa. The Union desired to continue to administer this territory in the spirit of the League of Nations mandate under which it had been passed over to her care, and General Smuts went to Lake Success to plead this cause in the United Nations. India immediately moved that South-West Africa should be placed under international trusteeship, and not even the personal prestige of the Union Premier was enough to prevent India's motion from being carried by an overwhelming majority.

In 1947 an exchange of letters took place between General Smuts and Mr. Nehru. General Smuts urged that the Indian High Commissioner should return to South Africa, and Mr. Nehru demanded in reply that South Africa should implement the United Nations resolution on the treatment of Indians in the Union. The deadlock remained unbroken when the United Party Government of General Smuts was defeated in the following year and a Nationalist Government under Dr. D. F. Malan assumed power.

The 1946 Act giving limited political rights to Indians in exchange for residential restrictions had not been implemented, and it was immediately revoked by the Nationalist Government. Early in 1950, delegates from India and

Pakistan arrived in South Africa at the invitation of the Union Government to discuss the possibility of holding a round-table conference between the three countries. A fair measure of agreement was reached on an agenda, but the delegates had scarcely returned to India before the Union Government announced a Group Areas Bill to delimit trading and residential areas for the different races in South Africa. All prospects of a round-table conference were wrecked, and when the United Nations General Assembly met a few weeks later, an acrimonious debate took place on India's dispute with the Union. The upshot was a resolution asking South Africa to suspend the Group Areas Act pending direct talks between the Union, Pakistan and India. South Africa repudiated the resolution on the score that it constituted interference in the domestic affairs of a member state.

As regards South-West Africa, Dr. Malan's Nationalist Government decided to give the Territory direct representation in the Union Parliament, and legislation was enacted providing for six seats in the Assembly and two seats in the Senate. Elections for these seats were held in 1950, and Nationalists were returned to fill all the posts. It was clear that both on the Indian question and in regard to South-West Africa, the Union meant to pursue her own independent course, no matter what resolutions might be passed by the United Nations.

Chapter 2

The Industrial Revolution

ON DECEMBER 3, 1948, Jan Hendrik Hofmeyr
died. For more than thirty years he had given himself unsparingly to the service of his country. During
the war years he had carried two men's burdens in the day-
to-day administration of the State, and he had faced
mounting criticisms of the liberal policies for which he stood.
The strain proved too much for his heart, and one morning
at a cricket match he collapsed.

With Jan Hofmeyr's death it seemed to most South
Africans that liberalism had also died. Like Hofmeyr
himself, liberalism was born in the Cape Province, and now
it had been killed by the hard, uncompromising, frontier
mentality of the North. 'The Cape liberal tradition is
trekking to the North,' Hofmeyr said in a speech shortly
before the war. And in the North it was ambushed and
overwhelmed.

What were the essentials of the Cape native policy which
Hofmeyr took over and sought to extend to the rest of South
Africa? They could be compressed into the two words
'Christian Trusteeship.' Hofmeyr believed that the white
man's ward must be encouraged to grow up. He supported
the Rhodes dictum of 'equal rights for all civilized men.'
He was prepared to set the standard of civilization high, and
he had sufficient faith in the white man and his civilizing
mission to believe that he would always be able to hold his
own in South Africa, despite the immense disparity in
numbers. Unlike the vast majority of white South Africans,
he did not fear for the future. But he recognized this fear of
being swamped by the black masses. He knew that fear was
the greatest psychological factor influencing native policies.
He did not want to force the pace of the black man's development, but he hoped for steady progress through education
and experimentation. He was prepared to admit that a

policy of ' apartheid,' or territorial segregation, might have
succeeded had it been adopted a century before, and had
the white man been prepared to pay the economic price of
such a policy. But he knew that now it was too late.
There was insufficient land available, while economic forces
were at work that could not be arrested.

The most important development of the years 1930–1950,
overshadowing all other developments and inexorably
determining the future of South Africa, was the beginning of
the great industrial revolution. This process is now at its
height, and it may yet achieve many of the ideals for which
Hofmeyr stood. South Africa can, indeed, consider herself
fortunate that this industrial revolution should have started
when it did, since without it the future for all races on the
sub-Continent would be bleak.

Let us consider the picture in 1932. South Africa was in
the throes of an economic depression. Partly for ideological
reasons, and partly on account of a too-rigid belief in
orthodox finance, the Nationalist Government had declined
to follow Britain when she abandoned the gold standard.
This resulted in a flight of capital from the Union. ' Good,'
said the Nationalist republican, ' it will break the British
imperialist money-power in South Africa.' But prices of
agricultural commodities fell and there was a general slowing
down in the nation's economic activity. The Union's
industrial sheet-anchor, the gold industry, was placed at a
serious disadvantage.

At that time there was a belief that the gold industry had
reached the peak of its development. Old mines were
nearing the end of their existence, and the possibility of
opening up new ones for exploitation appeared to be limited.
There were hopes that the life of the industry might be
prolonged by advances in the techniques of mining at deeper
levels, but even these advances would obviously have their
limits.

Meanwhile, throughout the length and breadth of South
Africa the soil was losing its fertility. Farmers had complained of the increasing severity of droughts, but it was
beginning to be realized that not drought but soil-erosion
was the real trouble. The soil in South Africa is generally
light and friable, and for many decades it had been wantonly

exploited. The destruction of natural bush, unscientific burning of the veld, over-stocking with cattle and sheep, and ignorant methods of cultivation were having disastrous effects on the countryside. The Department of Agriculture estimated that South Africa was losing her topsoil at the rate of one per cent. per annum, and that unless energetic steps were taken to fight erosion, the Union would become one vast dustbowl within a century.

Bad as the position was in the white farming areas, it was infinitely worse in many of the native reserves. Native methods of cultivation were primitive in the extreme. In the old days, before the white man came to South Africa, the practice was to cultivate a piece of land for two or three years, then to abandon it when it was no longer fertile. Given time, Nature would restore the soil. Tribal wars kept the population down, and a rough balance was maintained between man and Nature. But when the native people were confined to their reserves and there were no further tribal wars; when medicine became available to fight disease and veterinary science prevented the plagues of rinderpest, anthrax and East Coast fever that had periodically swept like veld-fires through the cattle herds, the balance between man and Nature was rudely disturbed. Further, it was traditional for a native to count his wealth in cattle, and the primitive African could not understand the evil effects of overstocking.

The net result was that the economy of the reserves deteriorated. Agriculture slowed down, and the menfolk were forced out into the towns in search of work. An impetus was thus given to the migration to the towns. Many native districts became dormitory areas, inhabited mainly by old people, women, and children. The men in the towns contracted diseases of various kinds and brought them back to the reserves—if the menfolk came back at all. A plague of inertia settled down on numerous communities, living among scarred hills and in valleys lined with gullies and denuded of their soil. This wasting process, both of human resources and the soil, varied in different areas, and according to the characteristics of the chiefs and their tribes. The Native Affairs Department began reclamation work and organized demonstrations of soil-conservation practices.

Attempts were made to persuade natives to part with their cattle, and stock-sales were organized. These efforts resulted in some successes, but the overall picture in South Africa is still one of increasing erosion and growing poverty in the reserves.

After South Africa abandoned the gold standard in 1933 and political stability was achieved through the formation of the Hertzog–Smuts Coalition Government, capital began to flow back into the Union in a steadily increasing stream. The six years from 1933 until 1939 saw many new factories erected. The mining industry boomed, and prices for agricultural products recovered. Then came the war, with its powerful impetus to industrial development. South Africa became a vital base for supplying the Allied armies in the Mediterranean theatre and the Middle East, and energetic steps were taken to boost industrial production. During the three years from 1939 until 1942, South Africa herself spent over £100 millions on war supplies, the bulk of which were manufactured in the Union. There was mass-production of clothing and foodstuffs, and more than 130 factories were fully employed on army equipment of various types. This gave a powerful boost to industrial development, and after the war most of the factories were easily switched to civilian purposes.

One important effect was to attract native labour from the towns. This migration of native labour to the industrial towns of the Union came not only from the native reserves and the protectorates in South Africa, but from the Rhodesias and Nyasaland. As the Union native tended to leave the farms and domestic employment to enter industry, his place was to some extent filled from across the Zambesi. Wage rates were higher in the Union, and the Northern native was attracted by reports of higher earnings, together with the prospect of adventure in the great towns of the south.

Yet while there was plenty of employment available for the native on unskilled labour, the colour-bar imposed by the white trade unions kept him from rising in the industrial scale over a wide range of occupations. Nevertheless, the sheer pressure of economics began to force holes in the colour-bar dykes. Industry was booming; there was a serious shortage of white labour, and an abundance of black labour was available. The fight to preserve the colour-bar in industry is far from concluded, yet it is obvious that gradually and unobstrusively white labour is being driven from its strongholds. And this infiltration of blacks into industry is, of course, to the great economic advantage of the white craftsman, though he refuses to see it. As the black man slowly rises in the industrial scale, national productivity increases and additional opportunities open up for exploiting the white man's initiative and skill.

The drift of the natives from the reserves of the Union to the towns brought serious social complications. One wave of this migration took place from the Transkei and the Ciskei, where the Kaffir wars of the previous century had been fought, into the industrial area of the Cape Peninsula. Thus in the middle of the twentieth century the Bantu moved down to further the industrialization of the Cape Peninsula, thus completing their great southward trek through Africa—a trek that had been halted by the frontier wars with the northward-moving settlers.

With the influx of natives into the towns, serious housing problems arose. Shack-settlements sprawled over the Cape Flats and around Johannesburg. On the Witwatersrand a squatters' movement produced a serious crisis. The riots and loss of life and the crime-wave that made Johannesburg almost a siege-town, were largely due to lack of housing and slum conditions.

One effect in the Cape Peninsula was to increase the difficulties of the coloured, or half-caste man. Previously the coloured community was the main source of unskilled and semi-skilled labour. Then the black man came in to undercut the coloured man in the unskilled jobs. The coloured man found himself between the black labourer at the bottom and the white artizan fighting to prevent him from rising into the skilled occupations. For some years the outlook for the coloured man appeared to be bleak, but gradually the tempo of industrialization eased the problem. It was discovered that the coloured man had a peculiar aptitude for certain types of industrial work, such as in the textile trade. Manufacturers began to regard him as a valuable economic asset, and there was an increasing demand for his labour.

An interesting example of this may be quoted from the diamond-city of Kimberley, where a textile manufacturer decided to establish a rayon industry. This manufacturer had fled from one of the countries behind the ' iron curtain ' in Europe, and had long been connected with the textile trade. He at first attempted to operate his Kimberley factory with white labour, but this proved unsatisfactory and uneconomic. Native labour, which was proving a great success in the cotton industry, was not as efficient in the more delicate and intricate rayon industry. Coloured labour proved to be the solution. In Kimberley is a fairly large coloured population, and coloured workers soon became highly productive weavers. The claim is now being advanced that this coloured labour force has attained the highest level of skill and efficiency in the rayon industry anywhere in the world.

But the greatest of all stimulants to the industrialization of South Africa was the discovery of rich new goldfields extending southwards from the Witwatersrand into the Free State. It soon became apparent that the new gold-mines would add at least 100 years—perhaps 200 years—to the life-expectation of the gold industry. Thriving new towns arose on the veld. The demand for steel, cement, machinery, and a wide variety of materials; the pressing need for housing, and for all the commodities needed to supply the many new urban communities, taxed the country's manufacturing resources to their utmost capacity. The steel industry was doubled, then trebled. New coal-mines were opened up. Plans were made for a big State industry to manufacture oil from coal. Base-minerals of all kinds were vigorously exploited.

In addition, one of South Africa's oldest industries—that of diamond-mining—enjoyed a healthy revival. The world demand for gem diamonds rose as the international situation became more uncertain, while new manufacturing processes increased the need for industrial diamonds. With the migration to South Africa of skilled craftsmen from Holland and Belgium, South Africa built up a promising diamond-cutting industry.

Between 1940 and 1950 South Africa became fully alive to the need for measures for the conservation of her soil.

It was clear that lack of water might easily become a limiting factor on industrial development. The main source of water-supply for the great industrial complex of the Witwatersrand, for the steel-producing centres of Pretoria and Vereeniging, and for the new Free State gold-mines, was the Vaal River. And it was essential to protect the ' sponges ' of the Vaal. It was necessary, too, to increase agricultural production in order to ensure adequate supplies of food. Shortages of food were a constant source of anxiety during and after the war years.

In 1946 a Soil Conservation Act was passed which was intended to touch off a national campaign to restore the ravages of soil-erosion and to encourage greater food production. A voluntary body, the National Veld Trust, was founded to stimulate public interest in the problem of conservation. Unfortunately, the difficulty of obtaining skilled technicians, together with administrative troubles and lack of initiative by Government departments, tended to retard the conservation drive. Yet it was generally accepted, at the time of writing, that this work of soil conservation on a national scale would have to be given high priority if South Africa was to take full advantage of the era of industrialization opening up before her.

This process of industrialization was also influencing life in the country districts. Labour shortages were forcing more and more farmers to mechanize. The tractor was displacing the ox, and the demand for skilled labour to operate and maintain agricultural machines was providing fresh opportunities for the native labourer to advance. This process was vividly described in a recent article by Mr. Bailey Bekker, M.P.:

' What many of us do not understand is that an economic revolution is taking place on the farms, and that traditional lines of thought are beginning to change. Let me quote a simple illustration to show what I mean. There is Oom Koos in the Ermelo district. He has a son of 25, educated at high school, with a course at one of the agricultural colleges. His son is running the farm under the father's general supervision. After a good deal of persuasion the son talks Oom Koos into buying a tractor. Next the most intelligent native on the farm is trained to drive the tractor. This is the beginning of a process of education. The native tractor-driver has to get a licence, and this involves more education and the passing of a test. Besides the tractor, he soon drives the lorry with the milk to the station and sometimes to the dorp. Then he begins doing responsible errands: signing for parcels at the station, drawing money from the bank, and shopping. All this means more education. The driver is now a cut above the ordinary labourer and his wages are substantially increased. He is encouraged to build a small house in place of the usual grass huts.

'This process of mechanisation, which has been going on almost unnoticed throughout the agricultural areas of South Africa during the past 10 years or so, has inevitably enhanced the value of skilled labour. And since the skilled labourer has a higher value, he counts for more on the farm. Ideas about him undergo a subtle change. Ten years ago if you mentioned the word education for natives to Oom Koos he would fly off the handle. To-day he has definite ideas about educating natives on vocational lines. Thus mechanisation is influencing many changes on the Platteland—the country districts—changes in thought as well as in habits and values. Let us remember, then, that the industrial revolution through which South Africa is passing at the moment, is affecting the country districts as well as the towns.'

Jan Hofmeyr saw that all these economic trends, in the country as well as in the towns, must inevitably promote the liberal forces for which he stood. When he died, liberalism as a political programme had suffered its greatest reverse, and his own political stocks were low. Yet he refused to despair. A political cloud had, indeed, filled the South African sky. He knew that sooner or later it would pass. For, as he himself used to say, the weather in South Africa was marked by rapid and unexpected contrasts.

Chapter 3

The Focus of Power

IT HAS become a commonplace saying in South Africa that the political destiny of the Union will be determined by the Witwatersrand. This is true, not only of the white people, but also of the black people of the Union. It is true of the white people because half the white population of South Africa now live in the great industrial triangle of the Witwatersrand, Pretoria, and Vereeniging. Despite the 'loading' of the franchise against the voters in the towns, the Witwatersrand obviously commands the greatest concentration of seats in Parliament.

For twenty years there has been a steady migration from the country districts into the rapidly expanding towns of the Rand. And the main body of this stream has been Afrikaans. The Dutch churches have been concerned to maintain their hold over Afrikaners moving into the towns, and much time, energy, and finance have been devoted to this problem. In addition, the Nationalist Party established its own newspaper in Johannesburg. A great deal of political organization work was carried on throughout the 'industrial triangle.' During the 1938 general election the bulk of the Nationalist Party's electioneering fund was spent on the Witwatersrand. The result was that the Nationalist Party not only substantially increased its Transvaal representation in Parliament, but also won a majority in the Transvaal Provincial Council. This increase in the number of Nationalist seats won in and around the Witwatersrand was the decisive factor in returning Dr. Malan and his Nationalist Government to power.

In the early years of the population migration from the country districts into the towns, it used to be argued that urban conditions of life would mellow the Afrikaner and shake his attachment to the feudalistic outlook of the Nationalist Party. But this has not happened. The young

Afrikaans worker in the towns has remained loyal to his Church and his party. One reason for this is that the party itself has undergone an ideological change. It has embraced a National-Socialism similar in some respects to that of Nazi Germany. Another powerful factor is pressure from the other stream of migration to the towns—the black migration. In the 1936 census the native population of the Witwatersrand was stated as 670,000. By 1951—in only fifteen years—this number had increased to 896,000. These figures did not include the new industrial areas of Pretoria, Vereeniging, and Van der Bijl, where the increases were even greater.

The black migration to the industrial areas all through the war years and in the post-war period, had a profound effect, not only on the economics of the towns, but also upon people's thoughts. Lack of housing for natives resulted in squatting, the creation of ' shanty-towns,' and slum conditions. There were riots and loss of life. Crime flourished, and a wave of burglaries, assaults, and murders plagued such cities as Johannesburg. In addition, there was increasing pressure by the black worker on occupations traditionally reserved for whites. The older, tightly organized trade unions were able to resist this pressure, but in many unobtrusive ways the black worker was making inroads into the white employment reserve. Native Africans were employed as clerks, van-drivers, and in numerous occupations not controlled by the white trade unions.

It was easy enough, under all these circumstances, to rouse the fears of the white working-man, especially the Afrikaner who had recently moved in from the country. The Nationalist Party fought the 1948 general election almost exclusively on the threat to white supremacy by the black man. The slogan of ' apartheid '—the doctrine of separate existence—was coined by the Nationalists, and proved to be a potent cry. Nationalist leaders did not trouble to define it too closely. But it was understood by the electorate to mean separation of the races into definite territorial areas. The black man would be admitted into the white man's towns only on a temporary basis and only so long as his labour was needed. The black man would be encouraged to work out his economic and political destiny in his own reserves. This doctrine seemed reassuring to the white worker on the Witwatersrand, who was worried by the pressure of black labour, was anxious over the rise in the incidence of crime, the riots, and other evidence of what he took to be a growing ' truculence ' on the part of the native. It seemed an easy solution to say that the native must be pushed back into the reserves.

Yet another political factor must be mentioned. In 1936 Jan Hofmeyr uttered a warning in Parliament that General Hertzog's Native Bills, which were intended ' to settle the native problem,' would inevitably fail. These Bills provided that native political development should take place in a new body known as the Native Representative Council. This Council was elected by a complicated system of voting, and included representatives from both the country districts and the towns. The Council had no executive powers, but was purely advisory in character. It was, however, enacted that the Council should examine and report upon measures specifically affecting the native people, before they were introduced to Parliament.

Unlike Hofmeyr, General Smuts placed great value on the Native Representative Council. During the 1936 debate in Parliament, and later when he opened the first session of the Council, General Smuts forecast a great future for this body. But experience proved him wrong and Hofmeyr right. Inevitably the sense of frustration among leaders of the native people, which had been dammed up for years, poured forth in the Native Representative Council. And once the members of the Council had expressed their grievances, there was nothing constructive for them to do. They could only advise, and this advice was generally ignored. Year after year they sent forth recommendations to the Government that were not acted upon.

The actual proceedings of the Council were maintained on a high level. The standard of debate was excellent, and speeches were generally dignified and restrained. It is possible that the Council might have progressed had a realistic attempt been made by the Government to further its progress. There were many things that might have been

done: a special building might have been erected to house
this 'Native Parliament.' That would have given the
institution an air of permanence in native eyes. Instead,
the Council met in any available hall that could be hired for
the occasion, and the psychological effect was bad. Then,
the Council's members might have been given certain
privileges. Various minor functions of the Native Affairs
Department might have been delegated to the Council.
But nothing was done. On the contrary, many of the
discussions in the Council were viewed with unconcealed
irritation by the Native Affairs Department. Inevitably, a
sense of futility began to settle down on the Council's
proceedings.

In the end, the Native Representative Council—the body
intended to be the main outlet for legitimate native political
aspirations—went on strike. Its members announced that
they could see no useful purpose in continuing to meet.
That was a symbolic act, and its meaning should not have
been lost upon the white rulers of South Africa. Feelings of
frustration among native leaders were giving rise to a spirit
of non-co-operation. The blacks were drawing back into a
political laager.

Attempts to persuade the Council to resume its sessions
failed. Then in 1947 General Smuts admitted that the
1936 Acts had failed. ' Changes in the native way of life
have made this legislation ineffective,' he declared. He
went on to propose that the functions of the Native Representative Council should be extended. The Council should
exercise a measure of authority over the administration of
the native reserves. The five official members of the
Council, who were Europeans, should be replaced by
Africans. It would become a wholly Bantu organization,
with a Bantu staff and perhaps an executive committee.
Native Advisory Boards in the towns would be organized in a
congress and linked with the Native Representative Council.

But these proposals came too late. Leaders of native
opinion were thinking far in advance of such palliatives, and
they were in no mood to accept the proposals of General
Smuts, which they described as ' vague and disappointing.'
They asked for direct representation of Africans on all
legislative bodies.

The Nationalists made the most of all these troubles. It was obviously useless, they argued, to attempt to collaborate with the natives, who only made ' excessive and impossible demands in return.' The only course was to have separate development for the white and black races, with native political and economic development taking place in the reserves.

The 1948 general election proved to be one of the most bitter on record. In addition to urging their policy of ' apartheid,' the Nationalists launched a virulent and concentrated attack on Jan Hofmeyr. As the acknowledged leader of liberal thought in South Africa, they charged him with planning to break down all barriers between black and white. The old cry of ' Do you want your sister to marry a Kaffir? ' rang from platforms all over the country.

The United Party took its stand upon the report of a commission presided over by Mr. Justice Fagan, which had investigated the economic position of the native people. This commission brought out vividly the impossibility of separating natives from whites in the economy of the country. The commission also recommended that the problem of dealing with the influx of blacks to the towns should be treated as a question of national emergency, and that responsibility for meeting the position should be removed from the municipalities to the Central Government. Finally, the Commission emphasized the importance of providing adequate housing for natives in the towns.

However, the electorate was in no mood to listen to reason. The ' apartheid ' slogan and the attacks on Jan Hofmeyr had induced an emotional atmosphere in which racial prejudices carried the day. The result was a victory for the Nationalists. The campaign against Hofmeyr had been so bitter that for some weeks after the election his position inside his own party was in jeopardy. Some of his colleagues, backed by several English newspapers, blamed him for the defeat and urged him to retire. He met the attacks with a series of brilliant speeches that restored his position within the party. But he had felt the attacks deeply, and the strain of years of overwork was already taking its toll. His death occurred shortly afterwards.

Of the many tributes that poured in from all sections of

the people, the most touching came from the native and
coloured people. To many of them he was the one last hope
of co-operation from the white side. The immediate actions
of the Nationalist Government seemed to confirm their fears
that the white man was determined to screw down the safety-
valve. 'Apartheid' was applied to the railways in the form
of separate entrances and exits, and separate coaches were
provided for white and non-whites on suburban trains in the
Cape Province. Legislation was passed prohibiting mixed
marriages. After an attempt to persuade the Native Representative Council to continue its work on rigid lines had
broken down, a Bill was passed by Parliament abolishing
this body. There was a threat to remove Members of
Parliament elected by the natives.

The Dutch Reformed Church, meeting in congress,
demanded that the policy of ' apartheid ' should be carried
to its logical conclusions. The native must be removed from
the white man's towns and must be concentrated in the
reserves. The white housewife must be prepared to do her
own housework or employ a white servant. Native workers
must be kept to a minimum in industry, even if this involved
enormous cost. But the Government hastily replied that
its intentions were not so radical. A certain number of
urban workers would have to be retained on a permanent
basis. But natives in white areas would have no political
rights, and the native would have to seek his political destiny
in the reserves.

The Government then began to consider a scheme to
replace the Native Representative Council. The idea was
to create further councils in native areas on the lines of the
Bunga in the Transkei. These councils would be given an
increasing measure of authority within their areas. They
would ultimately be linked by a federal council which would,
in effect, become the Natives' Parliament. Urban native
populations in white areas might even be given some sort of
representation in this federal council. This plan had not
been fully worked out at the time of writing. Measures were
being taken to increase the tribal authority of the chiefs, and
there was a move to transfer control of native education from
the Department of Education to the Department of Native
Affairs. The whole drive was to separate black from white

wherever the activities of the two sections of the people had not become inextricably intertwined.

But to most thinking South Africans in the year 1951 it was clear that the attempt to apply ' apartheid ' had come at least 100 years too late. It was also clear that black–white relations—the so-called ' native problem '—would ultimately be decided, not in the reserves, but in the towns. No legislative measures could possibly stop the rapid process of native urbanization, which was dictated primarily by economic considerations. And as the native became urbanized; as he embraced the western way of life in urban areas, so would he increasingly insist upon a share in the determination of his own affairs.

The largest urban area, for the black man as for the white man, is the Witwatersrand, and this will continue to be the case for as long as the present industrial revolution is maintained in South Africa. It is therefore clear that the political destiny of the black man will be determined on the Witwatersrand, just as the balance of power between the white man's two main political movements will increasingly be decided by the way the vote swings in this great industrial region.

Chapter 4

The Future

W HAT of the future of South Africa? In the year 1952 it is far more difficult to answer this question than it seemed in 1930. At that time there were definite trends that appeared to point in logical directions: towards the goal of national unity within the British Commonwealth; towards a gradual, difficult, but progressive adjustment of white–black relations. On the economic side the picture seemed less clear. At the back of men's minds was anxiety about the too-great dependence upon the gold industry with its apparent horizon of only thirty or forty years. It was beginning to be realized that all was not well with agriculture, and there were doubts whether South Africa would be able to support a much larger population.

But events, during the succeeding twenty years, completely falsified all these expectations. The disruptive effects of World War II and the rise of new ideological concepts brought an era of national disunity. Powerful forces arose in favour of an independent republic, outside the British Commonwealth. A serious crisis developed in white–black relations. A sudden spurt of industrial development and the discovery of rich new gold-bearing areas opened up the possibility of doubling and perhaps trebling the population during the next half-century. The financial means were made available for fighting soil-erosion, conserving water, and rehabilitating agriculture.

If the forecasts of 1930 proved so completely wrong, how much more likely are the prognostications of to-day likely to be falsified by history. And yet we must at least indicate the trends, leaving it to the reader to make his own deductions.

It is wise, when looking at South Africa, to remember that things are not always what they appear to be on the surface.

A political observer, analysing the declarations of members of the Nationalist Government, and noting the autarchic direction of legislation since 1948, might logically deduce that the Union is moving rapidly towards a narrow, Herrenvolk dictatorship, with Afrikanerdom at the top of the pyramid and the black masses at the bottom. Judging, further, from Nationalist reactions to the deliberations of the United Nations, it would seem that this authoritarian State must be isolationist in character.

And yet, beneath the surface, there are other trends, important to the historian, though not so easily discernible. To begin with, it is by no means certain that the great majority of the Afrikaans people are anxious to diverge from the path of democracy. At the great celebrations to mark the opening of the Voortrekker Monument in December, 1949, Afrikaners gave an indication that in certain vital aspects of the Nationalist weltanschauung they were not prepared to follow their leaders. The celebrations extended over a week. Beforehand, every effort had been made by the Nationalist political leadership to turn the occasion into a tribal demonstration in its narrowest sense. But the hundreds of thousands of Afrikaners who trekked from all over the Union to camp round the Monument made their own decision as to the character of the celebrations. It was a friendly occasion, at which English South Africans were warmly welcomed and references to the need for racial collaboration were spontaneously cheered. The greatest applause of all was given to an English South African who spoke in Afrikaans. Thousands of natives mingled with the crowds and witnessed the proceedings without molestation or unpleasantness of any kind, although a Nationalist newspaper had solemnly declared that natives would not be allowed to attend. Pageants designed to emphasize the injustices of the past were received in silence. The mood of the great crowd favoured racial friendship and collaboration, and was against over-emphasis on the troubles of previous years.

It may well be that the present racialistic political divisions are more artificial than they appear to be, and that a national emergency or some unexpected political development will resurrect the spirit of the Hertzog–Smuts fusion of 1933.

A war against Russia, for example, would unify white South Africa, though it would tend to widen the gulf between white and black. An economic depression might result in new political alignments, as the gold-standard depression of 1931–1933 did.

South Africa's most urgent racial problem is, of course, the question of white–black relationships. The policies of the present Nationalist Government have hastened the movement among non-whites to join forces against their European rulers. Previously it was the accepted policy that the 1,016,000 coloured or half-caste people would be the special responsibility of the whites, and would progress with the whites rather than with the blacks. But the removal of the Cape Coloureds from the common voters' roll to a separate roll, the Act preventing mixed marriages, and the creation of a special Coloured Affairs Department of State, have driven the coloured people away from the white camp into an increasingly hostile black camp.

This opens up a frightening prospect. Leadership of the non-whites is drawing away from the policy of collaboration with the whites, and is advocating radical solutions to the racial question. However, there are two hopeful factors. First, the liberal spirit is growing among the white population, despite political appearances to the contrary. There is more tolerance towards the native people to-day than there was twenty years ago. The English-speaking Churches —the Methodists, with the largest native following of any Church in the Union; the Church of the Province (Church of England); the Roman Catholics; the Presbyterians and Baptists—have all gone on record strongly opposing the policy of 'apartheid.' These churches do not hesitate to speak out boldly, and their collective influence must count for something in the Union.

The other hopeful factor is the industrial revolution. This has its ugly aspects, such as the shanty-towns. It will undoubtedly provoke unrest, riots and disturbances, which may well assume racial characteristics. Though Native African trade unions are not officially recognized, they will increase in numbers and become more efficiently organized. Already Communist influences are evident among the trade

unions, and these influences may gather force. The black–
white struggle may become inextricably mixed up with the
struggle for improved working conditions among the
native people.

Yet, in the long run, the industrial revolution may well
provide the solution to South Africa's racial problem. It
will provide the Union with the financial means to tackle her
problems of soil-erosion, of food, housing, and health. It
will absorb the surplus black population which cannot exist
in the reserves and must inevitably form the great bulk of the
inhabitants of the towns. There is a real shortage of man-
power in South Africa which must increase as industrialization gathers momentum. The inexorable pressure of
economic circumstances has already opened gaps in the
industrial colour-bar, and the restrictive effects of this
colour-bar will be increasingly thrust aside in the future.
As the white worker finds that he is not threatened with
unemployment, but that, on the contrary, the increased
tempo of economic development is raising his standards of
living, his opposition to non-white labour will be lessened.

The big question is whether there is time for the yeast of
liberalism and the forces of the industrial revolution to take
effect before the threatening black–white explosion occurs in
South Africa. General Smuts was too late with his proposals
to extend the powers of the Native Representative Council.
Will other necessary concessions to native African sentiment
also be made too late? There are eminent historians in
South Africa, such as Dr. Arthur Keppel-Jones, who fear
that the hour is already too late for compromise.

I can write only as a close observer of the political scene in
South Africa during the past thirty years. And if I may be
permitted to conclude with a personal expression of opinion,
I do not take an unduly pessimistic view of the future of
South Africa We have suffered a series of political shocks
since 1948. But nothing has occurred to disprove the view
expressed by Jan Hofmeyr, a few weeks before his death,
that economic forces would in the end prove stronger than
the ideological urge of a group of Nationalist leaders
towards a Herrenvolk Afrikaans republic.

Index